Canada's Wheat King

Canada's Wheat King:

The Life and Times of Seager Wheeler

Jim Shilliday

2007

Canadian Plains Research Center
University of Regina
Regina, Saskatchewan S4S 0A2
Canada
Tel: (306) 585-4758
Fax: (306) 585-4699
e-mail: canadian.plains@uregina.ca
http://www.cprc.uregina.ca

The author may be contacted via the Canadian Plains Research Center at the above address.

Library and Archives Canada Cataloguing in Publication

Shilliday, Jim, 1928-
Canada's wheat king : the life and times of Seager Wheeler / Jim Shilliday.

(Trade books based in scholarship, 1482-9886 ; 20)
Includes bibliographical references and index.
ISBN 978-0-88977-187-1

1. Wheeler, Seager, 1868–1961. 2. Wheat--Breeding—Canada—History. 3. Plant breeders—Canada—Biography. 4. Agriculturists—Canada—Biography. 5. Farmers—Saskatchewan—Rosthern Region—Biography. 6. Rosthern (Sask.)—Biography. I. Title. II. Series: TBS 20

SB63.S42S55 2007   630.92
C2007-902954-X

We acknowledge the financial support of the Government of Canada through the Book Publishing Industry Development Program (BPDIP) for our publishing activities.

We acknowledge the support of the Canada Council for the Arts for our publishing program.

Cover design: Brian Danchuk Design, Regina
Printed and bound in Canada by
Index prepared by Adrian Mather (amindexing@shaw.ca)
The photo of the author which appears on the back cover is provided courtesy of the *Stonewall Argus*.

Contents

Dedication

To Beth

The closest we've come to divine inspiration

They are ill discoverers who think there is no land,
when they can see nothing but sea.

The Advancement of Learning, Bacon

Preface

Standing near the left bank of the South Saskatchewan River, a few miles northeast of Saskatoon—after tortuous manoeuvring of the car across stubbled wheat fields—we felt like pilgrims. Here was the site of the original homestead young Seager Wheeler and his mother had worked more than a century earlier. I had traced through his entire, dedicated life and now, to be in this place, was an emotional experience.

This is the story of North America's most celebrated wheat developer, whose varieties in the 1920s made up 40% of the world's wheat exports. Queen's University presented pioneer seed grower Wheeler with an honorary degree in 1920, and McGill collected his scientific publications. It is one of the most significant Canadian success stories never told. One of his wheat varieties, Red Bobs, was responsible for opening up the Peace River district of Alberta to successful grain farming at that period when immigrants were flocking into the West.

The federal government has proclaimed him a historic person, his farm has been designated a national historic site. Seager Wheeler played a major part in transforming the empty Canadian West into a prosperous region. More than 80% of Canada's wheat production—and much of that in the American mid-west—had been grown from his hardy strains. Although this work focuses on Saskatchewan, it also touches on developments in Manitoba, Alberta and British Columbia.

It has been written that the revolution that turned the semi-arid Canadian prairies into viable farmland had been accomplished through the "application of scientific methodologies to the art of farming." Seager Wheeler was one of the leaders of this revolution.

History has underestimated Wheeler's contribution to the success of the famed Marquis wheat. Glory was heaped on Dr. Charles Saunders as the "father" of Marquis, almost ignoring Wheeler's crucial role in stabilizing it as Marquis 10B. His improved strain was wildly popular and became the foundation stock of the Canadian Seed Growers' Association.

His most publicized accomplishment was being crowned World Wheat King an unsurpassed five times, from 1911 to 1918. The interest engendered by his triumphs was an acknowledged factor in Canada's success in luring immigrant farmers to Canada's west.

Sources include interviews with surviving daughters; the founder of the Seager Wheeler Historic Farm; relatives on the Isle of Wight; Seager Wheeler's unpublished memoir, notebooks and scrapbooks; newspaper and magazine articles of the time.

No biographer could have hoped to be so charmed by his sources, as he was by Wheeler's daughters Elizabeth "Betsy" Wheeler and Isabelle Blatz. We met in Betsy's Saskatoon apartment, strangers, Beth and I hoping to break the ice enough to get useful material, the daughters guarding the flame of their father's accomplishments and reputation. Their natural warmth and enthusiasm soon enveloped us, our tape recorder capturing fascinating stories, pealing laughter, retorts, and jokes to the point that Betsy, in subsequent meetings, happily turned on her own recorder. We have stayed in contact and are privileged to call them friends.

The Canada Council and the Manitoba Arts Council supported the writing of Canada's Wheat King through professional-writer grants.

The author also wishes to acknowledge the support of Brian Mlazgar, Publications Coordinator, Canadian Plains Research Center, for bringing this project through to publication.

The old site by the river had been difficult to find. The closest farmer's helpful instructions had pointed us across wide fields of autumn stubble that scraped disturbingly underneath the car. Yet, finally, there were the long stands of Manitoba Maple, offspring of those he planted so long ago, and the sloping riverbank he terraced for vegetable gardens and climbed up and down, summer and winter, to cross the river by boat or by trudging across the ice—sometimes risking his life.

Many months before, my wife Beth and I were headed up Highway 11 north of Saskatoon to visit the historic battleground at Batoche. We were approaching a little town named Rosthern, when Beth raised her eyes from a brochure and said, "I'd like to see Seager Wheeler's farm."

She could have said she'd like to see Old Macdonald's farm and been no less baffling to me. She assured me that Seager Wheeler had been an important farmer in pioneer times and his historic farm was nearby and sounded interesting. I had learned that what caught Beth's interest was always worth the time invested, and wheeled east towards what would become an absorbing pursuit for several years-writing the first full biography of this great Canadian.

Jim Shilliday
May 2007

— ONE —

In the Beginning

Seager Wheeler's forebears, fishermen, lifesavers, smugglers—parents separate—early life Isle of Wight, education at church school—religious non-conformism—Total Abstinence movement and influence of "teetotaller" Miss Nicholson—interest in plants, experiences that prepared him for what lay ahead.

Still in his teens, fisherman's son Seager Wheeler walked into the vastness of Canada's north-west, into a vacuum created by diverse forces—rebellion, threat from a "friendly" nation to the south, exploitive pressures from the east, powerful personalities and powerful ideas, and the deadly indifference of nature itself. He would persevere almost half a lifetime, then play a significant role in transforming the western lands into a sea of wheat that would become a mainstay of the Canadian economy.

Arriving in this world unheralded at Blackgang, Isle of Wight, Seager Wheeler departed the limelight two weeks, 11 months and 93 years later at Victoria, Vancouver Island, having done as much to open up the West, some said, as had the building of the Canadian Pacific Railroad.

Wheelers dwelt along a six-mile stretch of the southern cliffs of the Isle of Wight, facing the English Channel, from Ventnor in the east to Chale in the west. For generations they fished for mackerel, lobster, prawn and crab; they scoured the wave-ravaged beaches to salvage breached cargoes and wreckage from the merchant and passenger vessels that foundered regularly; and some of them lived on the edge in more ways than one, smuggling brandy and wine from France, a time-honored illegality.

Seager's ancestors were among the few literate Undercliff fisherfolk; they wrote reports and kept records for others. James Wheeler, the brother of his great-great-great grandfather Robert, kept a log of shipwrecks from 1746 to 1808, according to *Back of the Wight*, by local author Fred Mew. Generations of Wheeler men were legendary for risking their lives to save souls from those same foundered vessels.

Seager Wheeler's people were a vigorous line. His great-great-great-great grandfather, Robert Wheeler, was born in 1704, married Jenny Jollife in 1732, and produced six children, according to a family tree compiled by Dan Wheeler, of Chale Green, Isle of Wight, from county records and from entries in family Bibles. Seager's great-great-great grandfather Robert, married Elinor White in 1755, producing five children. His great-great

Cliff Terrace, Blackgang, Isle of Wight.

grandfather, James, born 1759, married Jane Jennie Searle in 1784; they had nine children. Nine children were the issue of great-grandfather John, not a seaman but a butcher, born in 1787, who married Hannah Calley in 1805. Grandfather William Wheeler, born in 1807, married Mary Young in 1834, producing 11 offspring, including Seager's father, Henry, born in 1837. Henry had brothers Frank, William, Maurice, Alfred, George, and sisters Elizabeth, Sarah, Lucretia, Ann and Agnes.

The Undercliff, near Blackgang, Isle of Wight.

Sheltered from intense north winds by chalk cliffs towering as high as 800 feet, the people along this coast enjoyed the best climate in the British Isles, warm in summer, mild in winter. Plants that couldn't exist in most other parts of the UK flourished here. A birdwatcher's, walker's and flower-lover's paradise, it was an environment that helped shape young Wheeler's future.

The road from Chale ran down to Blackgang Chine, a cleft in the cliff that, like a bad thought, scowled over Chale Bay stretching away in a sweeping arc. Looking out over Blackgang Chine's ruinous scene, from a ledge called Cliff Terrace, was a long stone structure called Low Cliff with four dwellings, the first the home of Henry Wheeler and his family.

Mrs. Wheeler was born Mary Ann Wood in 1843, at Whitwell, just under three miles northeast of the terrace. Hers was a non-seafaring family formerly from the mainland. The Wheeler children were Alice Amy, eight, five-year-old Minnie, and baby Percy Henry William, born in February 1867. Henry was short, dark-haired and wiry. Though just 30 years old, photographs show his round face already weather-creased. His wife, six years his junior, was taller, fair-haired, long-faced with an expression of calm endurance.

SOURCE: ELIZABETH WHEELER COLLECTION
The Chine, Blackgang, Isle of Wight

In the spring of 1867, as the British parliament passed the British North America Act establishing the Dominion of Canada, Mary Ann Wheeler was with child again and family lore says that her grandmother Sarah Seager, 101, who was born on January 3, predicted: "T'will be a boy. Mark me! Aye, and he'll be born on me birthday."

The old lady was right. A baby boy arrived the following January 3, 11 months after his brother Percy. What could be more fitting than to give him his great grandmother's name? So the fourth and last child of Henry and Mary Ann Wheeler was named Seager James Edwin Wheeler and his birth was registered on January 23, 1868, in the sub-district of Godshill in the county of Southampton.

Mrs. Wheeler doted on him, the last baby often being the mother's favourite. She remained by his side, encouraging him, for the rest of her life. But there was another reason for her protective motherlove: about two years after Seager was born, Henry had become romantically involved with Louisa Chiverton, from nearby Chale. The only course open to Mary Ann was to seek shelter with her parents. She gathered her children, belongings and pride, and left her unrepentant husband.

Her father, Cornelius Wood, 56, was keeper of a lodging house on Zig Zag Road, in

Ventnor. Maria Wood, 55, and her husband made them welcome until Mary Ann could plan their future. It's not known if Henry Wheeler took his paternal responsibility seriously enough to send money, but Seager's mother did washing and ironing, saved, and after a year or two, leaving Alice and Minnie with their grandparents, rented a house less than half a mile away, at 28 Albert St. Mary Ann continued to work as a laundress.

In 1874, according to the census, Henry Wheeler, still living at Low Cliff, fathered Ernest, born to "housekeeper" Louisa Chiverton. Ten years later, the next census showed, Elsie was born. Obviously, theirs was a lasting relationship.

At age five, Seager followed Percy and was registered at the National School, attending the Infant School and later the Boys' School. The "national" or church schools were almost universal in English villages. Religious and denominational quarreling had resulted in non-church schools being an alternative in big cities. But non-conformists in small communities usually had no choice but the church school, run by Anglicans, under the Education Bill passed two years after Seager was born, according to *English Social History*, by G.M. Trevelyan.

In step with the non-conformism of the times was the Total Abstinence movement, or "teetotalism." It flourished because drunkenness was a major cause of crime and the ruination of countless families. An attack was made on the drinking habits of all classes, in the mid-1800s, by the "Blue Ribbon Army," whose members pledged total abstinence and, of course, wore blue ribbons. The temperance movement was supported by all churches, and hundreds of thousands of "juvenile members" were enlisted to discourage them from becoming slaves to drink.

A few years later, one of these "teetotalers," Miss Cornelia Nicholson, 38, took a missionary interest in Seager and his chums. She and her father Cornelius, 77, lived at Ashleigh, an estate on the outskirts of Ventnor, attended by eight servants, including a coachman. They invited the boys to their mansion for Bible study. "My, it's a beautiful place," Seager told his mother. "Just like a park. And a butler greets us at the door." He would go on at length about the grand things he saw, and what they talked about. Later, Miss Nicholson encouraged him to be converted when he was 15 years old at a revival meeting of the Primitive Methodists. Miss Nicholson became a continuing influence in his life. They corresponded and she sent him books and advice long after he was gone from the Isle of Wight and a grown man.

Henry Wheeler, Seager Wheeler's father (early 1900s), wearing medal for saving a life at sea.

Studio photo of Mary Ann Wheeler (*née* Wood),
Seager Wheeler's mother, early 1880s.

Seager loved to read, particularly classic adventure stories. When younger, he had pored over the *Monthly Packet* and *Little Folks* magazines. And he learned to play the concertina, the sailor's instrument. He and his best friend, brother Percy, "shared an affinity like that between twins." They spent a good part of their free time and holidays hiking, swimming and boating.

Centuries-old wrecks still were locked in the sands below their home. After violent storms the boys would make their way down to the beach to see what had been torn from the ships' graves—old pistols, cutlasses, all kinds of exciting things. When Percy found a coin from Cromwell's time, they chipped the petrified material from its surface and it was a triumphant day when they sold it for one pound sterling. Sometimes, supplies for the larder floated in and they carried home such prizes as coconuts, boxes of oranges, cases of corned beef.

Later in life, Seager wrote of his boyhood rambles to Pelham Woods about a mile out of town in search of the first primroses, violets, hazel-nuts and wild plums. He would hike farther inland to watch farmers working their fields. He liked to roam amongst the beech trees, along meadow paths to the regal elms and ashes with clusters of bitter red berries. He became known for his collections of birds' eggs, stamps and old coins. Sometimes he explored the spots of luxuriant vegetation along the lower cliff closer to the sea, tangled brier, ferns, patches of wild thyme and flowers.

The first of scores of future articles about his activities came close to being the last. A local newspaper clipping from 1877 reported an incident that his daughters, Isabelle and Elizabeth, said he never told them:

> A number of boys were playing on the piece of land in Hambrough Road opposite the Vicerage [*sic*]. They were between 9–11. One of them, Seager Wheeler, was, boy-like, climbing the cliff which overhung the road and got into such a position as to not very easily be able to get up to the top on the grass again. Whilst endeavouring to do so, his companions, in fun, pushed him several times, the result being that the little fellow was compelled to release his hold and fell a distance of some 20 feet into the road below, breaking both of his arms and being severely shaken.

Like boys everywhere, Seager, Percy and their friends raided gardens and orchards, and were thrilled by the owners' pursuit, the closer the more exciting. "We wuz always too quick for 'em," Seager would chuckle in later years, head wreathed in pipe smoke, and reverting to dialect.

"Ah, they're bad boys," his grandfather growled the night Percy was caught with forbidden fruit and hauled off to the local jail for a few hours. Wheeler's youngest daughter, Elizabeth, recalled wistfully that her father's eyes would twinkle in remembrance: "But we wuzn't, we wuz just boys!"

— TWO —

The Big Decision

Seager leaves school age 11, messenger boy—shipwrecks, lifesaving, smuggling of spirits—works at
W.H. Smith book stall—ambition to serve in Royal Navy—letter from relative in North-West
Territories convinces them to emigrate to Canada—raise passage going door-to-door—in 1885 they
sail from Liverpool.

Fishermen's sons had to cut bait early. After passing second in his class with an illuminated certificate of merit, 11-year-old Seager's formal schooling was over. He had to go
to work. Mrs.Wheeler needed every penny her sons could earn to help feed and clothe
them. In any case, Victorian England offered little chance for a boy of his station to continue his education, regardless of how promising a student he might be.

Despite marine disasters that were an integral part of his family's history, his ambition
to serve in the Royal Navy remained steadfast, and he planned to enlist when he was of
age. But, until then he, like Percy, joined the small army of errand boys delivering parcels
and messages on foot in Ventnor and outlying areas. His first job was at a boot and shoe
store, where he also dusted shelves and kept the premises clean and tidy, for five shillings
a week. He worked from 7 a.m. to 6 p.m., Monday through Saturday. A year later, he
switched to an art and fancy goods store where he did the same job for the same pay, but
between deliveries he picked caterpillars from cabbages in the back garden, and snails and
slugs in the strawberry patch.

The proprietor left a coin on the floor one day, and when Seager found and returned it,
she explained that she was testing his honesty. He told his mother, who blew into the store
like an Atlantic gale and dressed her down for "underhandedness." Her boy would never
do anything dishonest.

Another year arrived, and with it another job, at W.H. Smith and Sons bookstall at the
railway station. When the train carrying London dailies chugged in at 7 a.m., Seager and
five other boys delivered newspapers to their assigned districts. His was west along the
coast trail leading to St. Lawrence, a round trip of four miles.

When the clerk married and bought a house nearby, Seager occasionally offered to help
him in the garden. Delivering papers was a job, but getting down on his knees working
with plants, seeing them thrive, was pleasure. A park was being made out of a woodland
by the town council and as he watched the workmen turning up the earth and planting

trees, he would write later, he wished that he owned a piece of ground where he could plant and tend growing things.

The Wheelers grew vegetables, and roses climbed across the boys' bedroom window and the front of the house. Seager wrote that he took cuttings from a euonymus hedge and other bushes and stuck them in the ground to see if they would grow.

Though their parents were separated, Seager and Percy are said to have visited their father occasionally and, of course, their half-brother Ernest. Henry gave Seager a book, a sea story, on his thirteenth birthday that he kept all his life. For years after Seager left the island, it is understood that he corresponded with them.

Seager now was a good-looking fellow, but his brother Percy was spoken of as "the handsome one." Seager was "nimble as a cat," and constantly talking, telling stories. The only boyhood photograph of him, at age 15 in serious pose, is in daughter Elizabeth's family album. "Though small for his age," she wrote, "perhaps

SOURCE: ELIZABETH WHEELER COLLECTION
Seager Wheeler studio birthday photo, aged 15 years.

even scrawny, he was wiry. The photo shows an open countenance and a smooth, broad forehead. His hair is light brown." His obvious good health contradicted the doctor's warning when he had whooping cough as a two-year-old: "He'll never grow up," said the MD, as he left his little patient gasping for breath.

In October 1883, Seager mailed the required character reference to C. Roach Smith, R.N., of H.M. *Training Establishment St.Vincent*, signed by the R.H. Smith and Sons clerk in charge, W.H. Ridgood:

> "Sir—We have great pleasure in certifying that Seager Wheeler has been in our employ during the past fifteen months and that we have found him to be honest, attentive, and willing in his duties and that he has given us great satisfaction."

If anything could have changed Seager's mind about taking the Queen's shilling, it might have been that terrible Sunday back in 1878 when he was watching from the cliff as the great naval training ship *Eurydice* plunged by, all sails set. As he apparently told Hopkins Moorhouse, who set it down in a 1919 biographical sketch, sailor boys were waving at the open portholes; it was a fine, clear day. Suddenly, a March snow squall bore down upon the scene. While 10-year-old Seager still was waving his cap, a dark mass enveloped the ship. After what seemed just a few minutes, the air cleared again. The sea was empty save for the tips of masts sticking out of the water. The *Eurydice* had been laid over by the storm and water had gushed into the portholes. There had been 328 cadets and officers on board, returning from a long cruise in foreign waters. Only two survived.

So five years later, undoubtedly thinking of a grand adventure ahead, he went to Portsmouth where the Boys' *Training Establishment St. Vincent* was anchored. He and several others were tested and examined, then told that since the ship already had its full complement of trainees, they should come back in the new year.

But he would never go back. He would never sail to India where Queen Victoria had just been proclaimed Empress, or round the storm-battered Cape Horn, or... . Hopkins Moorhouse's tale, recounted again and again in articles over the decades, said a sailor had taken Seager's measure with a tape, and reported to the officer in charge, who shook his head. "Sorry, admiral," the tale went, "it's not to be. Up and down, you're an inch short, and round about there's another inch missing. Next!"

That would have meant Wheeler was shorter than four feet, 10 inches, the minimum height required for boys aged 15 to 16 by the Admiralty circular of 1853. That regulation also stated an entry was subject to a survey of two captains and two medical officers. Boys had to be judged "of perfectly sound and healthy constitution and free from physical malformation or other defect."

Would he have had the necessary educational qualifications? According to the Royal Naval Museum Library at HM Naval Base, Portsmouth, "educational abilities appear not to have been taken into account, but school subjects were taught amongst 'seamanship' subjects.

"*St. Vincent* (was) mainly concerned with the training of boy seamen who would proceed to the lower ratings of naval vessels—although it was possible for boys trained at these establishments to be promoted eventually to officer status." Eligible boys "had to sign on for 12 years from the age of 18 (time spent in training did not count towards the 12 years)."

Moorhouse had claimed Seager was keenly disappointed at not being able to take up the life of a "middie," an officer-rank midshipman. But that was an unlikely route for a boy taken on by the *St. Vincent*. According to the naval museum's librarian, A. Wareham,

> "Naval cadets were distinct from boys, being the officer cadets who
> trained mainly at Britannia, Dartmouth and proceeded to Midshipman
> and officer status on finishing training."

Seager's life was not unfolding as planned. He passed the winter doing odd jobs and bringing home less money. That he would throw over his job before knowing if and when the navy would take him can only be attributed to a youthful lack of judgement, and possibly his mother's belief that it was time he made some decisions on his own. It was her tendency to guide him in most things, having a motherly concern for his welfare. This would manifest itself many times in the coming years when they struggled together to make a better life; she would give him full rein until it was time to suggest a tack, and then her son would readily agree to follow her direction. Theirs was a close relationship, based not only on kinship, but also on ambition and mutual respect.

The vacuum nature abhors soon was filled with new possibilities: Mary Ann Wheeler came across a pamphlet extolling the wonders and opportunities of Manitoba, Canada. Titles of Canadian Pacific Railway pamphlets included *What Women Say of the Canadian North-West*; *The Canadian North-West: What Farmers Say*; *Free Homes in Manitoba*. Their illustrations impressed Seager—farmers leading oxen, fields of waving grain to the horizon; a log house, smoke from the chimney rising straight into the sky. All this fired his imagination and filled him with longing for land of his own.

In the 1880s, travel books and other printed material had made Britons more aware of Canada in its own right, rather than lumping the country into an entity known as "America." In his introduction to *Letters from a Young Emigrant in Manitoba*, Ronald A. Wells wrote of the explosion of popular knowledge about Canada in Britain. This, he said, was a possible explanation for the gradual redirection of emigration from United States to Canada's northwest, along with "heightened imperial consciousness after 1885," and availability of good land. "The most effective written stimuli to migration were, of course, emigrant letters…"

Gus Lamonde, a relative of his mother's, had emigrated earlier. He wrote describing his farm at Clark's Crossing, just north of a settlement called Saskatoon, in the Northwest Territories. Seager's uncle, George Barrett, who was married to Mary Ann Wheeler's sister Sarah, was already there. In return for Barrett's labor, Lamonde provided room and board, and when the time was right would help Barrett apply for free homestead land and pay his $10 entry fee. He suggested that she send one of her sons out as well and, eventually, he could apply for a homestead, too.

The *Dominion Lands Act* of 1872 had set aside a huge chunk of North America previously owned by the Hudson's Bay Company, to provide free quarter-sections of land for immigrants who would build a homestead and settle. The Canadian government had opened immigration offices in Britain and the rest of Europe, offering assisted passages to selected applicants. Ottawa was busy signing treaties with various Indian populations. The West was open for settlement and land-hungry Europeans flocked to the land of opportunity.

Sailing across the Atlantic Ocean to the wild prairies of Canada was an exciting prospect for Seager. The navy didn't want him, but Canada did. How did his brother and sisters react to this proposal? Twenty-five-year-old Alice was eager to start a new life, but Percy, now 18 and a fisherman, wavered, wanting more time to think about it. Minnie, 22, a domestic servant now, was content to stay on the island.

Such a dramatic pulling up of stakes would have had great appeal for Mrs. Wheeler, who had been subjected to such embarrassment years earlier. And there was no way she was going to be parted from her Seager. The three of them would go to the North-West Territories of the "British colony" in North America. It was a decision that would have incalculable importance to the new country that Seager eventually would call "my Canada."

Their decision was made at a time when recasting of one's position in the class structure of English society was becoming less unusual. Religious non-conformism was rife. Authoritarianism—be it from the clergy, government, the gentry—was less likely to be accepted unquestioningly by those at the bottom of the heap. To better one's position, to own land, to take charge of one's own destiny, was a beguiling proposition.

An advertisement placed in *Isle of Wight Mercury*, by the Allan Royal Mail Line caught Mrs.Wheeler's attention, and she made inquiries. The line was licensed by the Canadian government to provide passage for immigrants, and advertised "the best and cheapest routes" to Canada, wrote Thomas E. Appleton, in *Ravenscrag*. In the U.K. it offered reduced rates for the initial railway journey to the port of Liverpool and arrangements for travel from the disembarkation point to western Canada in "colonist cars." Steerage or third-class sea passage cost six guineas (one guinea = one pound, one shilling) for adults, three guineas for children under eight. More than 18 pounds! It was a small fortune to Mary Ann Wheeler.

The Wheelers had to raise this passage money somehow. And they would need cash for food while travelling across half a continent to Moose Jaw, and then to keep them going while they were establishing themselves in frontier Canada.

That winter, the French schooner *Belle Monde* broke in half, spilling her cargo of coal briquettes amongst the rocks five miles from Ventnor. A local merchant bought the salvage rights and hired several boys, including Seager, for the job. He packed the coal into jute bags and carried them time after time on his back up the steep cliff. He was paid a gold sovereign (one pound sterling) and proudly gave it to his mother.

Mrs. Wheeler took in additional washing; Alice, a milliner now, sold hats, and also home-made baking. And, finally, Seager's mother squelched her pride and went door-to-door collecting "subscriptions." "It is what is being done these days," she insisted, "people contributing money to help those who want to go. Otherwise, none of us would be able to go." Henry Wheeler, apparently, was not prepared, or able, to help financially.

Friends and relatives were at the station to bid farewell. Boxes and duffel bags were in the baggage car along with a crate containing their little dog Pincher. Handkerchiefs and scarves still waved from the platform as the Ryde train plunged into the cliff tunnel. From Ryde, they took a ferry across the choppy 4.5 miles of Spithead to Southampton, and then all boarded the train for Liverpool.

A light snow was falling that Wednesday, Seager wrote in his travel diary, as they pushed their way through the noise and jostling of vast crowds of travellers and well-wishers on the landing stage. He would have been spellbound as he craned his neck upward to take in the mighty steamship RMS *Parisian*, flagship of the Allan Line built specially for the Montreal trade. She was a marvel close up, a huge stretching mass with five large lifeboats suspended along each side, two slightly swept-back funnels with smoke tendrils already twisting out, four masts, heavily rigged (builders hadn't yet been able to shake all the traditions of sailing-ship design). They boarded at midday and soon after, much to Seager Wheeler's satisfaction—for, of course, he was always hungry—were fed beef, bread and tea.

By 3 p.m., the mounds of baggage had been loaded, the gangways taken up. At 4 p.m., as a band played Auld Lang Syne, the crowd's cheers were obliterated by blasts from the ship's horns, many of the passengers crowding the rails waving as the *Parisian* slowly moved out until England faded into the distance.

— THREE —

To a New Life

Flagship *Parisian* comfortable, fast—starts travel diary—Quebec City—colonist cars to Montreal then westwards—eastern troops to Riel Rebellion in first stirrings of Canadianism—Owen Sound to Port Arthur by ship, train to Winnipeg—Moose Jaw, rowdy American cowboys—meets first Indians—walks with Metis freighters across 90 miles empty prairie and back—Mrs. Wheeler takes in washing, sister sells baking, Seager does odd jobs—joins Salvation Army band.

Meals aboard ship were a novel experience for Seager. Stewards carried food to the steerage deck where he and his fellow passengers lined up, clutching the cutlery, plates and pannikins they had brought with them. Newly-baked bread, salted butter, porridge and molasses, and lots of coffee started the day. There weren't enough cows on board, so bottom-of-the-ladder passengers went without milk. The main meal at 1 p.m. included soup, meat or fish, and potatoes. For supper, at 6 p.m., bread, biscuit and butter, tea. Biscuit—uneven squares of unbelievable toughness—was sailors' hardtack. Sunday was a special day for steerage and crew—dessert was on the menu.

By dark that second day, the *Parisian* was well out into the Atlantic. She pitched despite her projecting bilge keels, which did help dampen the roll. But most of the passengers, including the Wheeler women, were seasick. Seager had caught a cold but, "I was not seasick, nor was Pincher, he is all right," he wrote in a small notebook, putting down his impressions in the form of a letter to his brother Percy, which gradually became a travelling diary. "We had to sleep in hammocks with clothes on and my bones was one sided," he wrote in his homespun style. But below-decks was cramped, and fumes from coal oil lamps made his head ache.

"When I came to take out my concertina," he wrote, "I found the notes inside were loose, but I got some glue from the carpenter and mended it." His fellow passengers, after a few days getting their sea legs and rubbing shoulders, would have warmed to his pleasant, outgoing manner. It is easy to imagine them persuading him to play a patriotic tune—Rule Britannia, one of his favourites—a throng lustily singing the stirring words as they grouped around the young fellow, concentric whirls of open-mouthed faces about his pumping hands.

He recorded sightings of porpoises, sharks and whales. After a week at sea, he was excited to see icebergs emerge from the fog, some he estimated at three miles long. When he spotted Mother Carey's Chickens, delicate little dark-brown storm petrels with white spots, he would have known they were in for rough weather and, sure enough, "It was very squally, the vessel rolled about very much."

On the eighth day, the coast of Labrador came into view, parts of which "put me in mind of the Isle of Wight … one place just like Luccombe and the Needles and one place I thought was Highcliff and it put me in mind of when I went out with you in the boats at Atherfield." Next day, they entered the St. Lawrence River and on the tenth day, land still patched with snow close on either side, the water was calm.

"Such beautiful scenery up the river … pretty little shantys among the trees and a church now and then and boats and schooners along side the shore." His seafarer's eye noted that "[y]ou could almost touch the shore as we passed up the river, a wonderful depth of water for a great ship like the *Parisian*."

Just after noon, at Point Levee, the *Parisian* berthed alongside the low Allan Line sheds stretching the length of two of its steamships. Seager kept a weather eye for their luggage as cranes with huge nets hoisted baggage from the hold. Most of the 1,200 passengers boarded the Grand Trunk Railway train bound for Atlantic Canada. A tug took the Wheelers and 33 others across the river to another wharf at Quebec City. There, they boarded the train and stored their grips, boxes and Pincher, ready to set out for western Canada. The fare—$12 each—lightened Mrs.Wheeler's purse considerably.

Off they went to shop for provisions. After careful consideration, they bought six pounds of bread and four fish cakes, at the exchange rate of five Canadian dollars for one pound sterling. "We gave them five shillings in silver and we lost one-sixth on that," Seager wrote when they got their Canadian money in change. "Such a dirty place … most pavements of wood … very rotten and break down … all French people here."

The new cross-country railway line being built by the Canadian Pacific Railway had reached as far west as Manitoba and that part of North-West Territories that would become Saskatchewan. The colonist cars were huge compared with English coaches, a long aisle running the length with sections of facing seats on either side, accommodating 84 passengers. The facing seats pulled together at night to sleep two and, above, the ceiling pulled down to make an upper berth. There were no mattresses. And no privacy. Some people slept in their clothes. The women soon learned to improvise, hanging up sheets of newspaper while they changed.

Seager climbed into his bunk at 10 p.m., and ten minutes later the train lurched, squealed and lumbered off westwards taking them at 35 miles an hour towards their new life. He climbed down at 5 a.m. to stand between coaches and watch "pretty farms" go by on a warming, sunny Sunday. "Such a lot of dust came in during the night because the window was open."

They made their tea in one of the tiny rooms at each end of the coach containing a wood stove and water tap. After pulling into Montreal a little after 6 p.m., Alice and Seager went off to see the sights. "Such a curious place. I felt stifled, it was very hot. Such a lot of people … nearly all French. Was glad to get back to our car."

Moving again, the train stopped frequently at isolated communities to take on and drop off passengers and freight. One can imagine workers in the fields raising their heads to hear, above the clackety-clack of the locomotive pulling laden coaches over the rail joints, the tinny trill from an Isle of Wight concertina, strains of *Little Brown Jug* or *Two Little Girls in Blue*.

Staring through the smoke-smeared window at the endless expanse of lakes and woods of the Canadian wilderness, Seager would have wondered about what lay ahead. He was a boy, and had a boy's open-faced surety that the world out there held opportunities, problems to be solved, a future to be shaped.

"The shanties look so pretty when the smoke is coming out of the pipe in the roof," the young traveller wrote. "Such a lot of timber about, and rhubarb and corn … the young firs and spruces looked so pretty and, oh! such pretty little log huts." He also noted the many frogs, "just like birds whistling." He felt the heat and he took off his collar, tie and jacket for the rest of the trip. "It is 6:10 in the evening, but at Blackgang, it is 11:10 in the night," he wrote. Was he touched with homesickness already?

The transcontinental railway line had been whacked together quickly. At times their train had difficulty on the inclines and another engine had to be added. Four or five sections of the line north of Lake Superior still were not finished because of muskeg; during the past winter, veteran soldiers who had served with the British Army against the Russians said they suffered greater hardships on the train journey to the Canadian northwest "than they had ever experienced in the Crimea."

On a late spring evening, the Wheelers climbed down stiffly at Owen Sound at the southern tip of Georgian Bay, far south of the CPR's northern route that had so discomfited the troops. They would sleep and eat in a wooden building by the railway platform. There were 10 bedrooms, four bare bunks in each (Seager was used to having no mattress, but he was wound up and couldn't sleep). In the dining room, there were 10 tables, each seating 10. The kitchen was well set up with two wood stoves, two great kettles, frying pans and two pails and pans for dish washing.

Grocery shopping: three pounds of bacon for 25¢, potatoes, a three-pound box of biscuits—"Same as the toast biscuits in England"—for 25¢. The bacon was "just like pickled pork." This time, he didn't feel cheated by the money-changing: "I bought a gallon of potatoes and gave them a half sovereign and they gave me back the same amount in Canada money, so I gained 10 cents on it, that is, five shillings." Seager wrote again about the frog cacophony that sounded to him "just like a lot of crickets, only much louder and some sounds like a steam whistle." He noted banks of hyacinths in the first flower garden he had seen since leaving the Isle of Wight.

When they boarded the *Alberta* that afternoon, bound for Port Arthur (now Thunder Bay), they again found no mattresses on their bunks, "but we are used to it." Ice still clogged parts of the lake, and sheets of it stopped the ship—a two-master that steamed at 13 knots in open water—six times that night before it managed to force its way free. It crossed the top of Lake Huron, passed through locks at Sault Ste. Marie—"a very pretty place"—and steamed along the top of Lake Superior. They landed at noon, bought bread for 10¢ a loaf and sugar for 10¢ a pound, and then it was "All aboard!" for Winnipeg. That trip was a nightmare. More than 150 railway construction workers on board were all drunken roisterers. The men worked for weeks, Seager was told, then went to Port Arthur and spent "as much as $6 in one week" on drink. Then, broke or broken, they returned to work, until the cycle was repeated.

All the trains were carrying troops, supplies and equipment, so the weary travellers had to stay in Winnipeg until one was available. Gus Lamonde had sent a letter to Mr.Tremblay, the immigration agent, asking him to tell the Wheelers to telegraph on arrival. How relieved they must have been for confirmation that someone in this vast, strange country was expecting them. They had time to learn a little about life in Canada when they looked up several old friends from the Isle of Wight. They lived for a week in the immigration building, which would have offered the same comfort, or lack of it, as all the other immigration buildings.

Winnipeg was the best town Seager had seen so far in Canada with its fine wooden sidewalks; but step off and you sank ankle deep into sticky gumbo. The weather the first day was wild, with severe thunderstorms, and hail that hurt. Maybe it was the flatness, but "[y]ou never saw such storms in the Old Country. The thunder was awful, it did rattle." The day before, a "cyclone" threw a house 40 feet. And there were plenty of mosquitoes. "There are a lot of canaries here, and robins … a lot of half-breeds." Then, in an understatement that would prove wildly optimistic: "I don't think we shall go on to our land before the spring."

Winnipeggers, mostly real estate agents, land speculators, merchants and a few actual homesteaders, referred to their town as the Chicago of the North. A land-rush frenzy had gripped everyone. The same was true in Brandon and all the small settlements along the new railway line for more than 500 miles, such as "Pile of Bones," later renamed Regina.

Seager explored. He wandered well beyond the outskirts, observing unfamiliar sights, and probably asking the names of things from people he met along the way. "In the woods two miles out there are a lot of cherries blooming, large trees of it [perhaps saskatoons or chokecherries], and strawberry and raspberry and plums … beautiful ferns all along Red River. A lot of hedges, nettles high as your head and Houlees [coulees] too. Saw plenty of half-breeds and Indians. There are a lot of canaries, beautiful singing birds and robins as big as black birds."

Rolling west again, he was stirred by his first sight of treeless prairie a few miles west of Winnipeg. And his eyes were wide again near Brandon when they passed an Indian village, "wigwams like little tents. Chippeways." When they finally arrived at Moose Jaw on June 5, 1885, after a taxing nine-day trip, the Wheelers carried their belongings up the long flight of outside stairs to the second floor of the immigration hall and into an empty room that reminded them of a barn's loft. They made their beds on the floor and soon were sound asleep.

The hall was near the camp of a unit of the Halifax battalion. Wounded soldiers from last month's rebellion-ending showdown at Batoche were in the military hospital, a conglomeration of tents. Meanwhile, militia and regular army units farther north continued for the rest of June to comb the mosquito-infested woods and sloughs for Indians allied with Riel. The last of these surrendered on July 2.

Refreshed by a sound sleep, Seager eagerly explored the prairie, Pincher running and barking at his side. He was elated—free of shipboard confinement, free of the cramped, rocking colonist car, free to roam a spaciousness he had never experienced. The town extended two blocks from the railway station and was about the same width. There were no trees, but a few willows along Moose Jaw Creek. There was nothing blocking the view to the horizon in any direction.

Moose Jaw was not what he had expected. Where were the trees? Where were the wide grain fields, the settlers' cabins nestled in woods with smoke curling from little chimneys, the sense of fruitfulness and future well-being? This place was muddy and dusty, a tiny miscellany of mutable buildings and people—some of them dangerously wild—holding onto life by their fingernails. But Seager Wheeler, his eyes wide, probably relished it, intoxicated by its differentness.

The buildings were of slap-dash construction, nothing like those in Ventnor, and that was their attraction—the difference enhanced the aura of adventure. Seager met and talked to townspeople on the streets, in the drug store and the general store. He enjoyed exchanging stories with O.B. Fish in his blacksmith shop, and Mr.Bates at the Brunswick Hotel.

Here's how the NWMP constable John Donkin, a jaundiced observer, described the Wheeler's first winter home in Canada:

> "The town of Moose Jaw lies in a hollow of the prairie, and is the end of
> a section of the Canadian Pacific Railway. Here is a round-house for
> engines. The population is 500, and there is the usual scattering of hotels
> and stores, standing at intervals upon the unromantic flat. Ugly square
> objects, all of them, without the slightest pretence to architectural beauty.
> A prairie town is a more depressing object than a burnt forest."

Moose Jaw was "wild and wooly." Almost every night the Wheelers could hear gun-shots, and feared for their lives as bullets tore through the wood frame of their building while they lay on the floor trying to sleep. Cowboys from Montana brought up herds of horses and considered Moose Jaw their playground. A Mounted Police detachment guard-ed against smuggling of whiskey across the border by frontiersmen, and searched the grips and suitcases of suspect passengers arriving by train. Railway work crews got so drunk at times it was difficult for the CPR to meet construction schedules. How shocked Mary Ann Wheeler must have been by this rowdy place. But they would have to make the best of it.

And the books young Seager had read about red Indians came alive. American Sioux refugees who had fled the American army were camped just outside the town by a stream in a shallow ravine. He learned the chief was Black Bull, a relative of Sitting Bull whose warriors had massacred U.S. General Custer and his soldiers. Wearing a frock coat and black top hat, he limped, the result of seven bullet wounds, the story went.

One morning, Seager related in his memoir, Black Bull's wife came to the Holmes Block where the Wheelers now rented rooms, sat down and waited silently. His mother was star-tled. But she soon realized the poor woman was hungry and gave her food. There were more visits and the women became friends.

Black Bull's wife cried during one visit. She still hadn't recovered from the death a while earlier of her son. Mrs.Wheeler learned that the boy had died of tuberculosis, a dis-ease that had replaced smallpox as a killer of Indians. "The susceptibility of Indians and Metis," said John H. Archer in *Saskatchewan: A History*, "and the lack of treatment centres had led to an epidemic spread of the disease among Indians and in some isolated rural areas by 1905. The reputation of the territories as a health resort for consumptives may also have been a reason for the large number of tuberculosis deaths reported."

On his way one day to the Indian camp four miles out on the prairie, Seager laughed at Pincher's efforts to catch gophers. "They are like rats. They live in holes in the ground like rabbits. They sit up like a kangaroo." He likened some animals to what he knew: a garter snake as long as his arm looked like an eel; crawfish were "fresh water lobsters you couldn't tell from the sea lobster, but they are not so large."

Before the Halifax battalion broke camp and returned home, they treated their Indian friends to soup, bully beef and hardtack biscuits. "Then the Indians riding ponies bareback

arrived with guns and rifles, riding in and out firing their weapons and yelling and giving excited war whoops," Seager wrote. "It was rather startling to me and other onlook-
ers." There were many foot races and then photographs were taken. "After dinner there
was a Pow Wow. A Pow Wow is a conference on sports," he decided.

Seager didn't realize yet the trials suffered by the Indians who had lost their way of life
when the buffalo vanished. His assessment:

> "They are very ugly. They had a feed and it would make you almost sick
> to see what they eat. They will eat anything. I should like you to have seen
> them."

He was eager to get to Gus Lamonde's, to learn farming, to own some land. So he was
elated when Metis freighters transporting army supplies told him they were going to
Saskatoon, and then on to Prince Albert and Battleford. He could join them. He would
need food for a week, but the government provided the teamsters with biscuits, tea and
tinned meat, so Seager only had to take bread.

They set off on June 9, a warm, sunny morning—"You don't see such weather in the
Old Country." Everyone walked, whether the wagons were pulled by oxen or horses,
because the cargo rate was 14.5¢ a pound, and every extra pound carried earned that
much more money. They walked the treeless expanse of grass, badger holes, scattered buffalo bones and skulls, from just after sunup to nightfall, sometimes 28 miles in a day. "My
word, didn't the mosquitoes torment us!" Sometimes they had hardtack, bread and tea
without milk or sugar for breakfast, dinner and supper. Occasionally they soaked hardtack
and fried it with pork.

The trail was wide, and not as rutted as expected. The cavalcade of wagons and Red
River Carts was arranged so that each pulling animal, ox or horse, was tied to the rear corner of the cart ahead and walked in its wheel rut. In this way, the vehicles did not travel
in a single line and avoided making much-deeper ruts. The overall impression for Seager,
plodding alongside was: noise.

It was uncomfortably hot, and he pushed up the sleeves of his blue guernsey, stuffed
his red hat in a pocket, and his face and hands got browner as the miles passed. His thirst
raged the first day. Only a small amount of water was carried, and that reserved for tea.
At the "16-mile slough" he strained tadpoles from the brackish water by pouring it
through his handkerchief. Later, "I lay down and lapped until I was satisfied." He was
quickly adapting and felt like a true man of the trail now. "I walked 20 miles, you bet my
legs ached! The mosquitoes are a torment. Kept me awake nearly all night, my hands and
face is covered with bites as big as marbles." Next night, he woke to find he had been
sleeping on ant nests in the sandy soil.

The second day, they passed soldiers moving south, wagons loaded with wounded
from the "front." That afternoon, they came to a ravine, "like a chine, Walpen chine, only
much bigger," then the breeze sprang up into a gale and "the dust was so thick the oxen
could hardly face it. I was covered from head to foot with dust and then down poured the
rain. You can imagine what a plight I was in."

Half way along the 180-mile trail they met George Horn, on his way from Saskatoon to
Moose Jaw in a two-wheeled cart pulled by a pony, a second cart and pony tied behind. It
was no use going farther, he told Seager, because Lamonde was on his way to Moose Jaw
on another trail. He would hitch up the other pony, and Seager could drive the second cart.

That was more like it! Seager leapt onto the cart, caught on quickly, and bounced back to Moose Jaw in style, happy and now "brown as a berry."

"There is nothing to be seen on the prairie, not a tree or bush for 100 miles, a shanty in the distance now and then, it is like a sea—you can see so far and no farther … plenty of beautiful flowers," he wrote on Tuesday, June 16. There were wild roses that "smell sweeter than our garden roses … cherry trees, gooseberry and raspberry too and springs of clear water." He heard the howl of his first prairie wolf and he sent Pincher after an antelope but "it ran like the wind."

Back home, "Alice didn't know me. She thought I was a Half breed." He found Gus Lamonde and George Barrett listening as his mother brought them up to date on family news. The adults decided, to Seager's chagrin, that it would be best for him to wait until the following spring to go up to Lamonde's homestead.

The town's rowdies had stepped up their "wild and wooly" antics while he was away. He noted in his diary that two hotels had burned. And Alice had feared Indians were attacking when bullets whizzed by their building one night; soldiers were firing their weapons from the hospital tents. Another night, during heavy drinking by the troops, government hay stores were set ablaze, and two privates and a corporal on sentry duty were arrested.

The day after his return, Seager picked a bouquet of prairie flowers whose scent he rated better than any back home. They graced the table at dinner for the special meal his mother had prepared: spiced pork, potatoes, trimmings, and a finale of gooseberry pudding, the first home-style dinner they had eaten since arriving in Canada. Alice went to church and Pincher followed her. The minister tied the dog to Alice's seat and "he was very quiet."

It is not mentioned in diary, correspondence or memoir how much money Mrs. Wheeler had saved for the trip to Canada. But now she was obliged to take in washing, while Alice sold her home-made baking. Seager heard about a job emptying a boxcar of lump coal; the foreman of the section gang eyed his physique and grumbled, "This is a job for two men." But he let him try. Seager shovelled all day, emptying the boxcar. He was paid $6, a bonanza compared with his usual pay for odd jobs of $1 a day.

His mother, as she was wont to do, now introduced another element into his life, one that would stay with him to the end. The evangelistic Salvation Army had decided to establish a corps in Moose Jaw and asked her if her son would like to join. She decided that would be a good influence in such a wild town. And he would learn to play the cornet.

Seager was delighted with the red jacket of new recruits. "Oh my, didn't the folks stand and stare," his daughter Elizabeth remembered him chuckling years later, "this little straggling group going down the street beating the drum." And, he said, he liked their services because "they go out and they seek the lost."

This Salvation Army influence did not make a churchgoer of Seager in later years, not until after his retirement, when he attended their services, but his support was lifelong. He always was interested in religion, read the Bible daily, and collected inspirational poems and hymns that he played on his concertina.

Relaxing after a long walk one sunny afternoon in September, Seager lay at the edge of a high bank overlooking the creek watching garter snakes writhe across the water's surface and up the bank. He counted until he reached a thousand. After a rain, the snakes would crawl over the wooden sidewalks in town. "Sometimes they would crawl into the house, an odd one would get under the cook stove. One got used to them."

Later that fall he was hired, along with six other men, to dig trenches in the Moose Jaw Creek bed to allow water to trickle down to the railway station. They saw swarms of snakes on the banks. Despite scriptural admonitions, there was little regard for "God's little creatures." These were not the days of ecology and preservation. "We killed over one hundred, and others lying down deep in the wide cracks in the land, all sizes from about two feet to much longer."

He was delighted to meet a former school chum who had emigrated earlier, volunteered to serve with the Winnipeg Rifles, and had been in skirmishes with Chief Big Bear and his followers. He gave Seager a makeshift shotgun called a "Zulu," a single-barrel converted rifle.

It's doubtful Seager had used a gun before but, always game, he went hunting along Moose Jaw Creek; maybe he'd get a duck for dinner. "I was on my way home when two mallards flew down low towards me. I let fly at them and the next thing I knew I was on my back, the gun lying on the ground a few feet from me and the blood running into my eyes. I never looked to see if I had shot any ducks. I started for home. I was a sight when I went in and it frightened my mother. My forehead was raw and red, powder marks above and around my forehead. Fortunately, my eyes were not injured."

Several years later, after frequently feeling something under his skin against the bone of his forehead, he got his brother Percy "to make a small cut with a pocket knife and dig out … a piece of the brass portion of the shotgun shell, now turned black."

Seager did anything to earn money: house painting, cellar digging, carpet beating, feeding chickens. An opening with the CPR section gang at Parkbeg, two stations west of Moose Jaw, ended when "I took sick with the bad drinking water." Walking home east along the railway ties, he reached Caron where the section boss gave him a meal and told him to rest until the passenger train came in. "I've no money," said Seager. "Don't worry, just get on the train and sit down." The conductor didn't bother him. Seager, who liked things to balance fairly, figured he had worked for the railway almost a week for nothing and so didn't owe the company for his fare.

His introduction to farm work that fall was "stooking" sheaves on a half-section of wheat near town; thousands of sheaves had to be stacked in clusters to dry. He and another boy, Sam Waller, were given a tent, a tin stove, potatoes and bacon and left to get on with it. They pitched in determined to do a good job, toiled for many days, but set up all the sheaves on those 320 acres.

Home now was a rented "car house" on the edge of town, a one-storey structure with a low roof like a railway freight car, opposite Ostrander's Brunswick Hotel.

On New Year's Eve they were awakened by Pincher's excited barking. The Ostrander's stable next door was belching flames. Seager ran to the hotel to sound the alarm, then back to help his mother and sister lug and tug their few pieces of furniture and belongings outside into the snow. The stable burned down, killing some chickens and several horses. But the Wheeler's house was spared.

When Seager couldn't find work that winter, he often would skate up the creek snaring rabbits for the table, and trapping mink for their pelts. He polished buffalo horns, mounted them and sold them as ornaments.

Alice Wheeler was a natural entrepreneur. So, with her brother's help, she set up a bakeshop in a shack near the railway station where she made and sold cakes, pies, buns, tea and coffee. Settlers from the East, and railwaymen from the Moose Jaw divisional point enjoyed dropping in for conversation and refreshments. Seager hauled water from a well up the creek, which cost them 25¢ a barrel. "I helped her at times, doing little jobs for her and going up the creek for dry willows and tying them in a large bundle and bringing them home on my back to be used in firing."

Spring came to the great plains, and to Seager, as a revelation. Life's pulse picked up. The unbelievable cold and tedium of winter had ended, cheering warmth made the dark-water creeks run full and his spirits raced as well. A worker since age 11, he was a practical youth, but not devoid of dreams. His only goal in life was to build a farm with good land and a house, a place he and his mother would own and could truly call home. At last he could resume the great adventure of his life. Saskatoon settlers would be coming south for supplies and he could arrange to go back with one of them to Lamonde's homestead on the bank of the South Saskatchewan, and learn to be a frontier farmer.

— FOUR —

The Trek North

Spring of 1886, Seager walks 180 miles to Lamonde's near Saskatoon, works as farmhand—buffalo gone—Blow to head knocks out tooth—Alice marries.

Now, like a seasonal human migration, in mud-spattered carts and wagons creaking and listing from far-scattered locations, homesteaders arrived travel-weary at Moose Jaw to replenish supplies. On the boggy main street early that spring of 1886, Seager Wheeler approached Peter Robinson, who listened to his story and offered to take him back as far as his homestead just south of tiny Saskatoon.

They were going to trudge across the upper portion of the "Palliser Triangle." Capt. John Palliser had been sent out by the British two decades earlier leading an expedition to determine the agricultural potential of the Canadian plains. He had reported that there was a northern fertile belt west of Lake Winnipeg through the Clark's Crossing area into what later became Alberta. South of that he warned was too dry, that farming would be risky and delay settlement of the productive areas. He was proven partly wrong. More intensive studies later by Canadian botanist John Macoun predicted the area would become known as the best wheat lands anywhere. Palliser's mistake, he stated, was due to a hasty conclusion based on the absence of trees and scarcity of water. Rainfall, Macoun insisted, usually came when it was most needed.

So, from the 49th parallel all the way up to the left bank of the South Saskatchewan more than 180 miles north, the only settlements—apart from occasional one-room shacks—in the colossal emptiness of former Hudson's Bay Company lands were those in the southern District of Assiniboia, such as Moose Jaw and Regina in a narrow east-west belt hugging the new Canadian Pacific Railway line, and Saskatoon and a few other communities way up north near the bottom of the District of Saskatchewan.

The CPR had been built, at tremendous cost, because of feared U.S. ambitions above the 49th parallel—and financial interests in London and Montreal saw railway building as a way to revive the money-making ways of the old fur trade route. Then the U.S. had bought Alaska, making a territorial sandwich with Canada as the tasty filling.

In 1865, John A. Macdonald, two years before becoming Canada's first prime minister, growled of the west: "I would be quite willing … to leave that whole country a wilderness for the next half century, but I fear that if Englishmen do not go there, Yankees will."

The European settlers still were too scattered, isolated in nature's elemental indifference. Their field work was a dispiriting cycle of trial and error because advice on how best to make this virgin land productive was not available. To survive, many of these men and women had to revert to tribal times, searching out wild fruit and game to augment garden produce and grain. Collecting and selling buffalo bones or finding occasional work on more established farms often was the only way to earn desperately-needed cash.

Alice had married Theodore Ralph Goyet, a Moose Jaw barber, on February 5. So, when Seager started out for Saskatoon, his mother was left alone. By all accounts, she was more than able to fend for herself.

Hopes high, the half-pint kid from Isle of Wight walked into his future blissfully unaware of the hardship and disappointments that lay ahead. The terrain was open prairie to the horizon, few trees or bushes, except along coulees, creeks, or at the damp bottom of slopes. He scuffed along beside Robinson's wagon which had a few dry poles slung underneath for campfires, making about two miles an hour.

A favoured resting place was below the "Indian grave" in a ravine with trees, shrubs and a spring of clear water, a good place to prepare a meal and let the oxen graze. Robinson pointed out on the prairie's edge a shallow depression and a few scattered bones and told the wide-eyed Seager that an Indian had been dug out by a former rival. The aroma of wood smoke and frying salt pork filled the air, and as soon as the flour-baking soda batter was browned in drippings, they dug in. This was washed down with tea, the beverage of choice for prairie travellers.

The trail crossed the wavy prairie to a steep hill at the Big Arm Valley, all spangled with flowers—blues, yellows, reds and oranges—through tall and medium coarse grasses flourishing from the absence of the vacuum-cleaner effect of a once 60-million-strong buffalo population—tall bluestem and sloughgrass, knee-high fescue and blue grama. A stout pole was inserted between the spokes of the wagon's rear wheels to lock them. Bouncing and jouncing down the hill, a load of four-by-four timbers at the top of the wagonload loosened and one toppled onto Seager. "It hit me on the top of my head, a glancing blow, and one of my teeth dropped out and fell to the ground."

A shallow creek traversed the valley, and the ground was soft. Poles had been laid down and the teams were coupled and the wagons pulled across one at a time. Here was shoulder-high green alder on which the buffalo used to browse. Here also was red-barked dogwood the big animals had liked to munch, and that Indians sometimes wove into baskets; they used the bark for smoking and red dye. Higher up, fragrant juniper hugged the ground, providing berries Indians often threw into their pemmican for flavouring, along with the bright-red fruit of pin cherries.

In this place, after the evening meal, Seager Wheeler probably settled down in the flickering light of a buffalo-dung campfire, hauled out his little concertina, and challenged the surrounding sea of black wilderness, delighting his companions when he played and sang. Such uncommon entertainment! "She was an Irish girl...," he could have crooned in his distinctive Isle of Wight accent, "...she was homesick and wanted to go home." Then, "I'll take you home again Kathleen...," the words reaching across the vastness until they could be heard no more, and still the empty spaces continuing in every direction for mile upon mile, soundless everywhere.

At first light they followed the trail through a range of low sand hills covered with scrub brush. Here Seager saw his first wolf willow, a silvery-leaved shrub of medium height blossoming with small yellow flowers that gave off a pleasant perfume. He felt a now-familiar stirring for the things that grew naturally in this land. Later in life, the scent of wolf willow always brought back memories of this trek.

Once this had been prime buffalo land. The prairie vastness had trembled night and day as the shaggy beasts—more properly bison, but few referred to them as such—moved in herds of tens of thousands. They opened in front of a line of travellers in carts or wagons and closed again behind, like water around a ship. Their stomping and bellowing could be heard for miles. "Every drop of water on our way was foul and yellow with their wallowings and excretions," wrote one homesteader. "The path upon which the animals travelled resembled a war zone."

Five years before Seager arrived in the territories the buffalo were gone. But in his travels across the prairies, he often stumbled over decayed droppings, or bones of the wasted animals. Bison dung fuelled campfires for generations; their bones were the basis of a fertilizer industry for decades.

When the buffalo were no more, the Indians starved. The white men's indifference to their plight enraged the Indians and many of them had thrown their lot in with Riel's rebels. Following Riel's victory against the North-West Mounted Police at Duck Lake just two months before the Wheelers arrived in the area, Cree warriors—despite the reluctance of their leader, Big Bear—were inspired to massacre the tiny settlement of Frog Lake. Chief Poundmaker joined Big Bear. But, shortly after Riel and his rebels were routed at Batoche, Poundmaker and Big Bear gave themselves up, Poundmaker to Gen. Middleton, who had won the day at Batoche, and Big Bear to the Mounties at Fort Carlton.

Seager and his companions stumbled on through the sand hills to the high land overlooking the South Saskatchewan River at Elbow Valley, the present-day northern tip of Lake Diefenbaker, about 30 miles northwest of Moose Jaw. They crossed the valley, climbed the other side and here the prairie grass was knee high. They pressed on for the next 40 miles to Wilson's cattle ranch at Beaver Creek. There had been no water between Elbow and Beaver Creek and the travellers all leapt into the creek to wash off trail dust and then happily jawed with Wilson's sons, Russell, James and Archie.

The final 100 miles must have been mind-numbing because there is no further description of the terrain or wildlife in Seager's notes. At Robinson's, Seager gladly accepted his offer of a meal and bed, before going on to Gus Lamonde's. They caught fish, fried them, made bannock, and set their plates on a packing case.

"I was young and always hungry from living and travelling in the open air all day," wrote Seager in his memoir, written in 1949 when he was 81 years old. "While we were eating, I noticed a peculiar and not fragrant smell. I mentioned this to Peter. 'Oh,' he said, before I left for Moose Jaw I skinned a skunk on the packing case.'"

Next day, at last, Seager reached his uncle's place, eager to start work, to learn how to farm, to earn the right to his own land. There were about two miles of frontage along the river. He noted that the riverbank was high with large poplar trees and bush. High-bush cranberry, saskatoon, wild raspberry, and chokecherry bushes were plentiful.

George Barrett, 49, formerly a sawyer back home in St. Lawrence on the Isle of Wight's south coast, welcomed his young nephew. He would leave for Moose Jaw the following spring to bring back to their own homestead his wife Sarah, 49 (Mary Ann Wheeler's sister), and their boys, Percy, 17, Fred, seven, and Will, six. Coming with them would be Seager's grandparents, Cornelius and Maria Wood.

Seager Wheeler had taken the first step this year of 1886 in the journey towards his new life. Those qualities of character that would determine the course of his future—optimism, adaptability and perseverance—were being brought to bear.

— FIVE —

Learning to Farm at Last

Military still engaging Indians—Lamonde's homestead dreary—sows first wheat broadcast, scythes hay, ploughs with oxen—unrelenting mosquitoes, fleas; plenty of game—army donates food—Big Bear and Riel—taxing adventure on horseback.

The racing adrenalin of a new country in alarm had slowed. A superhuman effort of political will, popular clamor down east, and profit-seeking had turned a continent-wide strip of real estate into a nation—a fragile tapestry bearing the woven slogan "Yanks Keep Out!"

As 18-year-old Seager Wheeler looked out over the river valley of his new home this early summer of 1886, the 19-year-old country called Canada had just stitched itself together with a thin thread of steel and quelled the North-West Resistance in a fairly robust way. Just about every community from Stonewall, Manitoba, to Halifax, Nova Scotia, had sent eager sons to fight the insurgents in a flag- and fist-waving show of patriotism.

Throughout the spring of 1885, every trail leading towards the rebelling Métis and Indians in the Saskatchewan Valley had been glutted with swaying military supply wagons, troop transports and plodding, dust-covered men. After Batoche, the military continued to engage Indians, and remained alert in case of further flare-ups. Camps still dotted the region, with bored soldiers waiting to go home; the break-up and return of so many units had to be staggered so the fledgling transportation network wouldn't be overtaxed.

The South Saskatchewan River flows from the Rocky Mountain glaciers and over eons has carved a gouge in the landscape before pressing on to Hudson Bay. The sight of this watercourse, its high banks irregular with tall-grass tussocks, must have filled Seager with admiration. Its implacable surge suggested not the power or menace of a stormy sea, but the unruffled vastness of an aloof nature, an unyielding land.

But the Lamonde farmhouse skulked at the bottom of a ridge near the water, as though hesitant to disturb nature's design, A single large room in a log structure blending into the bank with its sod roof. Nearby, paralleling the riverbank, was a sod stable for his oxen, Duke and Dime.

This was not the kind of homestead Seager had envisioned; there was hardly any sign of progress, of man reshaping his world. It certainly was not the idyllic scene pictured on pamphlets advertising free land in the Canadian west—pretty cabins shaded by tall trees, huge horse-drawn wagons loaded with wheat, the settler busy at the saw horse, bucking the stack of winter firewood.

Seager was put to work in a wheat field hand sowing and harrowing with willow branches to cover the seed. Quick and agile, he cut tall slough hay growing on the flat with a scythe and gathered it with a hand-made rake, the frame, teeth and handle all made of tough willow wood. After raking, he made the hay into round cocks for curing, then stacking.

Summer's special misery was mosquitoes. He couldn't believe their viciousness, their unrelenting appetites. From early May until autumn, no relief. Such a torment, they were Seager's favorite yarn years later whenever he talked of the old days. With every swath cut, mosquitoes rose in squadrons and attacked. He was sure they had a particular affection for him and joked he was the dessert following anything else they had fed on. The blood of people from the Old Country was thick, he insisted, and the mosquitoes loved it. At day's end, he was covered with bites and sores and climbed into his cot moaning, only to be attacked by fleas. They came from the pelts of foxes, badgers, jackrabbits and coyotes. Gus, George and Seager would wrap their legs with tanglefoot and walk about the room, trapping plenty of fleas, but never getting rid of them.

Big, yellow mosquitoes swarmed at sundown and were unrelenting through the night. A wormwood smudge was lit beside the doorway after work, and the men sought relief in the billowing clouds.

While ploughing, they were engulfed in a black cloud of small, gray mosquitoes that moved with them and settled on their necks and hands, despite the axle grease they had smeared on. Sometimes the mosquitoes panicked Duke and Dime and they ran wild. Then Seager had to untangle them, the plough and the harness, and get them back onto the furrow. Hoping to ease the beasts' discomfort, they would tie a tin of smouldering wormwood—a gray-leafed prairie bush that produced pungent smoke when burned—on the yoke or on their collars.

On the higher land above the flats, Seager broke his first prairie sod with Duke and Dime and a walking plough. Reins were not used, and he just hollered "haw" or "gee" to keep the lumbering beasts on line. Lamonde led the oxen to line out the opening furrow. Then Seager was on his own. When the first furrow was opened up, a well-trained team would automatically turn back for the next furrow. When the ploughshare hit a stone buried in the ground, up went the handle and up went lightweight Seager. They usually ploughed from seven in the morning until nine at night. On a good day, a full acre was turned over.

Seager was up every morning at five, sometimes earlier. Lamonde worked him and Barrett hard, and at nightfall he fell exhausted onto his straw mattress. He recalled years later: "For a beginner, it was no fun. Life in those days was not all honey and not all jam for me."

His life might not have been so bleak if, as the record suggests, Lamonde hadn't turned out to be a sour companion, not inclined to sociable conversation. Seager was his cheerful opposite. His blue eyes always seemed to be taking in more than there was to see; he wanted to know, to understand. While George Barrett was at the farm, there were some pleasant times. But when he left the following spring, Lamonde apparently still didn't put himself out to make his young helper feel appreciated.

Seager eventually saw that few farmers really knew what they were doing. Greenhorns asked a neighbor for advice and ended up copying all his mistakes and bad habits. There were no federal agricultural representatives; government people were busy attracting homesteaders, and had little time or inclination to help them once they had moved out west.

Soil testing was unheard of: the farmer was either lucky enough to settle on good land, or he wasn't. All was hit-or-miss, and the formidable process of establishing a farm cost him about ten years of his life. Maybe a third of those homesteading before the turn of the century stayed on. The others failed the challenge, or made a rudimentary farm, sold it for a small profit and left.

"Part of the problem lay with the settlers themselves," Gerald Friesen wrote in *The Canadian Prairies*. "Late seeding, drought, early fall frost, and simple mistakes such as sowing seed broadcast on the surface of the soil, where it shrivelled in the hot sun, were a source of disillusionment to many. Thus, the mid-1880s were a nightmare to pioneers."

The sense of isolation was at times intense. The teenager from the Isle of Wight could stare at the wide horizon and feel he was adrift alone on an ocean. The honk of a solitary wild goose tugged at him: it, too, knew of separation, dissociation. Such tests of man are the anvil of a culture, a remodelling of his soul. Author Wallace Stegner, who grew up farther south in the Cypress Hills area, offered an idealistic assessment of the land in *Wolf Willow*:

> "Desolate? Forbidding? There was never a country that in its good moments was more beautiful. Even in drouth or dust storm or blizzard it is the reverse of monotonous, once you get out of the wind, but learn to lean and squint against it… It is a country to breed mystical people, egocentric people, perhaps poetic people. But not humble ones."

They didn't know how to make bread, so Lamond would bake bannock. There usually was a good supply of game to eat, bush rabbits—tastier than jackrabbits—in stew, boiled or baked. Prairie chickens were abundant, and a never-ending supply of fish—goldeye, pickerel, pike, ling, sturgeon—could be hauled from the South Saskatchewan. Gus grew potatoes and a few vegetables. But still, young Seager wrote, he was always hungry.

Three miles down river at Clark's Crossing ferry, the Toronto Rifles were breaking camp to return East. They readily gave handouts from huge stacks of supplies, wooden cases of hardtack biscuits, sides of excellent bacon, soaked pig jowls, cases of loaf sugar, bags of granulated oatmeal, tins of bully beef.

Temperance society settlers at Saskatoon were often hungry. Occasionally they would go to the camp and gratefully load their wagons with food that the military generously supplied because, on the frontier, you always helped a neighbor. In the summer of 1886, Lamonde got one big wagonload to put in the cellar and for the next few months he, George and Seager enjoyed a more varied diet.

Early that fall, Lamonde's thirty-acre wheat field awaited harvesting. It was on a flat near the riverbank, sloping up to the base of the rise north of the house. The grain was cut with scythe or cradle, Gus Lamonde, Seager Wheeler and George Barrett taking turns with one or the other. Flashing blades, curving sweeps with lots of waist rotation and muscle flexing, up the long row, down the next, row after row, hour after hour in the hot sun, mosquitoes and black flies.

The scythe laid the sheaves down in swaths that were then gathered together into bundles. The cradle—with several curved wooden teeth projecting above the scythe blade—collected and deposited the grain sheaves already in a loose bundle. "It was a back-breaking job, more especially for me as I was not used to it, but I did my share." Tying up of bundles with wheat stems was mostly left to Seager.

The grain was fair game for "wheat birds"—Seager's name for the English chaffinch, possibly meaning Canada's evening grosbeak—blackbirds and gophers; in the race to steal the most grain, wild geese and crows usually won flat out.

Neighborliness on this rugged prairie was vital. Living within reasonable travelling distance of the Lamonde farm were: Mr. and Mrs. J.F. Clark, who operated the Clark's Crossing Ferry three miles downriver on the east side; and E. Malloy and his family on the west side of the river at Clark's Crossing (he operated a federal government telegraph station). A little way north of Clark's Crossing was a settlement of Caswells, John, Joseph and Dave, and their families; four miles south of Lamonde's, on the riverbank towards Saskatoon, were the Hunters and, nearby, the Hoods.

A keg of whiskey led to a small adventure for Seager. As he told the story, Malloy employed a young man as line repairer between the crossing and Humboldt station, 60 miles to the east. Malloy sent him to the Métis settlement at Batoche for a keg of whiskey. When he returned, he admitted he had gone on a spree at Batoche. To cover his tracks, he had watered the half-empty keg. He was fired. Gus Lamonde was hired until a replacement could be sent from Halifax.

"Whenever there was anything to be done that Lamonde didn't want to do, he sent me." Malloy wanted a government buckboard delivered to the telegrapher at Humboldt. It would be a 120-mile round trip, no settlement nor homesteader between Clark's Crossing and the station. There was no road nor trail, just the telegraph poles to follow.

Seager harnessed the pony to the buckboard, loaded up with a saddle, tether rope and peg, blankets, some bannock, bully beef, a few sticks of firewood, and a tin pannikin for boiling tea. He packed firewood because it was open all the way, rolling hills from glacial churning, with occasional small ponds or "prairie potholes" fringed with willows where he could water the pony and make camp. So off went the fisherman's son into the sea of utter loneliness.

Late that afternoon a thunderstorm, its green-black menace coming up from the west, was gaining on him. Dark engulfed him as the storm caught up. He unhitched and tethered the agitated pony, and in the now howling wind spread his flapping canvas groundsheet, covered himself with a blanket. He ducked his head under and, resigning himself to his fate, hoped his low profile offered less of a target for lightning forks which split the blackness with terrifying intensity and were accompanied by crashing, ear-splitting thunder and slashing rain which soon soaked through his meager cover and ran in torrents around his body. Sleep was impossible.

Towards dawn came silence, save for a soggy whinny from the pony, bedraggled and dripping. Stiff and light-headed, Seager made a fire. He sipped hot tea, ate a little bannock and—no longer soaking, just damp—was on his way. Late in the afternoon, he drove up to Humboldt station.

Mr. Anderson welcomed him and—what joy!—Mrs. Anderson prepared a hot meal topped off with cakes and tapioca pudding. He hadn't enjoyed such treats, he wrote, since leaving Moose Jaw. The telegraph station, built in 1878, was one of the better buildings he had been in for a long time—log construction, chinked with mud and roofed with sod, but shaped just like a real house. Crooked stovepipes poked from the roofs of the main building and lean-to, and a Union Jack flapped from a poplar pole nailed near the peak.

The Andersons pressed him to stay overnight, not just to be hospitable, but because they enjoyed his company. Though he had never ridden before, the youthful daredevil in Seager was excited by the coming adventure, riding a horse on the way back just like a cowboy. He saddled up, tied on his kettle, bag of food, blankets, rope and tether pin. After a few false starts, he was mounted and feeling confident. He had watched others riding and had a general idea. He urged his mount into a reluctant trot.

As night fell, so did the rain. Easing their way down a hill, the pony slipped in mud and fell, throwing Seager. There was nothing to do but climb back up and go on until he reached one of the potholes. He camped and made a fire with some dead willows at the water's edge. After chewing some bully beef, and enjoying once again some cakes Mrs. Anderson had insisted he take, he brushed away the hot embers and curled up in his blanket. The heat from the ground soon had his wet clothing steaming. Exhausted, he slept.

It had been tempting for Seager to stay the night with the Andersons. It was a treat for a young bachelor to visit a home where the wife would offer a proper meal and, especially, fresh-baked bread. It was like talking to a mother or sister when they asked about your day, and if you were getting enough to eat.

Up at daybreak, Seager ate breakfast and, so stiff it hurt to climb into the saddle, followed the telegraph line. About two-thirds of the way back he noticed one of the black poplar poles had snapped, no doubt due to the storm. He tied the pony to the next pole and, without tools, managed to work out the stump and set the pole back in place. Preparing to mount, he was momentarily unsure which way to go. He saw heaving prairie in every direction. He checked tracks in the grass and figured out the way he had come.

Aching in every limb, the inside of his thighs chafed raw, he trotted on, arriving back at Clark's Crossing at sundown. A blithe spirit, Seager had enjoyed the whole experience. He was no longer a "greenhorn" in the saddle.

— SIX —

Toughening-up Process

Lamonde unsociable, works Seager hard—threshing with flails in winter—sleeps in bed fully dressed, frost on walls—always hungry—falls through river ice—sleeps overnight in snowstorm, snowblind—deadly winter blizzards—Spring 1888, Seager gives up hope on Lamonde promises, returns to Moose Jaw—brother Percy comes from Isle of Wight.

If Gus Lamonde had been friendlier, or better company after work, Seager might have enjoyed his apprenticeship more. But Lamonde's dour nature was so oppressive that even the light-hearted Seager often felt unwelcome, unappreciated and a burden.

There may have been a deep psychological reason for Lamonde's bitterness. In *Images of the West*, R. Douglas Francis said early farmers struggling to conquer a resistant land often were transformed into cold, calculating, and harsh characters, like the land itself. "The struggle required self-discipline, self-denial, and a sacrificial effort that carried over into other human relationships, creating the same lust for power and need to conquer that was required to subject the land itself."

Later that summer, Gus Lamonde decided to enlarge his riverbank dugout. They would dig an adjoining 12' x 14' hole, line it with logs, and cut an opening through the existing wall.

"As Lamonde always had lumbago or a bad back when work of this kind was to be done, it was I who dug out this deep hole," Seager recalled, rare criticism from a man who throughout his life was known for his amiable, tolerant nature.

After laboriously pick-axing and shovelling all day in the hot sun, he would have looked forward to resting after supper, or going down to the river to set lines for fish, snares for rabbits and prairie chickens. But no, Lamonde kept him at work on the addition and other projects. At times it seemed that Lamonde was devising jobs just to keep him working late at night. More digging—Lamonde wanted two more holes in the riverbank for a chicken house and a piggery, in line with the sod stable.

By the time the hay and wheat crops were in stacks that year, snow covered the ground and it was threshing time. The snow was cleared from the ground near the wheat stacks, sheaves laid on the ground and beaten with birch or chokecherry-wood flails.

The straw was built up in a ring surrounding the threshing floor, as a shelter from the wind. Fingers stiff from cold, the men threw shovelfuls of grain and chaff into the air to be winnowed in the wind. Then they bagged the grain. It was miserable work, swinging flails, getting rid of the chaff and bagging, all day long until dark, day after day. And it was disheartening going into a frigid house after all that work. "I do not know what amount of wheat we threshed as I then was not very interested," wrote the future World Wheat King.

Young Seager must have missed the gentle climate of those sea cliffs he had left behind. They ate, they stoked the stove as full as possible (poplar wood didn't last long) and they burrowed under blankets, wearing overcoats and moccasins, piling anything warm on top. By daybreak, the blankets were white with frost from body heat and their breath. Rime blanketed the inside walls. Anything in the room that could freeze, did.

In late winter, when their stored food was finished, meals were limited to bannock with milkless tea. The bannock was cut into squares, a precise amount for each man. If the always-hungry Seager felt peckish, he had to wait for the next meal.

Near the end of March 1887, Gus and Seager set off on a three-mile hike along the winter road, across the river, and on to Malloys to deliver some things they had picked up for him in Saskatoon. The ice appeared to be solid. Lamonde carried two fork handles. Seager, big sacks of sugar under each arm, stepped off the trail to walk around some jagged ice, plunged through, and one of the bags sank in the frigid water. As he made a grab for it, the relentless pull of the current tugged his legs under the ice. "Lamonde shouted in language not in the dictionary to let the sugar go and grab the fork handles. I managed to get hold of them and he pulled me out." Dripping wet, he quipped through chattering teeth: "There goes a packet of sugar to sweeten the Saskatchewan River."

As he sloshed onward, Seager's clothing stiffened and he could hardly walk. He put on dry clothes at Malloy's. He could always be cheered by food, and happily tucked in to a big meal with hot tea, then spent the night, warm and dry and full. Next day, his experience had become a "lark." And he had another story for his repertoire.

They ran out of flour for bannock early that spring, and decided to take a sleigh-load of wheat to be ground at the Duck Lake gristmill, on the east side of the river. They loaded the wheat, hay for the oxen, food and blankets, crossed the river at Clark's Crossing, then headed for Alex McIntosh's farm 25 miles farther on, where they would stop for a break. Seager led the way in an ox-drawn cutter sleigh with four bags of wheat. Gus warned him not to lose sight of the faint track in the snow. Soon the wind picked up and menacing gray clouds scudded overhead. They squinted into heavy, slanting snowfall, and as the day darkened, drifts built up. They pushed on until nightfall.

"There was no bush or any means of making a fire, it was just open prairie. We tied the oxen up to the sleigh. We had only one blanket apiece and had to lie down on the snow in our clothes. We lay rolled in our blankets side by side. In the night the wind got up, and in the morning there was a bank of snow between us."

They set off again, stiff and aching. They could not stop shivering. Towards dark, after two days of bucking snowdrifts, and another night curled in the snow, Seager complained, "If we don't soon get to McIntosh's farm it will mean another night out. I don't know if I can stand another night of it." Soon after, in the faint dusk light, he saw a pole fence. Years later, he recalled shouting with relief, "Here we are, a port in the storm!"

Hot food and drink warmed their bodies and spirits in front of the stove as they described their ordeal to Mr. and Mrs. McIntosh. She joked later that Seager and Gus drank fourteen cups of tea and ate all the food in the house.

Next day, they gave up the idea of continuing to the gristmill, and went instead to a nearby farm and traded wheat for flour. It was sunny and clear on the return trip. But Seager paid a price—keeping his eyes on the faint trail had left him temporarily snow blind.

Winter was the crucible. Death by freezing was not rare. Seager experienced the worst blizzard of the 64 years he would live in Saskatchewan the following winter. The storm raged for three days and nights, the temperature dropping to 60° below zero. All that time, Duke and Dime and the pony in the stable were without feed or water, while the men, huddled by the stove, listened to their bawling:

> "In those early days it was very dangerous to leave the house when one of these blizzards was raging. Although the stable was only a short distance from the house, owing to the fine, whirling, suffocating snow one could easily miss his way thinking he was going direct to the stable. He might miss it by a few feet or yards and once past, he was hopelessly lost."

By late afternoon of the third day, Seager felt his way past the chicken and pig houses to the stable. Nearly suffocated by whirling snow, he struggled to pull the door open, stumbled inside and fed the animals. Going out, he tried to shut the door, but the wind blew it off the hinges. He inched back to the house exhausted. Next morning, the wind had died, the sky was clear and cold. He took the animals to water at the well on the far side of the flat.

Back in Moose Jaw, his mother was worried stiff. Her correspondence, always beginning, "My dearest Seager," wrote Elizabeth Wheeler in a biographical sketch, *Lil Wheeler: Her Story*, would often contain a dollar bill or several coins, stamps, envelopes, and candies or nuts at Christmas.

"She sends him a cover for his bed, telling him to air it first, another time a shirt and trousers. When she cannot find his gloves she sends her own. 'Oh, how I thought of you in that dreadful blizzard, and all the days and nights, and how did those poor dumb things do.'"

Spring of 1888 came, and he had given up hope of Lamonde ever keeping his promise to help him get a homestead. His mother urged him to return to Moose Jaw, and that was all the prodding he needed.

"I had got neither satisfaction nor money from Lamonde, not even a postage stamp. Mother used to send me my stamps and clothing and sometimes a pound or two of tea with one of the settlers coming back from Moose Jaw. So I decided to return to Moose Jaw where I could earn some money sufficient to make an entry on the homestead I had in mind. This was opposite Lamonde's farm on the west side of the river."

Fortunately, young Charlie Lake, of Clark's Crossing, was driving his team of horses to Moose Jaw and he welcomed Seager's company. Two days from their destination, "We still had some flour and a tin of corned beef. I was the cook and the best I could do was, after we had made tea in the pannikin, use it to boil some water and mix in the flour and corned beef. It was pretty gluey but on the trail one can eat almost anything."

When he walked into the house after a two-year absence, "my mother didn't recognize me until I spoke, I was so bit up by mosquitoes and my face black from the smoke of the campfire and dust of the trail."

He was overjoyed to be reunited with his best friend, his 21-year-old brother Percy, along with his grandparents, Cornelius Wood, now 74, Maria, 73, George Barrett's wife Sarah (Mary Ann's sister) and her three boys.

The game immigrant boy now was a young man of twenty years, wiser, disappointed but more experienced, still short and wiry but muscled and much stronger. At first, he hadn't been used to the back-breaking labor, but he had performed manfully. He would come to appreciate in later years those first two years farming on the frontier, how they toughened him and taught him.

SEVEN

A Place of Their Own

Works two years to earn money for homestead—borrows $200 from Temperance Society, buys wagon, oxen, supplies—brother Percy builds boat, takes to farm site on Saskatchewan River—summer 1890, Mary Ann and Seager set out on 180-mile trip to first homestead, Seager walks—live in tents; buys milking cow.

Hurry up and wait was the story of the next two years. The siren call of a home of their own was as seductive as ever, but their priority was to make money.

Home was now a small house his mother had built on a lot near the outskirts, in a shallow ravine. She had little money, so presumably she had help from others. After working a while, Seager bought two adjoining lots, a questionable purchase, perhaps, when he was saving for a homestead, but obviously he couldn't resist the urge to plant.

"I dug some of this piece of flat prairie and going up into the creek, I dug up some wild currant and gooseberry bushes. After I had got the sod into shape, I planted these bushes and set up a lath fence around them. During a rain, the water from up the creek ran down the shallow ravine and was held in certain low spots. The following spring, I planted flowers and vegetables." This garden did very well, even the following year when hot, dry winds caused some local wheat crops to fail.

During a visit in 1945, "I noticed Moose Jaw Park and it occurred to me that it was somewhere about the place where our home used to be, and where I had dug my garden," he wrote. "I decided to start up from the lower part of the park where ducks were swimming in the pond. By following the ravine, I came to the spot where I first had my garden. There was a gardener working among the plants and flowers. I stopped and chatted. He looked surprised when I told him I had turned the first sod in the park."

This compulsion to plant, he said in a magazine article in 1919, went back to the Isle of Wight where "my early recollections are of the work of gardeners planting trees, shrubs, and gardens, floral and vegetable, transforming the wild plants into gardens and banks. I still have vivid recollections of those things and they left an impression on my mind that has never faded."

Some of the few grain farmers in his area were discouraged by the 1888 drought, and didn't plant the following year; but those who did were rewarded with a heavy yield. Seager realized that "next year" was the motto unlucky farmers had to adopt, in what author James Gray was to call "The Land of Beginning Again and Again."

After 18 months as an engine wiper in the CPR roundhouse, Seager switched to bridge construction work. He awoke in his work-train bunk the first night to find a man beside him, insensible, reeking of liquor. He didn't know if the drunk had stumbled into the wrong bunk or been put there as a joke, but he saw no humour in it. He never could abide drunkenness, and had seen too much of it on the prairies.

The bridge gang carried timbers for the carpenters and often repaired small earthen dams holed by muskrats. Seager didn't lack confidence and was convinced that the foreman always addressed him when issuing instructions. He liked the workers, enjoyed their rough and friendly rivalry. Some were from Ontario's Bruce County, others from Huron County, and each faction argued good-naturedly that their county was best. When there was an opening, brother Percy was taken on. Both were sent down to Virden, Manitoba, where their sister Alice now lived with her husband, Theo Goyet.

"We were sawing logs by the pump house and the foreman came out to chat. We asked him if he knew our brother-in-law, the barber. He did. So Percy said that he was not going to cut hair any longer. Why not? asked the foreman. He is going to cut it shorter, said Percy, trying to keep a straight face, before we both burst out laughing."

Shifting heavy timbers was harder work than Seager had expected. He could earn more money—$6 a day—loading box cars with buffalo bones gleaned from the great deposits on the surrounding prairies, which would be sent to the U.S. to be ground up as fertilizer and for bleaching sugar.

His last job was clerking in a general store. Since most of the money earned was used up in living expenses, it must have dawned on the Wheelers that they would be wasting time staying any longer in town. Seager sold his lots and put the proceeds with the little money they had saved. In Saskatoon, he contacted Thomas Copeland, agent for the Temperance Colonization Society that had founded the town, and took out a loan of $200, giving a lien on his future farm until the money was repaid. Forty-two dollars was deducted as interest in advance for two years.

There is little doubt that if the Wheelers had made the same move a year earlier, they would have been just as far ahead. The delay was just another cost of inexperience.

Land was free, yes, but homesteaders had to get to that land. And, of course, they must erect shelter, and try to plant enough vegetables for winter storage. They needed equipment, animals and supplies to keep them alive until some land was broken and the first crop planted and harvested. Settlers were told that $750 to $1,000 was the minimum needed to begin farming; those with $3,000 or more would find the going relatively easy. The Wheelers must have chuckled ironically.

Prices for equipment when the Wheelers arrived in the North-West Territories were as follows, according to *Saskatchewan: A History*: "double waggons, $65 to $75; Red River carts, $10 to $15; iron-bound carts, $30 to $35; buckboards, $50 to $75; waggon harness, $30 to $40; cart harness, $6 to $10; single harness $20 to $30; Canadian teams, $250 to $400; native ponies, $50 to $80; yoke oxen, $150 to $175."

On borrowed money, Seager was optimistic and ready for anything. He haggled over a second-hand wagon, and a team of broken-in oxen. And for $40, he bought a walking plough with a single cast-iron share—the most important implement for a homesteader.

The Temperance Colonization Society was not doing him any favor. It was one of several colonization companies that had sprung up with inducements from the federal government. The society was made up of Toronto Methodists who signed up 3,100 aspiring settlers for a site on the South Saskatchewan River. But to get a loan towards a homestead entry and equipment, the applicant had to sign the pledge, which Seager did, easily.

The teetotalling settlers were frustrated, though, in their zeal to create a drink-free community. The colony's grant of 200,000 acres, spread along both sides of the South Saskatchewan River, comprised just odd-numbered square-mile sections of land, said Douglas Hill in *The Opening of the Canadian West*. There was no way they could prevent hated drinkers from moving onto the free-homestead even-numbered land adjacent to each of their sections.

This situation arose from the federal government's decision at the time of Confederation to retain responsibility for all western prairie lands and natural resources, a source of complaint for generations to come. No other provinces lost control of their land. The constitutional move, many complained, was part of a National Policy designed to use the West to enrich the whole country, meaning Eastern Canada. The policy covered railways, settlement, establishment of the North-West Mounted Police, tariffs, freight rates and Indian treaties. Ownership of these lands was not handed over to the western provinces until 1930.

Way down in Ottawa, Sir John A. and his cabinet wanted to steal the Americans' thunder and blunt their expansionist thinking by offering free land to immigrants from the Old World. To help establish its dominance, the federal government instituted a land survey dividing the West into square-mile sections as was done in the U.S. The survey did not disturb the long, narrow Métis river lots established much earlier in Red River along the Assiniboine, the Red and several smaller streams.

In all, 25 million acres were set aside for the CPR and another seven million acres for other railroads, according to *The Canadian Prairies: A History*. Just over 56 million free acres ended up in the hands of homesteaders; another 60 million acres were open to purchase.

The dominion's settlement plan was struggling. It had attracted people such as the Wheelers, but the overall population increase of North-West Territories was slow. As Seager and his mother prepared to plod the trail north, many other English-speaking settlers were leaving, some having improved their land and sold at a profit, others finding the life too hard.

Now that the word was "go," Percy was almost as excited as his brother. A thought amused them: why not build a boat and carry it across the prairie? It would be handy—essential—with the South Saskatchewan River running past Seager's new property. Percy, being the family shipwright, eagerly started work. By the time he got the small craft built, an 18-footer with Isle of Wight lines, it was late spring. Now they would deliver the boat and prepare the site before their mother made the journey.

The Wheeler boys put the boat on the wagon in place of the box, loaded their supplies into it, and at first light, spirits high, hitched Buck and Bright and trundled off, squeaking and lurching, at the average rate of travel for oxen of 15 miles per day. About 10 days later, they crossed the river at Saskatoon by ferry. Mountie John Donkin wrote of 1884 Saskatoon in *Trooper in the Far North-West*. Promoters of homesteading often were carried away: "an illustration of Saskatoon … tall chimneys were emitting volumes of smoke, there were wharves stacked with merchandize; and huge steamers, such as adorn the levees at New Orleans, were taking in cargo." But the true Saskatoon was "six houses at intervals, and a store." Since the railway had arrived, there were now two stores in the village.

Another 18 miles and they reached their destination on the bank of the South

Saskatchewan River, in the District of Saskatchewan. "Upon our arrival at my homestead, Percy and I set up our tent and made a small jetty to which we tied the boat. For drinking water we used the river. For the jetty we cut some trees near the river and as at some time a big flood had washed away some bridges, we noted that some planks and boards were lying here and there on the shore. We took a few days towing the boat up the river and gathered what boards were stranded. When we got as many as we wanted, we fastened them together, picking them up as we came back and towing them to the landing place." Then they returned to Moose Jaw. Soon after, Percy went to Brandon to find work, staying for two years.

A few weeks later, Mary Ann Wheeler sat on a chair near the middle of the wagon box as it "set sail" on a north-by-northwest course heading into the sea of tall-grass prairie, her son walking alongside. She sat straight-backed and serene, buoyed by faith in her trinity—steadfastness inherited from forebears; her son's determination; unflagging confidence in herself. There's no doubt, this island woman harboured a stubborn will to survive and succeed.

This summer of 1890, after five years in western Canada, she sat surrounded by everything they could afford for starting a new life: bags of flour and other staples; an iron cook stove; two tents; pots and pans; axes and saw; hammer and nails; boxes of assorted goods and basic household items—and the all-important plough. They had been careful not to exceed the load limit for oxen of from 500 to 800 pounds. Little Pincher—an Irish and Scotch Terrier cross, "sharp and quick as a weasel"—trotted close by, tongue lolling, tail wagging, with occasional yelping darts away after prairie dogs.

"*To the West, to the West, to the land of the free, where rivers of gold run down to the sea*— these fancies as I then pictured them were far different to the stern reality, as it proved hard, uphill work for many years," Seager would write in *Farmers' Magazine* in 1919. "But I was young, and filled with an ardent faith and ambition. I found that (faith and ambition) was about all there was to live on."

Occasional numbered wooden pegs that government surveyors had pounded into the soil, to mark off each square mile, enabled newly-arrived settlers to find their quarter sections. Many of the farmsteads in the southern belt along the east-west CPR railway were taken up. Wheeler was heading across no-man's-land for the edge of the northern park belt.

During their creaking crawl along the trail at the oxen's top speed of two miles an hour, the Wheelers had seen not a single person, coming or going. Mrs.Wheeler had bedded down in the box each night, her son beneath the wagon. Squealing and howling coyotes close to their camp had kept them awake and his mother nervous. The travelling tired her.

At last, Seager could make out the site of their farm on the riverbank. Now, here they were, mother and son, at the land they had dreamed of since leaving the Isle of Wight seven years ago.

— EIGHT —

First Years in Own Home

Digs riverbank road to haul water—shelter built in riverbank—lives with oxen and cow—ploughs few acres—plants perimeter trees, builds stable-roothouse—barters for pony—survives first winter near starvation—builds better house—cuts hay, firewood.

A young man with Seager Wheeler's imagination and enthusiasm, placed beside a surging river on a heart-grabbing stretch of land all his own must have been bursting with eagerness to fashion a dream of years into reality. Here were the two of them, Seager and his mother, on soil laid down over aeons and subjected to prowling scouring winds and weather extremes, stretching beyond eyesight, suggesting promise of crops and a measure of comfort when worked by a competent person. The swells of the sea of grass hid a great variety of birds' nests, teemed with small animals, and fired the inquiring mind.

His sense of history was sharpened knowing that just nine miles northeast lay Batoche, scene of a recent epic Canadian struggle. He had no doubts about his abilities. He had learned much about survival on the prairie over the last five years. He had worked hard for Lamonde, and now he would work twice as hard knowing his efforts all were directed towards shaping a new life for his mother and himself.

What a vast property they now were taking hold of to make their own. A quarter section of prairie land, the northeast quarter, section 16, township 38, range 4, west of the third meridian—all of it theirs! And, once again, they lived on a "cliff" by a body of water.

They set up their tents and cook stove. They unloaded supplies and equipment, putting it all under shelter. They soon found that the tents kept rain off, but, "What a trying experience for mother to try and bake bread when the wood was wet."

Wilderness, yes, but not complete isolation. The Caswell farms were in the same general area, and Seager eventually would hire out to John Caswell at $1 a day for haying and threshing, $2 for stooking. Farming south of Lamonde's on the east side of the river were the Hunters and, farther north, the Barretts, Blackleys and Stevensons.

In the flush of their pleasure at being "home" at long last, Seager and his mother may not have analyzed the bleak, wind-swept prairie overlooking the South Saskatchewan River that July 20, 1890. There wasn't much natural cover. Not far from the tent there were bushes along the riverbank and trees at the bottom, near the water. To the west, there were few trees in sight for miles.

Here on this homesite they would soon learn more about the true nature of this harsh land that had known only wandering food gatherers from time beginning. They remembered the mortal dangers of the heavy seas off the Isle of Wight; but they would come to realize that the perils in this place were just as great. Not yet were there the wind-breaking obstacles of planted tree lots, shelterbelts, fences and buildings; the malevolent winter blizzards would howl across the frozen terrain unchecked for hundreds of miles. In summer and fall, high grasses stretching beyond the dry horizon could catch a lightning bolt and burn into thundering maelstroms of flame, neutralizing anything in their path. Each year, Seager would find, he had to plough fireguards around his homesite.

A few days after their arrival, Seager, Buck and Bright made the journey back to Saskatoon where he borrowed another $50 from Thomas Copeland. He paid $40 of this to W. Bates for a red shorthorn milk cow named Bossie. Six years old, she would prove a good milker, giving an average eight quarts a day.

In August, Bossie dropped her first calf, Daisy. Seager took his cows to John Caswell's for servicing, $3 per cover. In 1891, Bossie and a new cow Bess produced Jacko and Jumbo; in 1892, Bossie and Bess had Minnie and Sandie; Bossie, Daisy and Bess, in 1893, dropped Alice, Dick and Dave (died); Bess dropped Ralph in 1894; in 1895, Prince, Duke, and Bill joined the family. Prince was traded for Alma.

These details of daily life were kept in small notebooks starting in 1890. He noted, in 1896, sending $1.40 by post to The People Office, Milford Lane, Strand, London, for The People Musical Portfolio. The entries are cryptic, barely legible. "When dad was in a hurry," his daughter Elizabeth said, "he just scribbled."

On the other hand, a self-bound notebook he made in Moose Jaw, with a first entry dated December 28, 1889, displays handwriting that is flowing and clear. This volume, the first page illuminated by Seager in green, blue and red, contained clippings and hand-printed inspirational poems, Salvation Army hymns, musical notations and scales, suggesting that he had learned to read music after joining the Army.

Seager found living in tents an agreeable novelty for a while, rather like a character in the adventure stories he had enjoyed as a boy. But vital jobs had to be done before winter. Toiling for days with pickaxe and shovel, Seager fashioned a road down the riverbank wide enough to take his wagon, and angled so that the grade wasn't too steep for his oxen to haul barrels of drinking and washing water up from the river.

Where to build their house? They chose what appeared to be an old Indian camping spot on a rise of land by the riverbank. They considered a large ring of stones embedded in the ground and decided it had at one time anchored a teepee. Indians should know what's best.

Eagerly, he dug into the bank, as did the prairie dogs all about, forming the shape of a room roughly 16' x 12'. Digging the holes for Lamonde's buildings had been a thankless, back-breaking job, but now it was *their* house he was working on and he would have relished every swing of the pick, every shovelful he threw back. He cut poplar poles, hewed one side flat for the sills, and laid them down against the bank at back, and along the sides. The walls were filled in with upright poles, all spiked. "Pains were taken to stiffen the corners so that the building would be rigid." He was keeping in mind the heavy, blizzard-piled snowdrifts that would be coming for sure. Their floor would be the bare earth. He hooked up Bright and Buck and ploughed a few long furrows of virgin prairie, and cut them into thick sod strips roughly three feet by one foot to be laid over brush as a roof.

He plastered between the wall poles, inside and out, with a mortar of mud. He hoped it would be warmer than the larger room he had shivered in for his two miserable winters at Lamonde's. Perhaps unwilling to admit it, Seager basically was following his relative's example and owed him something for that.

The window he had brought from Moose Jaw went in the southwest corner where the stove, a table and chair (he would sit on a box) would be placed. At the same end, on the northwest corner, he left space for his mother's pole bunk.

"The door to the building was at the southeast corner facing the river. The oxen and cow were tied up to a manger on the north side, so that coming in the door at the southeast corner we passed the animals and went along the south wall to reach the kitchen on the southwest corner. It certainly was not very elaborate, but we would be sheltered for the winter. The animals helped in some measure to keep it warm."

It was rudimentary, but close to fire proof, cheap and quick to erect. It took skill to construct the shelter so it wouldn't collapse of its own weight. A major shortcoming was that a "soddy" was vulnerable to rain: a three-day downpour outside meant a five-day rain inside, the saying went.

But it was *their* soddy, and they were happy with it. They would live in the earth and grub in it. Mrs. Wheeler tried her best to feed them well that first winter with meager staples: flour, sugar, oatmeal, syrup, salt, baking soda, and tea. She baked bread and Bossie gave milk for rib-sticking porridge. She cooked whatever game her son could shoot and the vegetables she had stored. It was nutritious fare while it lasted, but the winter was long and supplies ran short.

Hungrily but good-naturedly, they may have recited a popular pioneer refrain: "Rabbit hot and rabbit cold, rabbit young and rabbit old, rabbit tender and rabbit tough, thank you, but I've had enough." That winter, Mary Ann Wheeler spent much of her time near the stove, keeping the fire going, cooking, reading, writing letters, patching and re-patching their clothing.

Because Seager planned to build a log house and outbuildings the following year, he cut trees on the other side of the river that fall. During the winter, he hauled the logs across the ice, snaked them up the road he had hacked out of the riverbank, and piled them. He hewed them flat on each side ready to set up after spring ploughing.

This Saskatchewan Valley was a region of few boundaries other than the North and South Saskatchewan rivers. It was a harsh land of high sky where temperatures could soar to 110° F in summer, and plummet in winter to 50° below zero. There was just a handful of villages not sited along the railways. These included Prince Albert, the biggest settlement in the territories, Battleford, Saskatoon, Batoche and Yorkton. Along the South Saskatchewan were a few settlements of Métis.

The same year that Seager made it to his homestead, the Regina-Prince Albert Railway designated a future townsite 38 miles north of tiny Saskatoon. On May 15, the track-laying train arrived and workers pounded in a sign between the rails and the infinity of flatness to the west, reading "Rosthern." This settlement-to-be and the young man from Isle of Wight would find their futures inextricably linked in what would prove to be one of the most fertile wheat farming areas of the Canadian west, the west which would come to supply more than 60% of the country's vast yield. Rosthern after the turn of the century would be the greatest shipping point for locally-purchased grain in the world.

The tough, unyielding winter went its way and the tough, unyielding prairie had to be ploughed. Turning his first sod, releasing the rich soil that had mouldered there for centuries, was an act of faith for Seager Wheeler, the most dramatic step towards establishing his farm.

"I had one of my [Barrett] cousins help me line out the first furrow." Bright was aptly named because once the furrow was opened he kept to it. Buck would wobble and step outside and Bright had to pull him back. Up and down the field, row after row the oxen strained with Seager clutching the plough's handles to keep it from tipping sideways. The cast iron ploughshare, only half an inch wide, turned over just a narrow band of soil, and at the end of that first long day he had, to his chagrin, broken just one acre.

Tough roots held together the turned-over strips, and it was advisable to let the sod rot through the summer so it would break up more easily the following spring and take the seed better. He broke only the area he thought he could manage, then started on the garden and construction work.

Writing and receiving letters were Mary Ann Wheeler's great pleasure. In some early account books, her penmanship was refined, and she was said to have a nice turn of phrase. She was delighted when a post office was established on William Hunter's farm four miles south on the other side of the river.

They were encouraged by the steady advance of rail lines webbing the vast western spaces. German, French, Danish, Swedish, American, Mennonite, Hungarian, Jewish and Romanian immigrants were setting up widely separated settlements. The frontier was quickening.

Later on, Seager would introduce himself to Mr. and Mrs. George Langley and their four sons when they got off the train in Saskatoon, after emigrating from London, England. Seager helped them find a farm near Osler, about a mile north. He also taught them how to trap for furs. George Langley's sons ended up farming near Maymont. Their father was elected to the legislature and, in 1912, became minister for municipal affairs.

Recognition as members of the Canadian conglomerate came in 1887 when North-West Territories pioneers took part in their first federal election. West Assiniboia voters elected Nicholas Flood Davin, owner of the Regina *Leader*, in 1883 the first newspaper in Assiniboia. The next year, two senators were appointed for the area. Then a federal Act provided for a 22-member elected legislative assembly and the struggle for responsible government in the territories began. In 1891, Ottawa increased the assembly's membership to 26 and, for the first time, they would be elected.

But the day-to-day problems facing settlers required local decisions. School districts were the first successful form of local government. Rural municipalities were too complex a system yet for the pioneer society, only four being organized so far, according to *Saskatchewan: A History*. There was no agreed-upon method of making a village into a town, so few towns were incorporated before 1901.

This summer of 1891, Sir John A. Macdonald fought his last election. The 76-year-old Conservative appealed to a fragile Canadian nationalism, putting his record and his dream on the line. Should Canada, he asked, be a strong, independent nation, or become increasingly dependent on the United States with no future but annexation as, he decreed, the Liberal insistence on free trade would make it.

The old warrior won, but exhausted himself. He died soon after, his shortcomings apparent to all, but was honoured for a stout heart, goodwill, and a consuming determination to create a Canadian nation.

During Seager Wheeler's second summer on his homestead, 11 Mennonite families set up a small colony near the townsite. They were families "seeded" from a larger Mennonite community in Manitoba. Although the "Rosthern" sign now was flanked by a railroad water tank, there was no railway station nor loading platform, no place to buy food or hardware.

Wheeler, recognizing the need for windbreaks, planted box elder (Manitoba maple) seeds around the perimeter of his garden. Then, by the riverbank, he built a sod stable with a root house at one end. He wasn't satisfied yet. "Now we had a cow, we needed a milk house. I dug out a hole near the house about 10' x 12' wide and 3' deep, set up a ridgepole and nailed light poles down to the ground. This left a grass shelf on which to put the milk pans to set cream. When the house was finished, I put in a concrete floor."

Barter was the norm in these cash-strapped times, so he traded a two-year-old steer to a Montana cowboy for a pony and her colt. The pony, Duchy—which lived to the age of 37—dropped a filly later that summer.

The Wheelers were ready to come up in the world. It was time to build a permanent house and get out of the riverbank, and there would be rafters to form a pitched roof with more headroom. This time, it would be large enough for a small living-room, kitchen, two bedrooms and a small storeroom that would double as a sleeping place on the happy occasion a visitor might stay over.

"Having hewed the logs ready during the winter time I was ready to start to set up the logs. First I laid down a sill, a thick heavy one all around on the ground. Then I set up the corner posts," held rigid by boards he had found in the river. "I set the hewed logs cut to length and spiked them down. As the logs were only the height of seven feet they were easily handled alone. I placed each log upright closely together and spiked each one in place top and bottom until the walls were up, leaving a space for the door and window, which were put in when the roof was on." The roof rafters sat close together covered with brush and hay. He cut sods that "were very pliable, yet tough, so that I could lift a sod length resting on my arms as they did not break if handled carefully. This made a reasonably warm roof. It was a pitch roof with gable ends of logs."

No mud for plaster this time. Lime cost 25¢ a bushel so Seager made his own. He dug a deep hole in the riverbank, made an opening at the bottom, and filled it with firewood. From the top, he alternately layered limestone picked up along the river, and wood until the shaft was full, then covered it with thin pieces of sod and started a fire at the bottom. Before long, he had a good supply of lime that he mixed with sand from the river's edge.

Also along the river were stands of a fine willow, about the thickness of a pencil, straight and clean to a height of 10'. He cut and stripped these and nailed them to the walls diagonally as laths. He plastered the walls smoothly inside and out. Then, to weatherproof the outside walls, he applied stucco, apparently mixing cement with plaster.

What a relief to be living above ground and able to move from room to room! The milk house was close by and cool enough in summer to keep the butter Mrs.Wheeler made and packed in wooden tubs. For breakfast, dinner and supper they drank their own rich, fresh milk with homemade bread and butter. They shipped by rail what butter they didn't need to Garland's Grocery in Portage la Prairie, Manitoba, in exchange for groceries shipped back in the fall. A couple of years later, they had enough excess that Seager could take eggs and butter to Sinclair and Leslie's store in Saskatoon.

Getting more land under cultivation, with so little equipment and no help, was frustratingly slow. So he did as much as he could and hoped for better progress the next year. He cut and stacked winter hay for the animals. Now, where to get the winter's firewood? He hitched up the oxen and struck out west, travelling all day before he found some poplar bluffs. After sleeping under the stars, and breakfasting on prairie chicken fried in bacon fat, he hefted his bow saw and started to cut and load a stand hit by a prairie fire and now hard and dry. He finished in moonlight, and set off at daybreak with two cords, arriving back home that evening. He made two more trips and after six days of marathon cutting had six cords, enough to keep their stove blazing all winter.

Seager needed 48 hours in the day to get all the jobs done on the homestead. How did Mary Ann Wheeler, now 49, fill her days? Well, her workload must have taxed her large store of resolve and ingenuity. She tended and harvested the vegetable garden if a hot, rainless summer, early frost, plundering animals and birds, or a prairie fire that jumped the fireguard didn't foil her efforts. She would have prayed for their continued good health, knowing that if an accident or a medical emergency arose—typhoid and smallpox still broke out in the settlements—there were no doctors or nurses nearby. She milked the cow, churned butter, baked bread, preserved food for winter, chopped kindling, kept the fire going, worried about her son, and encouraged his efforts, while striving in winter to give them both regular meals each day from sometimes scanty supplies. When they were out of flour, they ate boiled wheat laced with rich milk or cream, or boiled turnips. When they ran out of coal-oil and candles, they would open the top door of the stove and read by firelight or, sometimes, from the light of a wick in fat in a shallow pan.

In summer, nature was bountiful but competitive. There were few stands of wheat in the area, so geese would attack Seager's small crop. He would sit on the riverbank and shoot them as they crossed over. He did the same with sandhill cranes, which he called wild turkeys. Migrating geese flocked in such numbers that at times Seager and his mother, standing watching, could not hear each other speak. It was common practice to set foot-high stakes in a field and string them with binder twine, leaving openings at intervals. Confronting this barrier, the geese would walk along it until they came to one of the openings, honk happily, and step into snares.

In the fall, when prairie chickens were plentiful, Seager shot them from his doorstep. Later, when they no longer depended on them for food, he never hunted animals or birds. He caught many types of fish in the river, but his favorite was what he called ling, or buffalo fish. They weighed six to nine pounds and had few bones. They were eaten fried or smoked. "The fish was white and laid in flakes similar to halibut. The liver was delicious."

"I used to set a couple of lines with two hooks, one above the other, and a stone for a sinker thrown out into the river in the evening. We could usually depend on hauling in one or two in the morning. After they were cleaned, I cut them down the back and laid the two halves open and sprinkled a little fine salt on them. There I would leave them on a board until the evening when we smoked them in a barrel. They came out a nice light brown, equal or better than any finnan haddie as they were caught fresh. I certainly did enjoy them, and mother too."

One evening he set two lines for goldeye. Next morning, he hauled a line in and "realized I had something pretty heavy. It was a sturgeon. He was so big I was afraid he might get away. I left him there while I pulled in the other line and I realized I had another one as large as the first. They were some four or more feet long. I had a two and a half bushel cotton wheat bag and I put one in head first. His tail stuck out a foot or so. We tried to eat one but didn't fancy it so gave it to Lamonde. The other we gave to the telegraph operator, Mr. Malloy. He was delighted with it. That was the first and only time I caught sturgeon."

When the ducks were migrating, Seager walked out with his shotgun, shells in his pocket and optimistically carrying a two-bushel jute grain bag. When he came home and dumped the load of birds on the kitchen floor, Mary Ann probably cheered the hunter, and then the two of them would get to work picking feathers, saving the down for pillows and quilts. Then she would boil water in a large pot and dip the birds just long enough to loosen the tough wing feathers. After these and the pinfeathers were pulled, the birds were singed, drawn and washed, and ready to be roasted or preserved. Seager Wheeler didn't hunt for sport: he hunted to live.

— NINE —

Give It Your Best, Move On

No money for seed—early frosts hit Red Fife wheat—summerfallowing—wheat to gristmill for flour—Russian roulette on river ice—falls through ice—eagle grabs dog—herd grows—vegetables to 1893 world's fair—success with barley, brome grass—Lamonde quits—threshing gang tells of better soil at Rosthern—Percy back from Brandon with banjo—Mary Ann winters in North Dakota—Percy moves to Rosthern.

For some Canadians, "the Gay Nineties" was a decade of frivolity, but for the Wheelers it was a time of halting "hunt and peck" in their struggle to make a living from poor soil during poor growing seasons. They prized their wide-horizon sunsets, the sun-split azure skies, spring's ever-hopeful greeting from returning meadowlarks, and autumn's haunting Canada geese farewell—but on balance, the scales would tip to the sheer weight of a place that was not for them.

A patched and gaunt sodbuster in the Territories had one aim—to plant some wheat and sell it for cash. That spring of 1891, Seager Wheeler was ready to plant his first crop, so he made a deal with neighbor John Caswell to help him rake and cock his slough hay in exchange for some seed wheat. He had to make do with the only seed Caswell could supply, White Russian, an out-of-favour variety of soft grain imported years earlier into the Red River Settlement in the search for hardier stock.

Selkirk Settlers had been the first to sow wheat in the West, in their plots alongside the Red and Assiniboine rivers, but they had abandoned the soft White Russian and Club wheats for Red Fife a few years before Wheeler started planting. Red Fife flourished in western soils. But it was not early maturing, so was easy victim to early frosts, and the search continued for varieties more suitable to western Canada's climate.

Wheeler was gleaning practical ideas from other farmers. But, from the start, he went his own way when it came to handling the seed he was going to plant. There were so many factors he could not control, but he was determined that his grain would have all the growing advantages it was in his power to provide. He would strive to produce only the best.

Before sowing his first crop, he wrote later, he painstakingly picked over the bag of seed, removing impurities by the light of a coal-oil lamp at the kitchen table. He was following a line of thought that had occurred to him while working for Gus Lamonde, who had sown unclean wheat seed, and always had plenty of weeds and coarse grains come up as well. He planted in ground that he had given the best possible cultivation. And then he waited. Almost with bated breath, he waited for the first germination, those soft, green shoots. When they came, he watched and fussed, rooting out stray weeds and anything else that he saw as a threat to his first crop, on his first landholding in this wild country where he was pushing down his own roots. About this time, perhaps because it helped him to concentrate, he started to smoke a pipe.

He hadn't heard about it yet, but the year he arrived in the Territories, an important farming technique had been stumbled upon. En route to Batoche, Gen. Middleton had sent to the large Bell wheat farm near Indian Head to replenish his supply of horses, with the agreement that they would be returned to cultivate the land in the spring of 1885. They were brought back too late, and so the land lay fallow all summer. It was sown with wheat in the spring of 1886, a drought year. Wheat sown on stubble was a failure; but a good yield came from the land that had lain fallow, because the previous year's rains had accumulated and been saved for the next year's crop. Two years later, an experimental farm was set up at Indian Head and it soon reported that the best method yet developed for saving moisture in this dry territory was summer fallowing.

At this time, because Manitoba now was a big wheat-producing province, the Winnipeg Grain Exchange was established, an enterprise that would have a mighty influence on the lives of western farmers.

That fall, Wheeler decided it was logical to have most of his wheat milled into flour. As bracing coolness flooded the plains, he and his uncle George Barrett, and Gus Lamonde, each took a load of wheat 50 miles to the nearest gristmill. It was Indian Summer. He revelled in the calm, mild, sunny days and frosty nights travelling through a forest preserve, following the old Indian trail, shooting ducks, prairie chickens and rabbits along the way, cooking and eating them at warming campfires, then probably playing the concertina and singing until, finally, falling asleep.

They stayed in Prince Albert several days, sleeping under their wagons, while the grain was gristed into flour, bran and shorts, the by-product of wheat milling used for feeding pigs and cattle. Two weeks later, they were home again, each with a supply of flour to last the coming winter.

"By this time, I had grown potatoes, swede turnips and other vegetables. We were usually short of food except for bread, butter, cream and milk. Mother had some poultry by this time, but not many. In the summer the mushrooms were fairly plentiful which we used to fry and stew. Mother also made a good supply of mushroom ketchup."

If fresh conversation was not always available, a prized substitute now came into their lives. Their love of books was requited following the musings of Ishbel, Lady Aberdeen, and the alacrity with which some Winnipeg women responded to her ideas.

At the time the Wheelers trekked to their homestead in 1890, Lady Aberdeen, before her husband became governor general, had toured the west by train. She was shocked by the "settlement in the raw… May heaven preserve us from ever being fated to banishment to the far-famed wheatlands… Oh the inexpressible dreariness of these everlasting prairies… Nowhere yet on the prairies have we seen even a geranium pot, or a young tree planted…"

According to her biography, *Ishbel and the Empire*, she asked a group of women at Knox Church, in Winnipeg, "Could you not get the names of newcomers from the immigration agents and forward them from time to time such papers, magazines, books as you could get together. There must be many such in Winnipeg… And if you could add a packet of flower seeds you would foster the love of beauty which can lift up lives engrossed in material needs."

Her biographer, Doris French, wrote that within weeks the Aberdeen Association for Distribution of Good Literature to Settlers of the West had been organized. "Year after year, monthly parcels were sent to many hundreds of farm homes." After a decade, there were branches of the association from Halifax to Victoria. Ishbel persuaded the CPR to transport the parcels from eastern Canada without charge.

Although Miss Cornelia Nicholson occasionally sent books of a theological nature from the Isle of Wight—and the Wheelers were interested in the subject—they now enjoyed more variety in their nightly reading, thanks to Lady Aberdeen's efforts. Seager's daughter, Elizabeth, remembered her father as a great reader when she was growing up. "He was never idle," she wrote in *Old and New Furrows*. "In winter he bound magazines into books; he wrote, he read, he developed his own photographs. Every spare moment was spent in reading, even at the table for which we were often glad as it gave us a chance to say something. For if he were not reading he was talking, always telling us something: boyhood days in England; the glories of the British Empire; things he had read or seen or heard. Though his academic schooling was completed at the age of 11, he never stopped learning. He knew, or appeared to know, of what everything was made and told us."

Here on his own piece of land, Seager played a kind of Russian roulette with the fast-flowing South Saskatchewan River, unlike in most things, where he was careful. Was his risk-taking here a proxy for manhood, for accomplishment where progress was so difficult, the insouciance of youth? We will never know.

Desperately hungry—they had even eaten gophers—Wheeler couldn't cross the crumbling spring ice for groceries that Lamonde had brought them from Saskatoon. He "said nothing to mother as I knew she would not let me cross, but decided to take a chance and started across, stepping from one cake to the other … suddenly an ice block fell apart into long needles… I was up to my neck… I could feel the whole body of the ice blocks surging up and down and I with it." He had swum a lot in the sea and was good at treading water. "When I tried to get on the cakes they would loosen and fall apart. I at last got on a solid one… I turned back and my feet went so fast from block to block … my clothes were covered and stiff with ice, I could hardly climb the bank. Fifteen minutes later I saw the ice moving down the river. Next morning, the river was free of ice. It was foolhardy on my part, but in those days we had to take big chances." Was he embarrassed? That day's entry in his diary included a terse statement in smaller, fainter handwriting: "Fell in river."

He crossed the ice to Lamonde's early the following winter and, "with no one to talk to for so long," stayed too late and spent the night. Wheeler's relationship with Lamonde must have altered. Perhaps, now that they were equals, they had more to talk about. Wheeler returned home next morning, riding Duchy and with groceries on his shoulders. Sun had softened the shore ice and the animal went through, both of them floundering in the cold water. The pony swam gamely to the bank, but Wheeler, holding on to his groceries, had to one-hand his way to safety.

His next misadventure was his last, perhaps because his mother was watching. Their flour had run out, and Lamonde had got them some more. "I walked across the ice to

Lamonde's but again I stayed too long… My mother was sitting up our bank. I picked up the sack of flour on my shoulder and started across. I broke through and mother shouted, 'Never mind the flour, let it go!' But not me. I hung on to it and managed to get to shallow water and walk to shore." That was the last time, on foot or horseback, that he tried to cross the river ice in spring or fall.

When he launched his boat in summer, though, he considered himself master of the river. No matter the rough currents and waves when a strong wind blew and "made quite a little sea," he would shove off and row with certainty. At times, just as at sea, the boat would dip into the trough of waves and to those watching from shore, be out of sight. He might be a homesteader now, but the blood of those generations of seafarers still flowed in his veins.

"I was by circumstances a free ferryman. When neighbors from the other side wanted to cross they yelled for me and I went and brought them to my side in the boat. Most times I had to take them back later in the day." They sometimes asked him to row with their horses and cattle swimming in tow.

Once or twice a week, weather permitting, he rowed his mother across, accompanied by little Pincher, front paws on the gunwale barking, and the two walked the eight miles to and from the post office. They had tried shutting him in the house, but he usually got out somehow, swam the river, and ran to greet Mrs.Wheeler on her way back, so Pincher got his way and was a regular on the mail run.

The little dog was an ideal friend for those difficult and relatively lonely years. He asked for little, and offered devotion and companionship to both Seager and Mary Ann. He appealed to their senses of humour, and his escapades gave them much to laugh at afterwards, and stories to tell their friends. Some might say this enthusiastic bustle was an example of a little dog taking on the characteristics of its master.

Bald eagles with their seven-foot wingspan were seen all along the high banks of the Saskatchewan on the lookout for the plentiful fish and small mammals. Pincher was running just ahead of Wheeler one afternoon when one dropped down, sank his talons into the dog's back and, mighty wings swooshing, rose into the air, Wheeler shouting and throwing his hat. Pincher was wriggling and snapping and, about 15 feet up, the eagle let go and the little dog fell.

Not until the next day did they find him, burrowed into a straw stack, still shivering and whining, two holes in his back, one each side of the spine. Pincher soon got over his close call and went on to new adventures. He was a devoted friend, and a link to Wheeler's Ventnor boyhood, until his tail stopped wagging in 1900, at the age of 17.

Animals could supply comic relief from the intense business of staying alive in an unforgiving milieu. That spring, Buck had "blue lice" and Wheeler was told to rub kerosene oil in his coat. "When I had finished, he looked so comical. He had a leather strap around his horns with a tie rope. He staggered and the strap moved to one side making him look for all the world like a soldier in the early days who wore those round forage caps set to one side of their heads. Rolling along he reminded me of a soldier under the influence of liquor. We all roared with laughter.

"The next day (his hair) had fallen out in the night and he was bald, showing the blue skin. I was told that I should have put soapsuds with the kerosene, or milk. But there surely was no lice on him after that dose."

Word came one winter evening that Mary Ann's 79-year-old mother was not expected to live through the night. Wheeler attached his most reliable ox, Bright, to the jumper sleigh and headed across the river. "It was one of those starlight nights with a light misty sky when everything on the ground was white. If one left the faint trail they would never find it again. We saw a star and mother wanted to go towards it as she thought it was the Barrett house light. But I knew my directions. I led Bright almost all the way." They arrived just as Maria Wood died. Grandfather Cornelius Wood died a year later, and both were buried on the George Barrett farm.

In a few years the Wheelers had a small herd of cows and calves they free-ranged. Bright and Buck, on their Sunday off, would roam for miles south along the riverbank where there was greener, thicker grass. They were followed by the herd, and Bright would lead them all back to the boat landing and then up the winding path. This was fine until the vegetables were growing tall in the nearby garden. Bright loved vegetables. But so did the Wheelers. They couldn't risk losing one cabbage. So they kept a close eye on Bright when he neared their precious garden.

Wheeler had selected ground part way down the bank for his vegetables, and grubbed out the bushes and small trees. He made three descending terraces, levelled them and prepared the soil for planting. This site was a microcosm of the Isle of Wight's Undercliff, the higher riverbank protecting from the wind, the slanting bank absorbing the life-giving sun.

Silt from the river made the soil particularly fertile and, with Wheeler's natural bent for growing things, each year produced huge cabbages, carrots, beets, cucumbers, peas, squash and various herbs to flavor fish, fowl and salads. The second or third summer, he wrote, most of his potatoes weighed up to a pound each, and some were as heavy as two pounds, measuring 18 inches around. The year the first agricultural society was formed in Saskatoon, Joseph Caswell stopped by to ask for a collection of vegetables to send to the 1893 world's fair in Chicago. Wheeler included two squash he could just get his arms around.

"I had so many jobs to do and was so handicapped by want of equipment and cash, that I could not make much headway alone at bringing the land into good shape and getting more land under cultivation. It was a gradual, step-by-step process."

From the Indian Head Experimental Farm, Wheeler obtained seed of Canadian Thorpe barley introduced by Dr. William Saunders. The house was on a high riverbank that lost its snow cover early in the spring. Nearby he sowed the barley on new breaking and it ripened the last week of July, with large berries, plumper and meatier than he had ever seen. One year, the barley had grown rank and fallen flatter than if a "steamroller had passed over it." A few heads only were still standing, "and these I selected for a stiffer and stronger straw." He still was growing this barley 20 years later, with never a crop failure. It was a "sure cropper" that he had refined.

From 1911 to 1926, he would win 19 first prizes for his Canadian Thorpe in Regina, Denver, El Paso, Saskatoon, Peoria, Kansas City and Chicago.

It was disheartening for the Wheelers and the Barretts when Lamonde gave up the struggle in 1893. He owed money for farm implements and saw no prospect of making his farm pay. The soil, like Wheeler's, was mediocre, and he decided to try his luck in Winnipeg. If Wheeler knew what happened to Lamonde after that, he never mentioned it in his writings.

The Wheelers were struggling as well. In 1893 and 1894, Wheeler hauled his harvest, trip after slow trip, to Clark's Crossing, loaded the grain into a freight car, and got 35–40¢ a bushel in return. In September 1895, a barley crop bright green in the evening was dead black from frost next morning and there was nothing for feed or seed. He had to buy seed in Manitoba.

His second last wheat crop on the homestead was small, but excellent. John Caswell cut it, and Wheeler worked 18 to 20 hours a day for four days stacking stooks for the threshing machine.

"I went to work early with oxen and a basket rack made of poles eighteen feet long. I didn't have far to haul the sheaves as it was on a field close by. I had to do the job of two men. Not being able to be in two places at once, I had to climb up the rack and throw the sheaves down, then climb down and stack them, then up for more sheaves and so on. I built two big stacks. At supper time I quit for a bite to eat and then went at it again until midnight. At daylight, I was up again."

He was delighted when Percy came back from Brandon in 1896. His brother brought a new banjo, new tunes, and was raring to play. It was a happy winter, the brothers together again, Percy's banjo and Seager's double action concertina—which could be played in any key—enlivening the long nights. They often visited neighbors to play for dances.

But their mother had been invited to spend the season in Jamestown, North Dakota, where Alice and Theo Goyet had moved in 1892. Alice was due to have her third child. Seager and Percy drove her to Clark's Crossing, near today's Warman, to catch the train.

In her first letter home, Mrs.Wheeler wrote about the drama of her trip south. When the conductor, Mr.Elderkin, came to collect her fare—which the Goyets had helpfully sent—she couldn't find it. She must have lost the money on her way to the train. She broke down and cried. The conductor patted her on the back and went through the coaches to collect donations from the other passengers.

Mennonites had settled for 20 miles along the railway line between Clark's Crossing and Rosthern, and late in 1896 their small steam-threshing outfit came down to Osler and offered to do Wheeler's crop. There were only a few such outfits in the North-West Territories. They were kept busy because few farmers could afford their own machines.

The threshing gang's equipment rolled into his wheat field. The chug-chug of the engine's flywheel and a whistle toot announced that it was time to begin work. The steam engine puffed into position by the stacks, followed by a wagon carrying its fuel—straw. Florid from the heat, the fireman forked straw into the firebox. When everything was set up, the engine facing the separator, the heavy belt stretched full length and slapped into place, all the pulleys and belts snapped merrily into action, producing a primitive music, an orchestra of one cadence, one volume, a kind of allegro fluttertongueing. Bundles were dropped in, the grain was gathered.

The Rosthern gang stayed over, and relaxed drinking tea and swapping stories. "Percy and I played music the whole night through. We never went to bed. They surely enjoyed it." Buoyed by the good time—and maybe they wanted to attract musical talent to their town—they told the Wheeler boys of much better land at Rosthern. Percy decided to go there the next spring. He made entry for an abandoned homestead on which he lived and prospered until he died in 1944.

By spring, Bossy had dropped another calf. The brothers had broken in two steers over winter so that Percy would have a team to work his new land. He bought a second-hand wagon and lumber for a granary, at $18 a thousand board feet, and set off.

Mrs. Wheeler returned refreshed and in good spirits. What a holiday it must have been, getting to know her grandchildren and having another woman to gossip and laugh with. She had many stories to tell.

When she read Percy's enthusiastic letter from Rosthern, she agreed with Seager that there was only one course of action—follow Percy and buy some CPR land on "easy terms." If reports were correct, they would have better crops at Rosthern, easy access to the railroad; their lives would be more pleasant near a town, with more neighbors close by.

And there would be no river to cross.

TEN

Journey Into a New Light

Seager, 29, Mary Ann, 54, pull up stakes in 1897, move to Rosthern—hopes still high; live year in granary with Percy—Clifford Sifton woos immigrants—Saunders seeks earlier maturing wheat strain—grain elevators spring up—frontier Jubilee celebrations big success—Seager borrows $10 for payment on land, breaks first sod—cuts logs in winter for house—invents contraption to help in seeding; builds house—life shows promise.

They cast ghostly moon-shadows following the main trail, faintly visible in the quarter-light, which led from Saskatoon north to Batoche, across the river and beyond Duck Lake. Sitting straight and alert despite the late hour, reins tight in her hands, wool shawl about her shoulders, 54-year-old Mary Ann Wheeler drove the wagon. Seager rode Duchy, driving the small herd of cows, calves and Duchy's filly. They had set out in the May moonlight buoyed by anticipation and optimism, but must have felt a pang for the almost eight years of struggle with little return on the homestead by the river.

Lost in their own thoughts, Seager Wheeler, now 29 years old, and his mother rode on in their two-mile-an-hour world until dawn's faint light defined the horizon to the east. They stopped to rest the animals, stretch their legs and have tea and a bite to eat. As the sun rose, they continued the winding journey into a new light.

In 1897, after a dozen years in the "last best West", if their expectations had been tempered by painful adjustment, their hopes still were high. Toil, leavened with freedom and equality, was like a drug, difficult to give up. Their vision encompassed a simple but noble life where one might become a contented and productive being, in a pleasant place. The mother and son were not starry-eyed; they had seen that this land could, and often did, break the human spirit.

The new federal Liberal government's Clifford Sifton was sending out thousands of pamphlets to entice immigrants, soon would be sending millions. These pamphlets avoided negative words, using "bracing" rather than "cold." Men who worked in the West's climate were more virile, more apt to be of sound mind and body. The Wheelers saw this mythology for what it was—the West was no New Jerusalem.

The country they now were passing through had softened and was such a contrast to the place they had abandoned. Poplars were more abundant, prairie flowers were all about them, the scent of wolf willow pervasive, and at the edge of sloughs, and here and there, were tall trees—many of which would be doomed once cultivation became common. Wheeler pledged to himself that when he settled again, he would plant plenty of trees. He recalled the piquant flavour of wild plums when at a certain full ripeness back in the Old Country, in Pelham Woods, "kickseas" they had called them; he would plant wild plums, too.

Still adrift within an empty, indifferent pale, they wound towards an uncertain future, never envisioning the wonderful events ahead for Wheeler, and for his chosen homeland. The seeds were being sown from near and afar, although the harvest was yet years away.

Settlement was picking up in the North-West. Red Fife wheat was the dominant strain being planted, but it was subject to frequent early frost damage, particularly in the more northern regions. If only it had a growing period shorter by a week or 10 days, growers could beat the frost; wheat with excellent milling potential too often ended up as pig feed. Ottawa had recognized the need to develop a superior type of wheat.

Back in the mid-1880s, the government had asked plant breeder Dr.William Saunders to conduct a survey of experimental farms and stations in United States. Saunders's report, tabled in the House of Commons in April 1886, called for a Canadian program, and two months later establishment of five experimental farms was authorized. Saunders was named director of Ottawa's Central Experimental Farm, and land was acquired for farms at Nappan, Nova Scotia; Brandon, Manitoba; Indian Head, NWT; and Agassiz, B.C. By 1888, Saunders was busy, along with sons Charles and Percy, attempting to hybridize that better and earlier-maturing wheat.

In 1880, five years before the Wheelers arrived in the Territories, only 57,000 acres of western land were seeded to wheat, 6,000 in North-West Territories. By 1890, this had grown to 860,000 acres yielding more than 16 million bushels. The West, clearly, was good for more than furs, and the money-makers down east were catching on. But no one was talking about Rosthern, few had even heard of it. The district was considered too far north for wheat growing. No wheat could survive the frosts there. Manitoba was king of the wheat-producing provinces, Winnipeg was capital of the West, and in this more southern region, Red Fife still was seen as the wonder wheat of the country.

There were 90 grain elevators and 103 flat warehouses in the West at this time, with a combined storage capacity of 4.2 million bushels. Ten years later, according to Grant MacEwan's *Harvest of Bread*, there were 454 elevators and 126 flat warehouses. Farmers were being relieved of the time and effort required to load freight cars from wagons; to fill a freight car, for hours they had to shift 650 bags of wheat weighing 120 pounds each onto their shoulders and stack them in the railway car.

The market for Canadian wheat in Britain was expanding due to a long period of short-sightedness by British politicians who didn't care what happened to their agriculture sector. They believed that if farmers became unemployed, they simply would go to the towns for work. Latter-day Victorians were ignoring the future.

"The men of theory," wrote G.M. Trevelyan in *English Social History*, "failed to perceive that agriculture is not merely one industry among many, but is a way of life, unique and irreplaceable in its human and spiritual values."

The decline in British agriculture increased in 1875, when wheat acreage fell by a million acres. In the decade up to 1881, the farm labor force fell by more than 100,000. Whole regions were laid down to grass. This was followed by a second wave of agricultural depression from 1891 to 1899. When the demand for bread increased, Britain had to import more wheat.

Day was dying when the way-worn little expedition neared Percy Wheeler's farm five miles east of Rosthern. He was just three miles west along the trail from Gabriel's Crossing, that fabled ferry site on the South Saskatchewan that in earlier years was operated by the man who would be Riel's general, Gabriel Dumont. A half-mile before Percy's, they stopped for a meal and exchange of news with former neighbors, the Langleys. Some years after the turn of the century, Seager would buy this half section for $30 an acre to grow more grain and compensate for land converted to orchard.

Then, they pushed on to Percy's on the southwest corner of Section 2, in Township 43 A, Range 2 west of the third meridian. They stayed with him a year, until they settled on a farmsite of their own. Percy had not yet built a house, so the three of them lived in his new granary.

Civilization has many aspects, and 1897 saw new evidence of this in the West. Responsible government was established in the North-West Territories. Frederick Haultain was named president of the executive council of the Territories, in effect premier. Wilfrid Laurier, the first French-Canadian Liberal prime minister, had won office a year earlier. The country had gone through four Tory prime ministers in five years after the death, in 1891, of Canada's guiding architect, Sir John A. Macdonald. And now it was the Queen's 60th year on the throne, a royal spectacle never to be repeated, the first to be observed throughout the countries of what would become the British Commonwealth. Jubilee celebrations were popular throughout Canada. The sense of country and belonging was strong and everyone within many miles of Rosthern, though most were newcomers, "foreigners," eagerly took part in observing the Diamond Jubilee.

Rosthern was still very small, 40 or 50 residents, but the town was decorated, and a sports day was held followed by a dance. Seager and Percy Wheeler were two of the few English-speaking settlers but they left their granary home and helped organize the sports and provided music for the dance.

"It was a typical frontier gathering," said an article in the Rosthern history, *Old and New Furrows*, "Tobias Unruh, who had lived in Rosthern for many years was living at that time near the site of the present town of Hepburn. Mr.Unruh owned the only organ for miles around, and on the Jubilee Day, he loaded it into a wagon and brought it nearly 20 miles to provide music for the dance. Mr.Unruh played the organ while Seager Wheeler played the concertina." And, of course, Percy played foot-stomping banjo. For a long time after, the Wheeler boys were invited to play for all the dances in the district.

From Jubilee Day on, Rosthern grew and prospered. Farmers poured into the region. It was the beginning of the end of the depression that had begun in the early 1870s. South of the border, the wild frontier had been pushed into the western ocean, and before long Canada's northwest would be the attraction, the land of opportunity. American and European settlers would flow in at such a rate as to change the northwest from a sign of empty failure to a beacon of success and hope.

It would fall on Laurier to truly move Canada from colony to country. His minister of the interior, Clifford Sifton, had proved a wily pied piper to the world. In 1896, according to *Saskatchewan: A History*, just under 17,000 immigrants came in, the next year 32,000. Many were from the U.S. where Sifton opened nine offices and displayed the newly-developed hard wheat which had been grown successfully on the prairies.

Four miles out on the trail from Rosthern, after checking several likely locations, Wheeler settled on a CPR property—the southwest quarter of Section 3, Township 43A,

Range 2 west of the 3rd meridian—on the section adjoining his brother's farm. It was on a correction line (where, it was said, all the mistakes of the surveyors were dumped) and consisted of 190 acres rather than the usual 160. He paid $3 an acre, to be paid off in 10 yearly instalments.

The Wheelers were six miles south of the most historically significant and travelled route in the northwest, the Carlton Trail. This route, scored by the shrieking wheels of Red River carts, the hooves of horses and oxen, the plodding feet of buffalo-skin-clothed Métis traders, began at the Red River Settlement on present-day Winnipeg's Portage Avenue, and stretched more than 500 miles northwest to Edmonton. Red River and Edmonton were the two largest concentrations of human beings in the West, before the railways and telegraph opened it up. Lesser trails, such as the one crossing the South Saskatchewan at Gabriel's Crossing, and then skirting Wheeler's farm, linked up to the Carlton Trail. Others led northeast to Cumberland House and, by way of the now joined north and south branches of the Saskatchewan, on by water to Lake Winnipeg and then the Red River settlement.

The initial payment on his land was $10. Wheeler negotiated a loan of $10 from the CPR station agent, H.A. McEwan, promising to pay him in the autumn when he would sell a cow.

Repeating the steps taken on his original homestead, he first broke ground for a garden, and then as much as he could for the next year's crop. He and Buck and Bright broke 20 acres on a field half a mile long. He hired out to work for a neighbor in return for discing his broken ground. In the fall, he broke a little more land. The "prairie wool" virgin grass on his farmland was thick that year and he stacked as much as three tons to the acre for the animals.

He had no money to buy lumber for a new house, so he used what was at hand. When not ploughing, he cut logs at the river and hauled them to the house site. That fall and winter both he and Percy devoted most of their time to gathering more logs, and augmenting their food supply by shooting the abundant rabbits and prairie chickens. Dark, cold mornings heard them yelling to spur on their slow-moving oxen on the way to the river; and again in the evening, after a long day felling and cutting. They hewed their logs flat on two sides so they would be ready in the spring.

When the snow melted, and the trees leafed out, Wheeler made a deal with his neighbor, Jacob Friesen, to seed his first crop on 20 acres in return for half the harvest. But, having no seeder, subsequent crops still were seeded by hand. "Only narrow strips could be seeded at one time as it had to be plowed under quickly before the birds could eat it up."

But the result was uneven ripening of the crop. Wheeler did some serious thinking. He made a set of V-shaped runners from logs, several placed side-by-side, and fastened together. He hauled this contrivance over the ploughed land to make "corrugations" so that the broadcast seed would fall into these furrows and be more easily covered by the harrows. He made a drag of logs to finish the surface. Makeshift, primitive, but innovative; anything to get a more uniform crop.

"The pressing need for the bare necessities was imperative. We were concerned not so much in making a fortune out of the soil, as this was never thought of in even the wildest of dreams, as we were making a bare living. It was a problem to keep body and soul together, just a struggle for existence."

Wheeler started his third house. He laid poles for the roof and covered them with hay, then three-inch-thick sods. With no willows for lathing, he chinked the open spaces with wood. He mixed sand and white shell-littered clay from a nearby slough, and plastered both the outside and inside of the walls. The mixture set hard as stone and years later, when he built another house, the inside plaster was still intact. He whitewashed the outside with white clay. This ran a little in the rain. The end result was a snug house with parlor, kitchen, two bedrooms and a storeroom.

Now, mother and son had their own humble roof over their heads again. They had come to know their close neighbors, the B.J. Friesens and the Peter Abramses, enjoyed their company and appreciated their helpfulness. There was a pleasant town close by where his mother could go with him to browse, shop and exchange news with people they met.

Life was showing much greater promise.

— ELEVEN —

Life Blossoms at Maple Grove

Plants shelter belts—Red Fife frozen, misses farm payments—short of food—disillusioned farmers organize—CPR warns of foreclosure—good crop, back payments cleared—hires Henry Partridge—roof fire self-taught grain selection by lamplight—seeks wheat that matures earlier—band practice, music big part of life—borrows for machinery—hires another farmhand—mother dies, Seager and Henry on their own—secretary-treasurer of Rosthern council—decides to marry.

Thirteen years after coming to western Canada, Seager Wheeler, now almost 30 and penniless, again was starting from scratch. Yet, there is nothing to suggest he was discouraged. He threw himself into the struggle with his typical enthusiasm. Maple Grove Farm, as he called his new property, was not going to be left an unprotected, wind-swept expanse of prairie; once again he began planting shelter-belts—but on a grander scale—and, here and there, solitary tree and bush specimens.

This was the period in which he would set his life course. Learning by doing had meant false starts, but now he would pick up compass bearings and sail into smoother waters.

Nearly every tree and shrub was planted from seed. He started hedges of southernwood (a scented, gnarled shrub from the wormwood family), caragana, Russian poplar, and willow. Along the lane leading to his house—a long lane first used by oxen, then horses, and eventually cars, trucks and tractors—he planted Manitoba maple saplings.

In 1899 the Rosthern Agricultural Society was formed to exhibit purebred cattle, grains and produce. Among the first members was Percy Wheeler. There is no record of Seager's involvement until 1932, when he was listed as a director.

On January 22, 1901, the Wheelers would have said prayers when they heard that Queen Victoria had died at Osborne House, on the Isle of Wight. She was buried in her wedding dress, as she had said she wished to be dressed when she rejoined her beloved Albert. In Canada, 101-gun salutes were fired in nine cities; Toronto tolled its bells, business was suspended and all flags were lowered to half-mast; there were public displays of mourning. Many of the almost 3,000 inhabitants of Saskatoon attended church memorial services.

In the fall of 1901, nature threw a new curve at Seager and brother Percy. Their Red Fife did not begin the ripening process as early as usual. They waited days, with no sign of ripening, unsure what to do because both still were novices, and were learning through trial and error. More days passed until Seager, fearful of finding frost at every morning inspection, cut and stooked his crop. When the threshing machines went to work, what little grain they got was very lightweight. The reason: both fields were blighted with stem rust. They weren't alone in their misfortune; all the crops in the district suffered. It was so bad Percy set fire to his stooks.

After those time-consuming, boring and jolting trips between Clark's Crossing and Saskatoon, seated behind oxen with their measured, slow steps, Wheeler appreciated the relatively short five miles he now travelled to stores in Rosthern. At Unruh's, he paid $5 for a suit of clothes; 30¢ for a straw hat; four yards of patterned cotton cretonne for his mother's curtains cost 65¢. Two pounds of tea cost $1; four pounds of fence staples, 20¢; two pounds of putty, 20¢; seven window lights (glass panes), $1.75; tobacco, 25¢.

Most of the good homesteads around Rosthern had been taken up by 1902. But the settlers and land buyers kept coming and, of course, this forced up prices on improved land. So some farmers could now sell at a profit and establish new farms farther from town, and for the first time buy machinery with the money left over.

Western Canadian society was maturing. The demand grew for an organized farmers' group to counter perceived unfair practices, and a protest meeting was held at Indian Head, just east of Regina. A draft proposal for an organization was drawn up, and later approved by the territorial government. Thus the Territorial Grain Growers' Association was formed on February 12, 1902.

Way back in 1883, Manitoba farmers had protested they were being paid less for their grain than it cost to produce. Freight rates were "exorbitant" and tariffs "oppressive." Farmers had always been able to load CPR grain cars directly over the platform, but in 1897 the railway operators had decreed that all wheat delivered must go through elevators. The farmers saw in this the danger of price-fixing, fraudulent grading and monopoly. A government royal commission was set up to look into these complaints.

As a result of this inquiry, said John H. Archer in *Saskatchewan: A History*, in 1901 the Manitoba Grain Act came into law, applying as well to the Territories, and allowing farmers to continue loading directly over the platform and to oversee the weighing of wheat.

But that same year, all along the CPR's main line in the West, farmers harvested their best crop on record. They all rushed to ship their wheat before the huge quantities brought down prices. The railroad could not handle the volume. Elevators all along the line were full. By November, it was obvious the bumper crop could not be handled that year. Many farmers had to store their grain at home, as best they could.

Brinkmanship was still the norm for Wheeler. In early days at Maple Grove Farm, his Red Fife was frozen out two years in three, before it was ready for harvest. Frost-damaged wheat brought 25¢ or less per bushel. By 1902, he had three times missed the yearly payment of $60 to the CPR for his land. The railway's land company threatened him with foreclosure if he did not pay immediately. But because he had a promising standing crop of Red Fife, he explained his situation to the Imperial Bank manager at Rosthern, and asked for a loan to cover the three payments, suggesting a lien on the crop for the amount. The manager obliged, the crop was not hit by frost, and the loan was paid off. He never missed another payment.

At times they still ran short of food. And yet, their new location offered so much more promise that life would no longer be quite so trying. In 1903, another good crop finally put a little cash in Wheeler's hands, and he was able to buy a mower, discer, and harrow. He had always needed help, but couldn't afford it until now. And along came Osmond

Partridge, just 20 years old, who had come out with the Barr Colonists from London, England. Like many others, he was suspicious they were being hoodwinked and deserted the group in Saskatoon that April to find work. He got a job in Saskatoon cutting stovewood. But the inexperienced youth was unable to cut the amount his employer expected, and was fired. He went up to Rosthern where he approached Wheeler and was hired, at $50 a year plus room and board, a low salary even then.

Mrs.Wheeler found "Osmond" an unusual name. So she announced that she would call the young man "Henry." Her word must have been law, because that was the name that stuck all the time he was with Wheeler, as an employee and as a good friend. He married on Maple Grove Farm, fathered three boys, George, Leonard and Edward (who grew up to work for Wheeler) and a daughter, Esther.

Smoke jolted them awake one March night. The heavy paper lining the kitchen ceiling was ablaze. Soddy dwellers put the paper up to stop the dust that sifted into the room when the sod dried out. Desperately they ran to the barn to fill pails with water. Back and forth, slopping and throwing water until Wheeler was worn out. But Henry shouted: "We'll keep on!" and Wheeler rallied. A hole was burned through the roof. The kitchen was a cold place now but, fortunately, spring was not long coming.

Later that week, while cleaning seed grain, "I could see smoke coming out of the sod roof. We ran down and taking water from the well threw it on the roof near the stovepipe and kept it from spreading. We found that mice had made a nest close to the stove pipe coming through the sod."

The town of Rosthern enriched the Wheelers' lives in so many ways. No more "expeditions" for supplies; they made new friends there, and Wheeler could get involved in town affairs and take part in recreational activities. When Rosthern assumed the status of a town, it had a growing business section, including a Massey-Harris agency, a company now selling machinery from Winnipeg to the Rockies.

Although the Wheeler house had three layers of sod on the roof, it could leak. During a downpour, Wheeler awoke to his mother's voice announcing: "Here is the first instalment!" He found her sitting up in bed, umbrella held over her head to ward off a rivulet of water, and a great blob of mud on the bed cover. "She laughed and laughed." No wonder he admired his mother's plucky spirit! Defensively, perhaps, she generally saw the humor in a situation, a character trait that had made life that much easier for them, and which undoubtedly had rubbed off on him.

Still hanging over the Wheelers was the $250 he had owed the Temperance Colonization Society since 1890. "I wrote the company for a statement of my indebtedness. I received a bill for five hundred and nineteen dollars. I wrote for a detailed statement and they replied that if I sent $80 they would forward a statement. As I had no $80 to spare I went to Mr.George McCraney, a lawyer who had opened an office in Rosthern, to take up the matter with the company. After a time, Mr. McCraney advised me that it would be to my interest to sell a quit claim. On consideration I decided to do so. I sold it to him for $50 as I had no more interest in the homestead. I have never seen it since I left it."

In 1904, Wheeler got a 10-pound bag of "western wheat" from the experimental station at Ottawa. Western wheat was a cool-season, sod-forming range grass used for pasture, hay and erosion control. It was drought resistant, and had moderate alkali tolerance. He planted it on a clean, well-worked piece of summerfallow and was delighted with its growth, and the 60 bushels per acre of seed that he harvested.

He rigidly applied his self-taught process of grain selection, a dim path that called on unlimited patience, optimism, and rejection of the idea of quick return. And he needed a thick skin to ignore the titters of some locals when they heard how he sorted and fiddled with his grains of wheat by lamplight, far into the night. Now, with pipe in mouth and a pile of dead matches in the tin ashtray, he eliminated all weed seeds and foreign grain from his foundation wheat. By now he was obsessed with the idea of developing better methods of cultivation and a new strain of wheat that would give all farmers a better chance for success.

This kind of work was right up Wheeler's alley because he was, after all, a Victorian, a breed of people who had embraced the principle that science could solve any riddle facing man. This was the age of Arthur Conan Doyle and his creation, Sherlock Holmes, the fictional epitome of the scientific approach, applying observation and deduction to everyday problems.

He read about Dr. James W. Robertson's method of selecting by hand the biggest and best heads of grain and growing them separately in head row plots. Robertson was the founder in 1904 of the Canadian Seed Growers' Association, and former federal commissioner of agriculture and dairying. He had studied European methods of seed improvement, and decided a better system should be introduced into Canada.

A noted controversy before the turn of the century had lined up Robertson against Dr. William Saunders, Charles Saunders's father and Dominion Cerealist before him. Robertson insisted that selection of choice heads from among existing varieties offered the quicker and greater promise of plant improvement; Saunders contended that the introduction of new genetic factors by hybridization, followed by selection to fix the type, was necessary to effect radical improvement.

This confrontation foreshadowed similar disagreements between Saunders's son, Charles, and Seager Wheeler.

The technique of crossing wheats was simple for any botanist. The challenge came in choosing the best from the material produced and fixing its type by eliminative selection. Good judgement in selecting matings increased the probability of success, but chance played a large role in the result.

"The object in seed selection," Wheeler wrote, "is to purify the variety, to bring about uniformity of type, to select the most vigorous and high-yielding strains, to eliminate all other types and varieties, to raise the standard and quality, and thereby increase the yield."

Populating the West still was a major plank in the federal government's National Policy, and if a wheat variety could not be developed that would free farmers of the threat of frost, there would not be the deluge of settlers once hoped for. Dr. Saunders still was searching for an earlier-maturing wheat to beat the West's autumn frosts. He sent out samples of Preston wheat, and Wheeler switched to it for his experiments.

Saunders's finest Preston was not yet stable, Wheeler found. It showed a mixture of reddish and white chaff. The grain was both straw-colored and red. Season after season he kept planting and selecting. First, he selected the white chaff variety and, when that was fixed, he worked to separate the red grain from the yellow. "In short," wrote Hopkins Moorhouse, "after three years' work he had to pick over his entire stock of hand-selected heads—thirty pounds of grain—every kernel, until there wasn't a yellow one left; to do this he had to rub out each head separately by hand." By this means he secured a pure line and had sufficient seed to sow a small plot. And from then on, his Preston was true to type.

There now were two forces gathering strength to influence agricultural development of Canada's West, and the consequent building of a nation, one well established, the other just beginning. For now, in virtually unknown Rosthern, Seager Wheeler also was trying to produce a wheat variety that would mature early and escape frost, affording all farmers a decent chance to make a living. He had, as yet, little awareness of his potential for good.

Year after year he followed a system of sowing the best-cleaned, graded seed in separate, small plots. No one around him had ever heard of seed selection. For Wheeler, selection was begun almost by accident. He had handpicked his seed for his first crop to get rid of weed seeds and, when the crop ripened, his keen eye noticed certain stronger plants; seeds from these were selected and planted, and he saw a great improvement in yield the following autumn.

The little man from Isle of Wight had chosen a path few farmers had trod. Hand selecting grain and multiplying it called for unusual patience to follow up the work, each season, in detail. Required was an intimate knowledge of the different varieties to distinguish between false and true, and avoid errors of seed selection.

He began his seed selection and breeding with a quarter-acre plot. Each season, he raised his standard and, achieving the goal, raised the standard again, steadily increasing the size and improving the shape of the heads of wheat.

When he first grew Preston wheat, Wheeler saw how superior it was to Red Fife. It ripened earlier and was better developed. He was surprised how quickly it could multiply. "From a single head selected from Preston wheat, I have had an increase in one season of two and a half pounds of choice wheat. This amount, sown on prepared soil, would increase in one season by one and a half bushels. The third season … from 30 to 40 bushels. In four years, we should have 1,000 bushels … from the grain in one single head of wheat." Twenty pounds of seed on a quarter acre, he found, would in two years produce enough seed for a quarter-section farm.

But many of the farmers he wished to help thought he was barmy. It was reported that when he told them of his ideas, his hopes, they just smiled. They could not see beyond quick gain, putting plenty of seeds in large tracts of ground and selling the harvest at so much per bushel, the more the better. So he talked less about his ideas, this man of natural scientific bent and so little formal education.

"It was always my object to do things thoroughly on the farm as far as I was able," he wrote years later, "working to the best of my ability. I am a book farmer and an indoor farmer as well. We often hear uncomplimentary remarks passed about such men, but show me the farmer who does not read, and I will show you a poor farmer. Problems are worked out in the armchair by the fire as well as by observing during the day outside. I take one daily, three weekly, and five farm papers, besides other good reading material."

He was observant and deductive. The Mennonites from Manitoba who settled the Rosthern area brought machinery with them. They used a large, heavy roller to pack their land after seeding. After a couple of years, Wheeler saw this made the land too smooth and allowed the soil to blow away. He offered his opinion to the farmers. Only gradually did they do away with the practice.

Wheeler didn't just read about farming; he relaxed by reading almost anything—westerns, archeology, Biblical stories, *Argosy Magazine*, which he saved and bound. About this time he discovered a newly-successful British writer, Edgar Wallace, who had just broken out with his best-selling *The Four Just Men*.

Years of hard work had slowed Mary Ann Wheeler down. For her pleasure, Wheeler would order books from Eaton's in Regina. (Years later, Henry Partridge was quoted: "She was a great reader and would sit at the kitchen table with her cat, books and tea things and read, then she liked to discourse on the things she had read.")

Wheeler went to town regularly to evening band practice. The band likely was sponsored by the town and local businessmen, and he probably would have been reimbursed when he bought a $16 drum and sheet music for the group. He often played with them during intermissions of hockey games at the skating rink. In 1905, he went to Prince Albert with the band and the hockey team, for a tournament.

Wheeler still was borrowing money, if not from the bank, then from the affable Henry Partridge. A March entry in his 1905 journal shows he borrowed $200 from the Bank of North America branch in Rosthern repayable in eight months. From this he paid $151.25 to the Massey Harris dealer towards machinery, including a drill and a binder. In July, he borrowed $30 from Henry for a buggy. He borrowed from Henry usually in amounts from 50¢ to $5, and always paid him back within a week or two.

About this time, he took on an additional farmhand. Ernest E. Martin, of Prince Albert, 88 in 2001, recalled that his father, W.C. Martin, came from London, England, in 1905, made his way to Rosthern and, finally, Wheeler's farm. "There he stayed about a year and a half or so … talked a lot about Seager Wheeler, he would talk about soil, grain and fruits. At night they hand picked wheat taking out the poor kernels and so on. They would work practically all night, in the kitchen, by lamplight."

Music was an integral ingredient of Wheeler's life, whether playing the cornet and marching with the Sally Ann, in duets with his brother at local dances, listening to recorded favourites, lounging in his easy chair playing his concertina and singing for the family. The Rosthern band was a melodious counterpoint to the hard work and concentration of farm work. Musical expression was a break from the continuing routine of going to the bush for firewood, butchering pigs, crop experimentation and never-ending farm chores. Other diversions included going to town for municipal elections, council meetings and various civic activities, and friends visiting back and forth.

That same year, he and Percy played concertina and banjo for a town carnival. He bought prizes, and cloth with a loud check pattern for suits they would wear during their performance; he noted the carnival was a success, netting $46. He bought a gramophone (out of enthusiasm, or ham-handedness, he overwound and broke the spring the second day and had to send away for a new one) and they picked up tunes everyone liked from Wurlitzer records that Seager ordered by mail. He sent to New York for sheet music, all the latest songs.

His favourites, of course, still were from that golden age of British song, a particular Victorian social period covering war and patriotism, hymns and spirituals, life and laughter. Kingsley Amis and James Cochrane wrote, in *The Great British Songbook*: "They seem to reflect a people much given to sentimentality … but at the same time wary of emotional excess; respectful of institutions but prepared to poke fun at them; not inclined to sneer at ordinary life or humble aspirations, in fact ready to salute merit there … deeply patriotic without much jingoism or undue sense of superiority."

Rosthern's population was 918 when, in 1905, the Province of Saskatchewan was born, along with the Province of Alberta. Gerhard Ens, of Rosthern, was the only new MLA of non-British origin. Prime Minister Sir Wilfrid Laurier and Governor General Earl Grey were in Regina for celebrations that included long parades, longer speeches, red-white-and-blue bunting, Union Jacks, the Mounties' musical ride and swearing in of the lieutenant-governor, followed by a grand inaugural ball.

Wheeler was convinced the land in the Rosthern district was the best in Canada. It was, in his words, a fibrous loam, not too heavy and not too light, a medium soil of clay and sand, a mixture with a chocolate subsoil down to a white clay. Such soil well worked, he found, was very retentive of moisture. He soil-tested some summerfallow with an auger and there was moisture down as far as the auger went. There were no stones. Good water was found at depths of 20 to 25 feet. Unbroken land had a dense grass cover. There were many poplar bluffs and he allowed those on the farm to grow up, for all-season protection.

Early that autumn of 1905, Mrs.Wheeler told her son she wanted to go and look at the beautiful stand of Preston wheat just ripening. He noticed on the way home that she was tiring. "She was always interested in the crops. She was so pleased. I little thought it would be the last crop she saw." It also was the first full crop Wheeler had ever been able to sell for cash money, rather than barter.

On April 2, 1906, Mary Ann Wheeler, after spending a sickly winter, weakened and died, aged 63 years. There is no record of what caused her death. Always looking out for her son's welfare, she called in Henry Partridge shortly before her death. Henry had been thinking about going to the States with a friend. "You know," she said, "there are a lot of rolling stones around these days, and you're better off to stay." She confided she was worried about Seager, who was having such a struggle and asked Henry to promise that he would stay to look after him. He kept his promise, for more than 40 years.

"Osmond was with my father and Uncle Percy at her bedside. She asked them to put on the record, "We Shall Meet Beyond the River," and her last words were, "I'll come out a long way to meet you," wrote granddaughter Elizabeth.

She wrote in a brief biography of Henry Partridge in *Old and New Furrows*: "When visiting the farm many years later, Mr. Partridge walked over the old haunts with a feeling of satisfaction, knowing he had kept his word. 'She was a nice old lady all right.'"

His mother's death was a hard blow. She had shared all of his effort and hardship with fortitude and good humour. "She did not live to enjoy the better comforts," he wrote, nor to bask in the reflected glory of her son's coming celebrity.

Their neighboring friends, the Friesens and the Abrams, eased the situation by looking after all of the funeral arrangements. "She was laid to rest on a lovely spring day. The prairie crocuses were all in bloom, masses of them, as we passed along the trail to the small cemetery (just a quarter mile from Maple Grove Farm). It was sunny and warm, one of the earliest Easters I can recall," Wheeler wrote.

With heavy heart, he did his best, with Percy's help, to provide a suitable memorial for their mother in the wind-swept, grassy Bergthal Cemetery. They fashioned nine posts from six-inch square timbers with chamfered corners, pyramided tops. Painted white, these were sunk in the ground until they stood four feet high. The posts were joined with a heavy metal chain passing through drilled holes. This stout construction lasted until the 1940s, when a grass fire swept the area. Now, a slight depression in the ground is the only indicator of her final resting place.

Mary Ann Wheeler's legacy, she probably would have argued, was her son Seager. It is difficult to imagine any greater influence on his character than her devotion and attention, and her own great strengths—fortitude, honesty, determination, and an ability to laugh at fate's practical jokes.

Wheeler and Henry Partridge now had to look after themselves. In between work in the fields, Wheeler baked bread, and churned butter at night. They got along as well as they could, but "baching" wasn't easy.

The fine stand of wheat that Wheeler's mother had admired for the last time—Preston A, a selection he had developed—harvested an outstanding crop. Despite the heavy work schedule, he still played in the band in 1907. That same year, the town built a bandstand on CNR grounds south of the station. Sunday afternoons in summer the band held concerts, the stirring music wafting far out over the treeless terrain, drawing in nearby settlers. He is believed to have taken over as bandleader a couple of years later.

Rosthern's first council meeting was held in 1907, and the first item on the agenda was the need for a Town Hall. The motion passed and the new hall stood that same year, at a cost of $24,782. But no action was taken on the idea of building an electric light plant because the four 1,000-candle power gasoline lamps installed on streets three years earlier, at a cost of $18 each, still were doing a good enough job.

In 1975, *The Saskatchewan Valley News* reproduced a Rosthern town tax receipt dated in November 1908, made out to F. Henschell for $4.80 on three quarters of land. It was signed by Seager Wheeler, secretary-treasurer.

Earlier that same year, Wheeler had announced he was going to build a new house. He had decided, at age 40, to marry.

— TWELVE —

Marriage and Seed Selection

Lilian Martin comes from Leicester—Seager asks for hand—Seager builds new house, they marry—cousin teaches him photography—L.H. Newman, of Canadian Seed Growers Association, instructs in scientific seed selection—Seager innovates and transcends teacher—works on Preston and Bobs—new buildings—first prize for Preston at Regina—exhibits sent across Canada and U.S.—befriends John Bracken.

While Seager Wheeler tilled the soil at Maple Grove farm, a young woman toiled in a factory in Leicester, England. Separated by more than six thousand miles, they were joined by a single, invisible bond—a common future.

Agnes Lilian Martin was born in Humberstone, Leicester, in 1882, to Benjamin Martin, 26, and Hannah Bennifer Martin, 27, from Grimston, Norfolk. Benjamin was a gardener, a music store proprietor, and a builder of reed organs.

Besides her sisters May Ruth and Maud Mary, Lilian had two younger brothers, Gerald Harry and Benjamin Bennifer. Maud and Lilian left school in their early teens, as was usual for the time, and worked in clothing factories. On their Sundays off, Lilian told her daughters years later, she and Maud loved to let down their hair and bicycle off into the countryside, admiring the farms and fields. This must have been after church service, because Lilian was a lifelong Anglican.

When Benjamin Martin's health declined in his late forties, his doctor advised him to move to another climate. He decided to try the Territories of the Canadian west which so many were talking about at the time, both as the land of opportunity, and for the clean air and brisk climate considered "salubrious" for those with respiratory problems. His wife Hannah, who was not strong, probably believed the change would benefit her as well.

Hoping there would be a market in the new west, Benjamin carefully crated an organ, and packed the parts to build several more; Hannah took equal care in packing her fine linens, probably in tissue paper and plenty of lavender. They and their two boys sailed for Canada in 1904. Until they were established, it would be best, it had been decided, for the girls to remain with their grandmother.

Martin filed for a homestead just northeast of present-day Maymont, about 50 miles due west of Rosthern, and north of the North Saskatchewan River. Possibly with the help of his sons, now about 17 and 19 years old, he put up a frame building 14' x 16', and the

four of them crowded in—along with the organ. The crates of organ parts and trunk of linens had to stay outside, and to Hannah's sorrow her treasured reminders of a gentler lifestyle soon were damp and mildewed. Before long, Hannah was homesick, lonesome for the companionship of her lively daughters, and this possibly contributed to her health declining further.

Maud and Lilian wrote in 1905 that they wanted to rejoin their ailing mother and the rest of the family. They did not care if the Maymont house was small. They would gladly sleep on the floor.

Their aunt Ruth and grandmother set to work sewing stylish outfits for the young women. But just three weeks before they were to sail, they received the shocking news that their mother had died. Their father had made the casket and buried her near the house. When Maymont's All Saint's Anglican Church was built in 1908, Hannah Bennifer Martin was reburied in its cemetery. Aunt Ruth and their grandmother set to work again, sadly making appropriate adjustments. When 22-year-old Lilian and her 26-year-old sister arrived at Maymont in April 1905, they wore mourning clothes.

SOURCE: ELIZABETH WHEELER COLLECTION
Lilian and Maud Martin, in Lincolnshire, 1890s.

According to *Sod to Solar*, a history of Maymont, the Martins lived in the original frame house for a year, and then a larger house was built. Martin served as chairman on the first board of Keystone School. He installed an organ in the school and played for church services held there.

Benjamin Martin was a musician and organ builder, not a pioneer. He had tried, but Canada apparently was too much for him. The rough country had taken his wife. When he thought his sons' and daughters' futures were assured, he planned his return to England. Maud married Wheeler's cousin in 1907, and Lilian would marry the following year.

When Percy Barrett left Clark's Crossing to start anew, he chose Maymont, where in the early 1900s he opened the first photography studio. Occasionally, Wheeler travelled there to visit his cousin, and he got to know others at social gatherings where he probably entertained with his concertina. Percy taught him how to take photographs and to develop and print them, a skill he would later put to good use in his work.

Romance was in the air when Maud Martin married Percy Barrett. Wheeler's discerning eye had settled approvingly on her sister Lilian, whom he called Lil. It's unlikely that he had entertained the idea of marrying during his first years in Rosthern. He would have been too poor to support a wife, and too busy establishing his farm. He would have considered his house too humble for a bride. Besides, his bachelor life was comfortable thanks to his mother's cheery nature as she cooked and cleaned and looked after him and Henry Partridge.

But now, the equation had changed. Events and Miss Lilian Martin had refocused his priorities. Although he did not write about his feelings in his diaries and memoir, it is reasonable to deduce that he was taken by Lilian's manner and appearance. She was said to be well turned out, thoughtful and friendly. Photographs of the young woman show classically-strong features, well-defined eyebrows, and thick, lustrous dark hair. A good listener, she was, by all accounts, impressed by his philosophy of farming.

And what were her impressions of him? Unfortunately, there are no diaries or letters extant, but she might well have found him to be delightful company; he was a spirited conversationalist with a ready sense of humour. But Lily, as some called her, was 14 years younger and a few inches taller, and was being courted by another fellow closer to her age.

So Wheeler, as he did with everything important, persevered. When he proposed in 1908, Lilian told him that she needed time to consider. Apparently not swept off her feet by either of her beaux, she asked for her father's advice. He was direct: "I would trust you with Seager Wheeler to the ends of the earth." And that was that. Wheeler did have that effect on people.

He had a little money put away now after some good harvests, and bought lumber for the new house that he made a priority. In the fall, when the grain ripened, it had to be harvested. But they continued to saw and pound nights, from September until November, into the small hours after working in the fields all day. "Grain, then, was threshed from the stack (of sheaves). The grain had to be stacked in time before the first week in October when we usually had the first fall of snow, and I was anxious to get it done in order that the sheaves were still dry and not heated in the stack. Also, I never had a stack of grain that let the rain in. It was always in good condition when threshed."

He had followed the typical progression on successful prairie farms, from a "soddy" to a small frame house and, later, to a larger two-storey house. In a biographical sketch, "An Admirable Life," Elizabeth Wheeler wrote: "When my father had driven the last nail, Osmond (Henry) said, "'He threw down the hammer. He was exhausted.'" Finished, the house stood one-and-a-half storeys. The southeast corner had an "interior" porch, a built-in notch protected by the roof above and giving entrance to the house, a distinctly Isle of Wight architectural detail.

MISS AGNES LILIAN MARTIN AND

MR. SEAGER WHEELER MARRIED AT MAYMONT

A pretty wedding occurred in the new Church of England at Maymont on Thursday, Dec. 17th, the contracting parties being Miss Agnes Lilian Martin, daughter of Benj. Martin, of Maymont, and Seager Wheeler, a well known farmer of Rosthern. The bride, who was prettily gowned in cream voile with lace trimmings was given away by her brother, Benj. Martin. Miss Ethel Wynne (sic—Ethelwyn) Bean, of Maymont, assisted the bride. She looked very attractive in a gown of red velvet. The groomsman was Mr. Percy Wheeler, a brother of groom.

The ceremony was performed by the Rev. Donald Schoffield, of Maymont, in the presence of about 25 invited guests. This being the first wedding in the new church, the young couple were presented with a handsome bible by Mr. Schoffield.

After the ceremony, luncheon was served at the home of Mr. and Mrs.

Seager Wheeler stacking hay, an art so perfected, he claimed, that he never built a stack that let in water.

> Percy Barret [*sic*], where a dance was held in the evening. The wedding presents received by the young couple was both numerous and costly. Mr. and Mrs. Wheeler left the next day for Rosthern and will reside on Mr. Wheeler's fine farm east of town.

When they arrived at Maple Grove Farm, the new Mrs.Wheeler hung her trousseau of fur-collared coat, dresses and the stylish hats she loved upstairs beside her husband's clothes. Theirs was a partnership that would lead to successes never imagined.

The proud husband now sported a heavy moustache, which took on added droopy prominence on his spare frame—a condition marriage changed, when before long he would be described as "stocky." In the field, he generally dressed in the British farm workers' fashion, collarless dress shirt under suspenders, vest with watch chain, or suit jacket and trousers, but seldom in the overalls favored by many farmers in Canada. He wore several types of caps and straw hats on his balding head, often donning an unblocked fedora, and in cooler weather, threshing or haying, he might sport an English-style peaked cap with high crown.

Wheeler was secretary of the Local Improvement District for six years, until just before it was replaced by the formation, in 1912, of the Municipality of Rosthern. He also had the government contract to plank-drag the road from the corner of his farm to the town,

SOURCE: ELIZABETH WHEELER COLLECTION
Early aerial photo of Maple Grove Farm in the 1920s.

almost five miles. To maintain the road, he used the municipal drag, pulled by a four-horse team. Instead of cash, earnings from this work were deducted from taxes, with a limit to how much he could "work off."

Throughout their long life together, it is clear from family reminiscences that Seager and Lilian were well-suited to each other, and happy. Everyone who knew him said he was a devoted husband. "Oh, he's so good to me," Lilian would tell her daughters in later years. To be considerate of those he loved was an integral part of Wheeler's character. Could that, in part, be ascribed to seeing the mother he loved treated shabbily by his father?

Food still was important—those early days of near-starvation were not forgotten—so he must have been charmed when his wife's soft voice invited him to try her delicious omelets or snow rice pudding. She usually cooked a traditional English Sunday dinner of roast beef and yorkshire pudding. Then, contented Wheeler would sit in a cloud of pipe smoke, play hymns on his concertina and sing.

It was a momentous fall day in 1908 when Wheeler spent hours with L.H. Newman, who dropped in to see him. It was a pleasant afternoon, smoke curling from his pipe, the two men sitting on shade-dappled ground, beside stooks of selected Preston wheat in a seed plot near the house. Newman was giving Wheeler his first informed lesson in scientific seed selection. He outlined wheat genetics and "propagation of seeds in individual short rows, from which single heads were selected and separated for planting in long rows, then in plots, in successive years." Neither would fully realize this lesson's significance for several years.

But the meeting was serendipitous, a turning on of the light bulb for Wheeler, a message akin to that expressed in the Coronation Service: "Here is wisdom; this is the royal Law… ." Wheeler was a natural, a quick study. Newman's instruction was sucked in and absorbed by a man whose whole being was focused on the subject. He soon would apply the lesson and then innovate like a student who transcends his instructor's capacity to teach.

"I hired a man to take me out to see a seed grower and he happened to tell me about a man named Wheeler who was fussing around with seed grain," wrote Newman in a 1920 newspaper article. He was curious, had lots of time, and drove out to see him.

"He pumped me for fair. He was interested in everything about wheat. At that time, Wheeler had a nice selection of Preston, which he called Preston A." Newman said he told him about the newly-formed Canadian Seed Growers Association, of which he was director. Wheeler enthusiastically joined the association right there. A defining, life-shaping decision had been made: he would become a grower of registered and elite seed.

"I was working along lines of my own, but as soon as I became a member I saw it was systematic, something for which I had been looking."

Elite Stock Seed, he explained in a book, is the highest pedigreed seed obtainable, available only in small quantities. "As this seed is the progeny of hand-selected heads, and usually grown on small plots of one-quarter of an acre, the yield from each plot may average anywhere up to 10 to 12 bushels. It is not in the interest of the producer of this Elite Stock Seed to sell it, as it can be multiplied into first generation registered seed.

"The amount of Elite Stock Seed produced each season restricts the area that will produce first generation registered seed. A few acres only, averaging around five acres, can be sown with Elite Stock Seed from a quarter-acre plot. This will multiply into anywhere from 100 to 200 bushels of first generation seed. It is to the interest of the producer to hold all his (seed) for propagation before he disposes of any for sale. In some cases there may be a few small parcels of Elite Stock Seed which may be purchased by growers who are interested in seed selection, such as members of the CSGA, or beginners who want to start out with genuine foundation stock."

He was opting for accomplishment and service over riches. He realized how painstaking the work would be; he did not realize, until two years later, just how strict were the rules that would be applied.

"When I got back to Ottawa," wrote Newman, "I telephoned Dr. Charles Saunders. For some years we had been watching the development of the new Marquis wheat which was still in the nursery plots, and suggested that Wheeler would be a good man to work with Marquis. Seager Wheeler was the first farmer to whom Dr. Saunders entrusted the precious Marquis."

Wheeler implemented Newman's suggestions. He established additional seed plot areas. "The smallest, in which he planted his first-stage headrows," wrote Edward Mills in a well-documented paper for the Historic Sites and Monuments Board of Canada, "were located in the garden area beside his house, which he had previously enclosed with a series of sheltering hedgerows; the long-rows were established in one-quarter acre plots situated around the perimeter of the farmstead area; larger plots, ranging in size from one to several acres, accommodated the larger third-stage seed crops.

"These larger plots and fields were defined by shelterbelts and hedgerows. To improve the fertility of his soil, Wheeler routinely planted various forage and vegetable crops such as alfalfa, corn and potatoes in his plots. His firm belief in the value of composting these crops to build up the nutritive content of the soil accurately anticipated later agricultural theory on soil conservation measures."

Wheeler expressed his attitude in a 1919 article in *Farmers' Magazine*—My Method of Producing New Wheat: "After I had become associated with the Canadian Seed Growers' Association, I became impressed with the big possibility that lay in individual plant selection. My experience in the work has shown me that there are greater possibilities than are generally realized and that it is possible to create or originate new varieties with equally good results as that obtained by cross breeding.

"It would not be an easy matter to define just where and when I improved the conditions of soil and seed. I was selecting the better and riper parts of the field for seed, and carefully cleaning and grading to the best of my ability.

"In spite of setbacks each season, there was always that try-again spirit… At harvest time it was a pleasure to bind the nice, clean, shapely sheaves… I began to pick out some of the largest heads and to sow the seed in odd corners of the garden, without any definite method of seed selection other than that of experiment. Naturally, I began to realize that here was something worth while, and a prospect of growing a wheat that in season would ripen before a frost could seriously injure it."

A 1925 *Maclean's Magazine* article described these efforts: "Night after night, weary with long work in the fields, he sat up in his kitchen, spreading seeds on the rough table, examining, comparing, selecting certain kernels and writing down infinitesimal details concerning them. These details, in turn, he used with later productions, for purposes of comparison. He formulated endless tables and rough books of statistics."

The long, narrow experimental rows of growing wheat near the house now contained selections of Red Fife, Preston and a new variety named Bobs. The wheats were planted in headrows, single lines of plants so that each stalk grew distinct, for easy observation. Wheeler walked the lines, inspecting each head. When a plant showing exceptional or new and promising characteristics caught his eye, out came his pocket knife and the plant was cut just below the head and put away with others in a sack to dry until winter, when the sacks were laid on a hard surface and beaten with a stick. Then the kernels were screened. These were carefully sorted, put away in envelopes and precise notes made. Next spring, their seed was grown again. After about eight years, it was possible to evolve a permanent type.

Wheeler now realized that a new type of wheat could be thrown off time after time and the average farmer would not notice. But he was watching and, "I see them each season. They strike my attention at once as worth investigating. So I shell the head, and the next spring the seed goes into my headrows to be watched with others as long as results show that it is worthwhile."

There were other things Wheeler and Henry Partridge had to attend to if Maple Grove Farm was to become efficient. In 1909, they built a 14' x 24' shanty-roofed stable for $125, and a 12' x 24' pitch-roofed granary, for $130. The next year, he enlarged the stable half again for $100, built another in 1911 for $75, and two more granaries, for $250.

As he persevered in his work, Wheeler was beginning to get good results. His brother Percy and a few close friends urged him to start exhibiting at the local winter and summer fairs. But, sure exhibiting was done by farmers better than he, he declined. In 1909, he attended the first provincial seed fair held at the collegiate building in Saskatoon.

Back home, he pulled out his pipe, packed and lit it, and mulled over what he had seen. His grain was every bit as good. The next year, he decided none of the exhibits at the Regina fair came up to the standard of his wheat. His natural modesty was pushed to the background as he decided he should be showing the world—or at least, Saskatoon—how he, Seager Wheeler, was improving crop production. He had seen new methods of preparing exhibits and he realized that the appearance of the wheat played an important part in winning prizes.

Well, in 1910 he didn't exhibit in Saskatoon, but went instead to Regina:

ROSTHERN WHEAT SCORES AT REGINA

> At the provincial seed grain fair in Regina this week, Seager Wheeler, of Rosthern, secured first prize for group exhibit of Preston wheat. In the seed wheat class Mr. Wheeler took 7th place. It will be a source of pleasure to know that the Rosthern District is maintaining its high place as a wheat growing centre, and Mr. Wheeler is to be congratulated upon his enterprise.

The Regina *Leader* reported that his Preston wheat was

> "splendidly arranged in a glass case and contained wheat heads and bulk grain raised from hand-selected seed, and by way of comparison, wheat grown in the ordinary way, together with a sample of Red Fife wheat. This novel exhibit created a great deal of interest ... and Mr. Wheeler was kept very busy explaining his method of raising such splendid wheat.

> "The exhibit was so good that Mr. Wheeler was induced to turn it over to the Provincial Department of Agriculture by whom it will be exhibited at all of the leading exhibitions in Canada and in many points in the United States. The department will everywhere make known the fact that the wheat was raised at Rosthern."

Wheeler had sent in his field notes on a plot of Beauty of Hebron potatoes, and his Preston wheat records, to the Canadian Seed Growers' Association. The association replied that, considering the bad weather, his records were creditable and "you are to be highly complimented on the success of your work... We are glad to note the excellent record of your improved Preston wheat, as shown by your reports, photos and samples."

In 1910, Wheeler became a full member of the Canadian Seed Growers' Association, and his hand-selected seed that year was eligible for registration. He now learned how meticulous and precise seed growers had to be, after he applied for certification of registration for 20 pounds of hand-selected, 350 pounds of improved and 3,000 pounds of general crop seed:

> "seed must be selected by hand at least three years before it is eligible for registration. The product of this registered hand-selected seed is then eligible for registration as improved seed. The product of improved registered seed is eligible for registration as general crop seed ... only your hand-selected seed is eligible for registration, as this is your third year. Next year the product of your hand-selected seed plot will be eligible for registration as improved seed, and in 1912 the product of your improved plot will be eligible for registration as general crop selected seed."

John Bracken, a professor of field husbandry at the University of Saskatchewan who Wheeler met at the Regina fair, was generous with advice and encouragement. "He was the most capable man in his line of work in Canada," wrote Wheeler. Bracken's careful, conservative approach to farming methods "led to the axiom: 'What Bracken says, goes.'" Bracken later went on to become premier of Manitoba, leading a coalition government, and then leader of the federal Progressive Conservatives.

Bracken never became prime minister of Canada, but the Rosthern-Saskatoon-Prince Albert area had an astonishing record for being represented by prime ministers, possibly more than any other Canadian riding. Three of the country's most influential prime ministers successfully ran in the area that included Rosthern—Wilfrid Laurier, Mackenzie King, and John Diefenbaker.

It is difficult to understand why history books generally ignore the fact that Laurier and King were ever elected in a western riding. In the federal election of June 23, 1896, Laurier ran in the then North-West Territories constituency of Saskatchewan (Provisional District), a riding that included Rosthern—largely made up of Liberal supporters—to show his support for the Métis. Laurier's narrow win with 988 votes over Conservative James McKay, 944 votes, made him prime minister of the country.

Mackenzie King, whose occupation was officially listed as "gentleman," won Prince Albert in 1926. He represented the constituency for 19 years, being defeated by the Co-operative Commonwealth Federation (CCF) in 1945.

John Diefenbaker won the Prince Albert seat in the Commons in 1940. He won again in 1957, forming a minority government, and came back in the 1958 election with the largest majority in Canadian history.

Wheeler was a strong Tory in later years, his favorite politician John George Diefenbaker. He had no use for the CCF. According to his daughter Elizabeth, he believed that socialists depended too much on the hard work of others.

Now the surge of immigrants to Western Canada flooded, and the CPR pushed rail lines into most of southeast and east-central Saskatchewan. Homesteading increased from 6,689 in 1899 to 30,819 in 1905—the majority of it in Saskatchewan—and almost 45,000 in 1911. From the Missouri River to the Volga they came to set up a polyglot quilt of settlements—British, Dutch, French, German, Hungarian, Doukhobor, Hutterite, Mennonite, Black American, Ukrainian, Scandinavian, Polish, Jewish.

The farmers of Saskatchewan were hardly aware that they were making their province into the great wheat-producing area of Canada—the "Breadbasket of the Empire." They were on the threshold of a development that would bring unbelievable fame to their province—and to one of their own.

— THIRTEEN —

Big Bang Alters History

Saunders isolates Marquis, sends seed to Seager—U.S. editors, professors visit farm, best wheat they've ever seen—world demand for bread wheat grows—Canada becoming "land of elevators"— Seager enters Marquis seed in 1911 New York show, wins Wheat King of World— $1,000 richer, pays off mortgage—honour to province and country.

Compounds can lie inert and uninteresting until they are mixed together and provided with a spark—and then there's a big bang. Something similar to that was taking shape on the North American continent in 1911, the diverse ingredients brought together to await the spark being men in different pursuits: a government plant scientist in Ottawa; two railway tycoons, one in Canada, the other in the U.S; and a largely unknown Saskatchewan farmer.

The scientist was Dr. Charles Saunders who was striving to develop a new variety of wheat. This wheat that altered the history of Saskatchewan—and changed Seager Wheeler's life forever—would be named Marquis. At the Agassiz experimental farm in British Columbia, plant scientist Percy Saunders, Charles's brother, in 1892 had crossed the popular Red Fife with various imported wheats of early-ripening habit, including Red Calcutta. From a single head of this cross of Red Fife and the hard, red Indian parent, the descendant Marquis was isolated in 1903, in Ottawa, by dominion cerealist Charles Saunders, producing twelve wheat plants in 1904.

Saunders used his primitive but effective test for gluten strength—he popped several kernels into his mouth and chewed them. The sticky consistency convinced him the wheat might have good baking qualities. By 1906, the hybrid had yielded 40 priceless pounds. The next year, he entrusted the Indian Head experimental farm in Saskatchewan with 23 pounds for test production in Canada's harshest climate—and crossed his fingers.

Superintendent Angus MacKay placed the treasure on a granary shelf. A couple of nights later it was gone, stolen. Panic! How to explain such a loss to Dr. Saunders?

According to author Grant MacEwan:

> "Suspecting the thief was a man working on the experimental farm,
> MacKay posted a written appeal, suggesting that the lost seed might
> very well hold the hope for an improved variety such as was needed by
> western growers. The granary door would be left open that night, the

writer of the appeal added, and nobody would be on guard. To MacKay's great joy, the bag of wheat was back on the granary shelf next morning, undamaged…

"The new wheat grew well in 1907, and being at least a week earlier than Red Fife, it escaped a fall frost which damaged the other variety growing nearby. Also, it proved to be less vulnerable to rust in a season that was cool and wet. In each of the next two years, harvest results confirmed the wheat's superiority. Late in 1909, MacKay advised Saunders that he had complete confidence in the wheat and believed the time had come to share it with western farmers. Marquis was released to government stations (primarily) in time for planting in 1910, but the supply was limited and the demand was great."

When L.H. Newman had suggested Dr. Saunders send some Marquis to Wheeler for trial planting, the scientist was reluctant. It was not his policy to send seed to a private individual; university-trained officials at government experimental farms understood the principles of the trial process. Would a self-taught farmer be capable of such a task? Then, won over by Newman's high regard for this fellow, he agreed to send five pounds of the precious new seed that still was being tested in government nursery plots.

Wheeler was not an excitable man, but that April 21, 1911, as he stepped onto the deeply friable soil of the seed plot near his house, he must have felt a pang of anticipation he had not experienced before. Some of Dr. Saunders's pedigreed seed was sown on a mere one-twentieth of an acre for close observation. The rest of the seed went into larger plots. All the growing areas used were part of the first land ploughed by him in 1898. For 14 years they had been subjected to annual crop rotation, an innovation for the area. The first crop had been oats, followed by potatoes, barley, summerfallow, wheat, including his Preston, and so on. Wheeler wasn't *mining* his soil—as too often was the case with other western farmers—but improving it. The soil was in better shape than when he first turned a furrow more than a decade earlier.

Wheeler followed the growing routine he had perfected over the years: cultivation, selection, observation.

 After running his seeder across the furrows left by the cultivator last fall, making sure the seed was buried no more than an inch, to prevent double rooting, the soil was packed, putting the seed in direct contact with the moisture. Then, seated behind his horses, a thin wisp of smoke trailing back from his pipe, he pulled a homemade roller over the plot. When the grain was up four to six inches, on a hot, dry day he and the horses moved in over the solid and uniform seed bed pulling drag harrows—once again homemade—to break up the soil crust and kill weed sprouts. He had found that such cultivation did not injure the grain, while harrowing on a loose seedbed sometimes smothered or pulled some grain out.

"I plant a crop in four operations, where other farmers generally make five," Wheeler said at the time. "It seems to me that many of them waste a great deal of time and effort needlessly churning up the soil—losing the moisture, pulverizing the soil and inviting soil drifting." His crops invariably out-produced the average of the Rosthern district. "I am working," he said, "for the improvement of crops in western Canada, not only in the quality of the grain, but also the yield. This can only be done by careful study, hard work, through the hand-selection method."

All was not toil. Often, Wheeler went into town at night to attend a meeting or, more frequently, for band practice. Then, in 1911, the Orpheum Theatre was built and brought movies to Rosthern. He and Henry Partridge sometimes would go and watch the jerky scenes to the chords of a player piano.

In October 1911, an official of the seed growers' association wrote to Wheeler asking him to include his grain case as an exhibit at the next fair. The previous year "that exhibit was the best advertising which the C.S.G.A. has ever had at a Provincial Seed Fair. For not only did you explain the work of the Association, but you had the material to illustrate the different stages of improvement which you had been able to bring about." The letter quoted their grain inspector, Mr. Coglon: "Mr. Wheeler is the most interesting and most enthusiastic member I have found so far."

A party of farm editors and professors from Illinois, Nebraska and Ohio, and an editorial writer with Hearst's *Examiner*, came up to Canada to have a look at the 1911 crops, under the auspices of *Canada Monthly*, a Winnipeg farm publication. After stepping down from the train at Rosthern, they were driven out to Maple Grove Farm where they would meet Wheeler who, according to their guide, "farms with his brains." It didn't take the Americans long to see that was the simple truth.

Here was a man who analyzed every aspect of the growing process. They were impressed that he applied generally unknown, or ignored, principles of conservation that, they agreed, would ensure his land would be "as good twenty years from now as it is today." They walked out into the golden stalks, turned the hard, firm, well-colored grains over in their palms, studied the sand-and-clay loam and asked questions. Their host with the shrewd, bright eyes promptly answered—pausing frequently to relight his pipe—with the ring of conviction in his voice, "no bluster or brag," one visitor commented. They all agreed Seager Wheeler's wheat was the best they had ever seen.

The world demand for good bread wheat was growing, especially in Britain. Two main types of wheat were grown in Canada, hard red spring wheat for bread making, and soft winter wheat for cake and pastry flour. The hard wheat—called that because the kernels were harder to crush—contained lots of gluten, the gluey substance that allows dough to rise and hold its bread-loaf shape. Spring wheat is planted in the spring and harvested in the fall; winter wheat is planted in late fall and harvested in the late summer.

Wheeler knew how important his work was in trying to find an even better hard wheat for Canadian farmers to grow. He probably did not realize how important it would be to development of the West, and to the pocketbooks of the East. In the coming years, every Canadian would be indebted to wheat.

As Grant MacEwan pointed out in *Harvest of Bread*, wheat quickly became the lifeblood of Canada. The weather and wheat were what everyone talked about; "most promissory notes were dated for payment on the first day of November, because farmers would have their wheat returns by that time." Babies were given names such as Garnet, Fife and Marquis in honor of wheat varieties. Down east, "Manufacturers and business organizations studied western crop reports and planned operations accordingly. Farms were sold for specified amounts of wheat, and governments in power aimed to hold general elections at times when wheat growers had the least cause for worry or complaint." Said MacEwan:

> "The marketing of 300 million to 600 million bushels of wheat has brought
> employment and benefit to Canadians far beyond farm fields ... additional

wages created for men in railroad service, lake and ocean shipping, elevator operation, milling, baking, banking, administration, manufacture of
farm machinery and other essentials, distribution, sales… There seems no
limit to the stimulating influence of a big western crop."

Canada was becoming "the land of elevators." By 1890, elevator space on Lake
Superior totalled 4.5 million bushels and was expanding. Eventually, huge storage space
became available at Lakehead, Pacific, Churchill, and other terminal points. With all the
country elevator space, it was possible to carry over 500 million bushels at the end of a
crop year with little hardship on the growers who, often in the past, had to hold their grain
at home, where it could deteriorate.

Wheat was native to the Middle East, but thrived in Canadian soil. Interestingly, that
"desert" triangle south of Wheeler's farm that Palliser had rejected as unsuitable for growing wheat, consistently has grown the best wheat produced anywhere in the world.

In the first half of the 1900s, prairie family farmers were justifiably proud of what they
were doing; outside conglomerate pressures had not started reducing their status to the
level it has fallen today. But the unfairness of their lot in the marketplace began early on.
A pound of wheat yielded enough flour to make a twenty-ounce loaf of bread; so the retail
price of bread depended little on the cost of flour, wrote Grant MacEwan. This disparity
between the price that farmers got for their grain, and what retailers could charge for
bread, has always existed.

"Producing the raw materials for a nation's bread should be seen as the most essential
and crucial of all occupational undertakings. And if there are advances in the price of
bread, the wheat growers cannot be blamed for thinking they are entitled to some part of
them," wrote MacEwan.

L.H. Newman had been watching the performance of Marquis in government plots for
the last three years. When Wheeler's Marquis crop was filling out its heads, Newman
came by to inspect and found it "in beautiful shape." He told Wheeler about the American
Land and Irrigation Exposition in New York, scheduled for November 3–12, in Madison
Square Garden, for entries from anywhere on the continent, and urged him to prepare an
exhibit. He also was encouraged to enter the New York show by Dean Rutherford, of the
University of Saskatchewan.

Wheeler's attitude towards these urgings was described in a pamphlet issued by the
Canadian Pacific Irrigation Colonization Company, Ltd.:

> "But when it came to sending samples of wheat to New York land show
> to compete with the finest wheat… Wheeler could not see that he had any
> chance whatever. However, urged on by encouraging and begging letters
> from the different associations in the province, he finally decided to pre-
> pare and send an exhibit of his best crop."

He even wrote to F. Hedley Auld, director of the college of agriculture at the University of
Saskatchewan, asking if it were possible to submit more than one entry. And he was curious how far down the scale he would be when it was all over.

In early 1911, the New York show's $1,000 gold cup prize for the best spring wheat was
limited to U.S. exhibitors. The president of the CPR, Sir Thomas Shaughnessy (American
born), proposed to the American president of the Great Northern Railway who was running the show, Jim Hill (Canadian born), that the prize be opened up to Canadians.

"Nothing doing," responded Hill, who had been a CPR director and once operated a steamboat line on the Red River, from St. Paul, Minn., to Winnipeg. "United States citizens only," according to various reports of the time.

"All right," countered Shaughnessy, "the CPR will offer a prize of one thousand dollars in gold for the best bushel of hard red wheat grown on the continent!"

His company sent brochures to all farmers' organizations on the prairies, with key phrases in shouting red ink: "One Thousand Dollars in Gold," and "Canada Must Win". It called on agricultural societies, United Farmers' societies, boards of trade and town councils to stimulate interest and help bring "honor and glory" to Canada, which had to remain "Mistress of Wheat."

The CPR brochure took on a wheedling, almost pleading tone: "If Canada loses this contest, it will be a serious blow; we have advertised this Great West by our ability to produce the best wheat in the world, and, if at an exhibition of this kind, we have to take second place, we will be shorn of one of our greatest advertising assets." In the district where the winning wheat was grown, land values would go up and "the winning of this prize will induce settlement all over the Dominion."

CP donated a silver trophy and $25 cash to three provincial seed fairs, at Regina, Saskatchewan, Lacombe, Alberta, and Winnipeg, Manitoba, for the best 200 pounds of Hard Red Spring or Winter Wheat. Entries competing would be eligible to enter the New York contest, and indirectly would be competing for the $1,000 in gold. Other farmers, who didn't compete in the provincial fairs, could also send samples of their best wheat, in case they were superior to fair exhibits.

So, how poorly would he do at the show was Wheeler's frame of mind when, on August 28, he went into the plot to cut the grain, satisfied that this Marquis was indeed a good strain of wheat. Wearing cowhide gauntlets to protect his arms from scratching by the sturdy stems, he stooked the cut grain, eight or nine sheaves to the stook, and left them to dry.

"It had to stay in stook a long time, as wet weather had set in and we had one of the heaviest rains I ever saw in September," he wrote in *The Farmer's Advocate* of January 14, 1912. "The ground was covered with water. I had to wait a long time for the grain to dry out enough to allow me to thresh it. As the time was limited to enter the grain at New York, the first opportunity I got I took some of the crop to my brother, Percy Wheeler, who has a home-made contrivance to thresh out small plots of grain. The grain was fed in handfuls and when threshed was sifted from the chaff and cleaned by a fanning mill and prepared for entry at the New York show. If I had not cleaned it thoroughly I would not have stood any chance in such keen competition as developed at the all-American contest. It was cleaned in the same manner as for seed purposes. There were no broken grains in it, no immature grains, no useless impurities and no smut. Some grains were slightly weathered but this was a circumstance over which I had no control."

He was astounded to find his crop, grown on a strip of land measuring 15' x 155', had harvested at an average of 80 2/3 bushels an acre. He had never heard of such a yield. He and Percy made fine, wooden cases with glass tops, to display his exhibits.

His grain samples reached Calgary on October 4, a month before the show. A few days later, Canadian Pacific Irrigation acknowledged receipt, and the tension built. "We will have the sample examined by our Superintendent of Agriculture, Professor W. J. Elliott, and other competent authority, and if the sample is considered equal to three which we

Undated photo of Seager Wheeler in selected strain of Marquis wheat, showing the upright character of stems and heads.

have picked out and are now preparing for the exhibition, we will be glad to enter your grain… You will hear further from us within the next day or so."

Then, October 10, a telegram from Elliott: "Your wheat excellent if you have 125 pounds equal to sample express at once to undersigned will enter same at New York for you."

On October 26, a letter from Elliott: "I have your wire of October 14th, and beg leave to state that your sack of wheat arrived just an hour or two before our train left for the east. We managed to get same aboard, and it is now on its way to the big show."

The *Saskatchewan Valley News* trumpeted to its readers:

ROSTHERN WHEAT GOES TO NEW YORK

SEAGER WHEELER ENTERS IN
WORLD'S PREMIER WHEAT
COMPETITION FOR $1,000 PRIZE
OFFERED BY SIR THOMAS SHAUGHNESSY

Rosthern wheat has been entered for the $1000 prize offered by Sir Thomas Shaughnessy, president of the C.P.R. at New York this winter for the best wheat raised between the Panama Canal and the North Pole. The wheat which is of the Marquis variety was raised by Seager Wheeler, a well known Rosthern farmer who for some years has been doing considerable experimenting in the raising of wheat varieties…

As there was very keen rivalry in the province for the privilege of entering this the premier wheat competition of recent years it became necessary to limit the entries. Consequently, all wheat had to be sent to the

Department of Agriculture, Regina, where the choicest samples were picked out and forwarded to Calgary from where the grain was shipped direct to New York ... no small satisfaction to Mr. Wheeler for the trouble and expense he has been put to to cultivate wheat of such high quality."

Late the night of November 5, 1911, drifts of snow around the little frame farmhouse were just visible in the faint light from a window where Lilian and Seager Wheeler sat by the coal-oil lamp on the kitchen table. Upstairs asleep was their daughter, May Dorothy Minnie, born on October 5, 1909; Lilian was expecting their second child, who would be born May 9, 1911 and named Ella Marquis. Although that summer they had won $100 when a professor from Montana judged them winners of first prize in the Good Farms Competition held by the Rosthern Agricultural Society, they still were on shaky ground financially. Forty-three-year-old Wheeler's experimental work took so much of their meagre income. How did Lilian feel about this? It's clear that she had an unshakeable faith in her husband, and believed wholeheartedly in the value of his work.

Then came the spark that set off an explosion, a sensation felt across North America and picked up around the world, because it was a time when men who endeavoured and succeeded were acclaimed heroes. Wheeler described that night in a local newspaper interview:

"My wife and I that very evening had been discussing our financial situation, which was indeed anything but satisfactory... I lacked the ready cash to carry out experiments I was making. I sadly wondered what I should do; we went to bed late, disheartened.

"About 11 o'clock a knock on the front door sent me grumbling downstairs to see who it was; what was my surprise and joy, on opening the telegram which the boy delivered, to learn that we were richer by $1,000, and in possession of ample means to enable me to go on with my work. It brought me near to tears, and seemed the very hand of Providence. It taught me to have faith, and that hard work, perseverance and unfaltering courage—the essentials of all true farmers—are the surest ways to success."

Speaking was the Wheat King of the World.

The telegram he held in his hand said, simply: "You have won shaughnessy Thousand dollar prize for best Hundred pounds winter wheat grown in the World. Norman S. Rankin, Can. Pac. Ry."

Astounding! His shock soon gave way to realization of what this wonderful news meant: now he would be able to use the CPR's money to pay off what he owed the CPR for his land. Since coming to this country more than a quarter century ago, he had owed money and been almost constantly broke. Now, now he would pay off his mortgage and at long last have some money in the bank. And now, he could concentrate more fully on his work.

Neither Wheeler nor his wife got much sleep during the night remaining. The Wheat King was up at the usual time, 5 a.m., and had made his own breakfast as usual; it was his firm belief throughout the years that Lil, as he called her, should not get up early to fix it for him when her own days were so busy. He had finished his chores and was in the

SOURCE: THE AUTHOR

Telegram informing Wheeler he was the Wheat King of the World, an accomplishment that would eventually affect commerce in all of North America, and in Europe.

kitchen when a crowd of men from Rosthern stormed up the road in sleighs, horses snorting clouds, and into the farmyard. Gerhard Ens and H.A. McEwan asked Wheeler to come outside. It was at this point, he related years later, that he first learned of his win at New York. But it's more reasonable to accept his first version, given no more than two months after the win.

Gerhard was the Ens who had arrived at Rosthern siding with the first Mennonites. So he was a first settler, first postmaster, first Justice of the Peace, first representative of the Rosthern constituency in the provincial legislature after the province was formed in 1905. Ens, McEwan and the others grabbed Wheeler, shouting jocularly that he was wanted by the police. They picked up the grinning farmer, pipe clenched protectively in his teeth, and carried him shoulder high in a victory march about the yard, laughing, singing and shouting hurrahs. He had brought honor and recognition to them, to Rosthern, to Saskatchewan, to Canada.

Tiny May Wheeler tottered at the doorway watching, and cried. She thought the men were taking her daddy away.

— FOURTEEN —

Sudden Fame

Rosthern inundated by telegrams, mail, reporters, photographers—newspapers, magazines wire for stories—Seager handles pressure with aplomb, judging, writing articles, lecturing—immigration department sends seed samples to U.S. and England—Isle of Wight newspapers proud—English farmers write for land prices—Rosthern banquet covered by Cora Hind—CPR banquet in Calgary.

An immense sea-change had occurred. Life's tide had deposited Seager Wheeler high and exposed, and his eyes were dazzled by the unusually bright light. The adulation was universal and immediate; more gradual, but just as imperative, would be the gush from outside to fill up the open spaces where such good wheat could be grown.

Shaughnessy's shrewd move, the gold he put up for the world wheat king's prize, had proved to be "seed money" for a huge return—big profits down the line for railway and shipping companies, an impetus to immigration, and eventual transformation of the once questionable status of the West to its recognition as the British world's breadbasket.

That same night of November 5, the editor of *The Enterprise* in Rosthern got a telegram confirming Wheeler's triumph. Next day, the town was abuzz, people talking of nothing else, everyone rushing up to congratulate him when he appeared at the newspaper office. "I simply can't realize it, it doesn't seem possible that I have won," he said in an interview, when shown the editor's telegram from the railway's Winnipeg office.

"Mr. Wheeler received the news in his own modest way, remarking that he was very glad the prize came to Rosthern as it meant much to the district in advertising value." The interview went on to praise Wheeler generally as a farmer.

"Seager Wheeler's farm is one of the best kept in the Rosthern district. This year he won first prize in the Good Farms Competition which included every feature in farming and the care of the land, buildings, fencing, etc. After driving over his farm it is easy to realize just why the judges awarded the prize to Mr. Wheeler. A long driveway lined on both sides with trees leads up to a modest but well kept farm home with the barns comfortably adjacent. But everywhere is noted cleanliness and good care. He farms only 200 acres believing that a man cannot farm more and do it well. And the 'doing it well' has been the characteristic feature of Mr. Wheeler's life."

His operation more nearly resembled an experimental station, the piece added, and "the grain raised on his farm has been much sought after for seed purposes." Wheeler was a "modest, unassuming man with the appearance of the student rather than of a man engaged in a commercial pursuit... His extreme modesty was more than ever apparent."

Said the paper in an editorial:

> Rosthern is now before the eyes of the world in a way that has not happened in our history. The town that produces the best wheat in the world is being heralded not only through the Dominion of Canada (for it is a national as well as a local triumph) but through the United States and Europe—almost we might say wherever newspapers are published. It is a wonderful achievement and the credit belongs to a man who has given years of his time and energy to producing a quality of wheat that cannot be beaten anywhere. A few weeks ago Seager Wheeler, a very modest and retiring man, was even doubtful if his wheat would pass the initial examination... To say that Rosthern was jubilant is putting it mildly, indeed. There wasn't a man, woman or child in the neighborhood but thrilled with joy. And the modest winner who has brought so great an honor to the Elevator Town made himself a real big man in the eyes of everyone when he said he was "glad for Rosthern's sake."

Another editorial, possibly written by an English immigrant, stated that a feature of Wheeler's triumph "is the fact that a good deal has been said from time to time in a slighting way of Englishmen as farmers in this country. Mr. Seager Wheeler, who is an Englishman, has won from competitors all over the continent."

The telegrapher and the postmaster were kept hopping as messages for the "wheat wizard" poured into Rosthern from all corners of the globe. Daily, strangers got off the train asking how to get to Seager Wheeler's farm, or "the wheat king's farm." The Lieutenant-Governor, George W. Brown, and his party arrived on foot one afternoon early in December, huffing and puffing through deep snow and 40-below temperatures to pay their respects. His sleigh had become stuck a fair distance from the farm. Someone had loaned Brown an extra coat that was tied around the middle with a piece of rope. "But a cup of tea, which he appreciated, warmed him up."

Hopkins Moorhouse, in his biographical sketch, described the hectic time following the New York Triumph:

> "Telegrams and letters of congratulation came in an avalanche from every direction—seventy-five a day. Newspapers and magazines wired for the story of his success. Reporters and special writers came in clusters and singly and walked all over the place. Photographers came and took his picture when he wasn't looking: they caught him in dusty overalls and his oldest and most weatherbeaten broad-brimmed straw hat—at work in his fields; they made him dress in his Sunday-to-meetings and sit at tables, toying carelessly as it were with empty ink-bottles out of which stuck sprigs of the championship wheat. Civic and other official bodies lured him to banquet-places and dined him and wined him and were kind to him. Everybody lined him up with the benefactors of his district, his province, his country. It was all true, too—the biggest advertisement Canada had had. Seager Wheeler would have died if it hadn't been for his pipe! But he survived it all, though greatly bewildered by the harassing

attacks of sudden fame. So many demands were made upon him that there was no time to attend to the cattle or the farm work, he objected plaintively."

Moorhouse was one of those writers ofttimes "intoxicated by the exuberance of their own verbosity." In the middle of winter, it's unlikely Wheeler would have been working in his fields in dusty overalls and straw hat. He would not have been as "bewildered" as Moorhouse claimed. It was, Wheeler admitted, "enough to set a man in a whirl." But the years leading up to this moment had been a period of gradual though unconscious preparation. He had read widely, he had met knowledgeable and influential people. He had a natural love of communicating, buoyed by his own brand of ethical and spiritual beliefs. He was considerate, outgoing, intelligent and, with a little practice, soon was able to handle with aplomb the demands he faced to judge, to lecture, to write articles, to personally handle an immense flow of correspondence—and to continue with his life work.

He told the *Herald* newspaper that he would try to answer all farmers' letters because, "to learn more about farming would mean thousands of dollars for Canada."

Little more than a month after his coronation as the world's wheat king, Wheeler was asked to address a meeting of the Rosthern seed fair and institute. He stressed the importance of good seed of uniform size, ploughing at uniform depth, harrowing and dragging. He told how he had prepared his winning exhibit and urged better fanning of seed.

The Dominion Immigration Department wired Wheeler asking for 100 bushels of the prize-winning Marquis for exhibition in England and the United States. The manager of the Mutual Life and Citizens' Assurance Co., an Australian institution, of London, England, asked for two bushels of the wheat to be sent to Australia for "advertising purposes." Branch managers of the Bank of British North America, in Toronto and Montreal, both Rosthern men, wired him to say they were proud of his accomplishment, as did Canada's agriculture minister, horticulturists, professors, agricultural and seed-growers' associations, MPs, MPPs.

November, what a month! Friends and neighbors honoured him with a banquet in Rosthern. Then the big one, the banquet hosted by the CPR in Calgary where Wheeler would be presented with his $1,000 in gold coins, and the New York show's blue ribbon.

Back on the Isle of Wight, proud relatives and friends, and islanders generally, read in the Newport *County Press* about Wheeler's triumph and victory banquet at Rosthern. It was held at the town hall on Tuesday evening, November 21, 1911, by Rosthern's fledgling "Board of Trade." There were more than 200 men and women present, including Lieutenant-Governor George W. Brown, Mayor H.W. Weatherby, three Saskatchewan cabinet ministers, representatives of municipalities, agricultural colleges, agriculture and commerce. Public figures from across Canada, including the Governor General, His Royal Highness the Duke of Connaught, sent regrets.

Introduced by Mayor Weatherby as "a very modest man who has never sought honours," Wheeler rose and gave tribute to Charles Saunders and his Marquis wheat, "the excellent qualities of the Rosthern soil and the fine climate." The gala event ended with boisterous singing of "For He's a Jolly Good Fellow," followed by "three cheers and a tiger, and a demonstration such as few men ever received in Rosthern."

The menu was impressively printed on embossed paper tied with a white silk ribbon and featuring, of course, sheaves of wheat. There were 14 toasts listed. The revellers could choose: Raw oysters on half shell and lemon; mock turtle soup; spiced ham and chili sauce, turkey and cranberry jelly, spring chicken and currant jelly, ox tongue and olives, domestic goose and crabapple jelly; cream mashed potatoes, corn on cob, French peas flagelet; young lettuce, gherkins, chow chow, mixed pickles, olives, assorted sauces; shrimp au terrapin salad, fruit salad, mayonnaise chicken salad; apple pie, mince pie; champagne jelly and whipped cream, banana ice cream with water ice wafers; vanilla Charlotte russe with lady fingers, cream tartlets, bride's cake, white mountain and golden spice cake; sweetmeats, oranges, grapes, apples, raisins, almonds, mixed nuts, bananas, figs, dates, celery, tea, coffee.

Cora Hind, the astute Winnipeg agricultural writer whose every printed word about western crops came to be pored over by financiers as far afield as Montreal and Chicago, travelled almost a thousand miles to cover the Rosthern banquet. She was Commercial and Agricultural Editor of the *Manitoba Free Press*:

> "The haphazard methods of farming which have prevailed in the Canadian west to a most alarming extent are responsible in a great measure for many of the losses from crops from which the country is suffering.

> "…the famous crop was grown on land prepared only as Mr. Wheeler prepared all his land for seeding. And when you read of the primary struggles of this man without any great means or educational advantages, you realize how often he must have been 'faint yet pursuing.'"

Later, she pointed out that Wheeler's achievement was all the greater because "Rosthern has been known as a Number Two district; that is, the bulk of the crops raised there have seldom gone over the Grade No. 2 Northern. It was therefore a very great triumph… ."

November 29 in Calgary was a mild, snowless day when Wheeler arrived with the MLA for Rosthern, Gerhard Ens, as "chaperone." They met with CPR officials and, sipping cocktails, went over arrangements for the next day's banquet, hosted by the Calgary Canadian Club, to make "this first public acknowledgement of a national success a brilliant function." Much of his time was spent fielding questions from excited reporters of the two daily newspapers.

Wheeler was a congenial man, one who could join in the fun and let his hair down, as shown by his account of the Calgary banquet, held at Cronn's Café the evening of November 30:

> "At the banquet there was only a very select gathering … the mayor of Calgary on my left, Mr. Ens on my right… I don't remember what the eats were but do the champagne in long glasses which the waiters wouldn't allow to get down very far, and kept filling them up. I had never had champagne before, but I do know it tasted good, but did not affect me in any way. I remember how the waiter leaned over Mr. Ens and I and filled our glasses saying 'Slip it into you boys.' The fact was the waiters had been helping themselves in the cellar and they had to lock the cellar up before things got on too far. Anyway it went off fine, Mr. Ens getting up to make his speech, which I am sure was the best he ever made."

Wheeler was presented with his $1,000 in gold coins by Calgary's mayor. There were fifty $20 coins on black velvet lining a large case of Morocco leather. Inside the cover was the CPR's beaver monogrammed in gold. The menu, in the shape of a wheatsheaf, included green sea turtle soup, chicken, halibut, prairie belt salad, Saskatchewan young turkey, Rosthern dressing, B.C. champion potatoes, and plum pudding with brandy sauce. Next day, the Rosthern men were taken on tours of the city, and Senator Pat Burns showed them his packing plant.

With all the publicity, Wheeler was concerned about getting his treasure of gold coins safely back home. He popped them into a cotton bag and secured it inside his waistband for the return trip by train.

Norman J. Rankin, a Calgarian and permanent secretary of the Western Canada Irrigation and Colonization department, had attended the New York show. Despite three Canadians making a clean sweep, grabbing first, second (W.J. Glass, MacLeod, Alberta) and third (T. Maynard, Deloraine, Manitoba) of the big wheat-growing prizes, he said, many Americans were ignorant of the resources and whereabouts of the Canadian West. An alfalfa exhibit had been flanked by a card stating it was grown in Alberta, and a newspaperman asked if Alberta was a new brand of fertilizer; in response to a query, a woman showed off her knowledge: "Oh, yes, Canada is near Scranton, Pennsylvania."

Not long after, another piece appeared in *The County Press* at Newport, Isle of Wight, this time referring to the Calgary award banquet, where "Western Canada's Wheat Wizard" was celebrated by "the greatest banquet ever attempted in the northern section of Saskatchewan." The article eulogized Wheeler as a man with ambition above simply making money, "He is a man above that. He thinks more of improving the quality and quantity of a head of wheat than of all the money in Canada."

More than three decades later, L.H. Newman wrote to a historian who was interested in the origin and development of Marquis wheat. After Wheeler won in New York, he explained, "Two enterprising gentlemen, whose names I had better not reveal, bought all the seed of Marquis Wheeler had, at eight dollars per bushel and capitalized on it handsomely. It was this distribution by these men, facilitated as it was by the publicity given to Wheeler, that gave Marquis its first real boost. From then on this variety did not need any encouragement but went forward like a prairie fire on its own merit."

Newman was correct. Entrepreneurs quickly showed the profits that could be made on a good, and popular, wheat. In the fall of 1910, the Mooney Seed Co. of Regina bought several hundred bushels of Marquis from a farmer who had propagated some small samples of the wheat he had obtained from the experimental farms in Ottawa and Indian Head. The company, of course, then propagated this seed and had 20,000 bushels ready for sale in the winter of 1911–12. Fired by Wheeler's success, there were ready buyers at $3 per bushel. The next year, Mooney's easily sold 100,000 bushels. It was estimated that, if Saskatchewan farmers had been raising Marquis wheat generally in 1910, it would have meant an additional $15 million in income for them.

Meanwhile, the CPR was busy capitalizing on the great publicity Canada and Saskatchewan were enjoying. Twenty-four of Wheeler's glass cases were to be sent to various parts of the world for exhibition in an immigration drive, and 12 already were on their way, with the others, containing the winning Marquis display, to leave shortly.

Letters to Wheeler were flooding in from English farmers asking about Rosthern's soil, the price of land, and general climatic conditions. Some of them had already decided to emigrate to Canada, but hadn't made up their minds about where to locate. The local newspaper commented that, "There is a great amount of work for the Rosthern Board of

Trade to undertake and the importance of this great victory for Rosthern makes splendid material for advertising the district." Early that spring, the town began sprucing up, constructing wooden sidewalks, designing a park, planting boulevard trees, and painting buildings.

Most of the complimentary messages Wheeler received in the next few months asked for something. Some wanted Marquis seed samples or supplies of seed, and hints on how to become successful wheat farmers. Some wanted personal information, or articles written for publication, all of course with deadlines just days away. Others rather brazenly backed up their requests for his wheat or valuable time with appeals to his patriotism, his sense of duty to other farmers. A few were demanding, brushing off his request for patience. He spent an unaccustomed amount of time writing replies, as well as articles. For a man with so slight a formal education, little of his material needed editing. It became evident he had a natural awareness of publicity methods, and that he had greatly perfected his hobby of developing and printing his own photographs.

F.H. Reed, representative in Regina of Canada's department of agriculture, seed branch, wrote to tell Wheeler that it was his duty to speak at the annual meeting in Saskatoon of Saskatchewan members of the seed growers' association, in February. He also wanted him to speak at the Ottawa annual meeting a week later, and the two speeches could be the same. "Although I understand your natural reluctance to appear on a public platform, yet I feel that you owe it as a duty both to yourself and to your fellow farmers."

He heard from his old friend L.H. Newman. And Dr. Charles Saunders, dominion cerealist and "inventor" of Marquis, sent three letters in a month. He said Wheeler's harvest average yield of 80 2/3 bushels was "extraordinary and I am glad that my personal acquaintance with you makes it possible for me to believe … the general public might regard them as erroneous." This yield was so much higher than Saunders had ever observed that he could not mask the slight air of the "professional" talking to the "amateur," and asked Wheeler to send further particulars of the planting to back up his claim. Disdain for Wheeler's lack of formal education was suggested from time to time over the years, in newspaper interviews and comment. By his third letter, Saunders could lighten up and joke: "I am glad to know that although you have scarcely time for your meals at home you are having a series of banquets which may partly make up for this deficiency."

Saunders joined the line-up for seed, requesting about half a pound of the prize-winning Marquis for his "permanent collection of special samples." In future, he said, he would send very little Preston or Huron to Saskatchewan, and "will limit ourselves almost altogether to Red Fife for the southern districts and Marquis for farther north." How could he know that Marquis, as amended by Wheeler, in future would be grown all over the continent?

One opportunist proved a benefactor. W.S. Grieve, of Cross, Goulding & Skinner, Winnipeg agency for Victor and Berliner gramophones and Victor records, reminded the prize winner that he had been contemplating purchase of a Victor-Victrola for some time and "We think that this would be a fitting way in which to celebrate the event. What do you think?" A lover of music, Wheeler thought it was a fine idea and before long, recorded music from a newer machine filled the Wheeler home, particularly enhanced by a larger sound horn he and his brother Percy made, painted to resemble a morning glory blossom. The first horn they made was so large that they couldn't get it through the door, so they made another.

Seager Wheeler with gramophone, and horn that he and his brother Percy made.

In the meantime, requests and tributes flowed in from all sides. A telegram from Thomas Kirk, a Boiseman, Montana, farmer, stated:

> "Send me one bushel of your seed wheat which won the prize at New York if you have it if not let me know where I can get it will pay ten dollars and express must be good and clean ship by express COD."

The *Grain Growers' Guide*, Winnipeg:

> "You have done a great deal to raise the standard of the grain growing in Western Canada…ask you to write an article for us to publish in our 'Progress Number' on December 6th…we would like for you to write an article for us of about 2,000 words or more…an article on your farming experiences in general, containing all the information you can give on wheat growing. We would like also to have a photograph of yourself as well as one of your home, and another good view of your farm. We cannot afford to pay very much … but we will be glad to pay you $15.00 for a good article… ."

The Canadian Pacific Irrigation Colonization Co. Limited, Calgary:

> I take pleasure in enclosing you a photograph of the three winning wheats which will doubtless be of interest to you: also a few copies of our little folder *"Canada Mistress of Wheat."* Ten thousand of these are being issued … and 5,000 scattered through the state of California by the Calgary Board of Trade excursion… I shall send you in a day or so, a little pamphlet, thousands of which we are sending out all over the country. You

will see your smiling countenance, a picture of your gold, and some of your grain…At least 10,000 of these will go over the country.

The *Farmers Advocate*, Winnipeg:

> "The article and illustrations covered slightly more than three pages. We have forwarded the copy to … *Country Life in Canada* and have told them that you requested that it also be sent to the *Grain Growers' Guide* and the *Gas Power Age*… If you have no serious objection we would like to get this article of yours out in folder or booklet form. Our object is to distribute them from our tent at the large fairs during the coming summer, and possibly at some of the Conventions this winter. We think we can make up something that will be a credit to you as well as to ourselves, and something that can be distributed to advantage throughout the West in an endeavor to spread the gospel of thorough farming."

Porte & Marle Jewelers, Winnipeg, who initially had actually asked Seager to send them his leather case *and the gold coins*:

> "We are in receipt of the presentation case for prize wheat, also sample of wheat, for which kindly accept our thanks. We have asked our bankers to procure the gold pieces. When same arrive we propose displaying the goods and the wheat in a prominent place in our window."

R.O. Armstrong, Pastor, Virden Methodist Church, Manitoba Conference:

> "I wrote a short account of your work for our Sunday School papers, under the head of "*A Bloodless Battle.*" The work that you and thousands of others are doing is the fulfilment of the old prophecy of the era when men would turn their spears into pruning hooks, and their swords into ploughshares."

The Canadian Northern Railway Company, Winnipeg:

> "The Canadian Northern Railway Company is making preparation to exhibit extensively in the Industrial Bureau which has been established in Winnipeg, and contemplate putting these exhibits on view at the various State Fairs and exhibiting throughout the West. We naturally feel that our exhibit would not be complete without a sample of the World's Prize Wheat, which was grown by you on the line of the Canadian Northern Railway."

Mrs. A.V. Schroeder, *Der Nordwesten*, the leading German newspaper in Canada, Winnipeg:

> "I have been writing a fine article about your winning the $1,000 prize and about your farm in German for papers in Europe…the photos are exceedingly good and clear and show up so nicely to anyone who understands anything about farming, the fine crop, the size of the heads and straw that it ought to be a good advertisment of our adopted country, which I like as it is giving fine opportunities to everyone who likes to work. Though it is pretty cold just now!"

Campbell Soil Culture Co., Lincoln, Nebraska:

> "[W]e are in receipt of the *Phoenix Harvest* number of December, 1911, which contains a very well written account of yourself and your prize wheat. Will it be possible for you to favor us with a photograph of yourself, and of the field, together with the four heads shown in the lower left hand corner of Page Twelve? We wish to use this in the April number of the *Scientific Farmer*."

The *Winnipeg Telegram*'s Western Editor:

> "The *Telegram* would greatly appreciate if you would forward to it (1) a photograph of yourself and of your farmstead. They will be returned uninjured (2) an account of some of your work and experience in raising wheat and your opinions of the best varieties for the west methods of cultivation, etc. An account of your success and how achieved should be of great value to Western farmers. I should be glad if you would act as our correspondent for your district and will pay $3.00 per column for all news matter sent in."

And then from his cousin, Percy Barrett, in Maymont:

> Just a few lines to congratulate you on winning the prize. We were pleased to hear you had got it, but the Lord knows it was coming to you anyway, for you have worked for it and stayed with the game thro all kinds of hard times. Hope to see you soon, Yours Ever, Percy.

FIFTEEN

The Michelangelo of Wheat

Experiments with Red Fife, Preston, Red Bobs, oats, barley, potatoes—develops Kitchener wheat—"no man in Canada enjoying greater notoriety"—visitors from U.K. invest $2.5 million in farm-land—700 visitors to farm on weekend—develops Marquis 10 B in 1912, official standard—80 per cent of all wheat grown on prairies and States, extends growing boundary north—develops Red Bobs which out-yields Marquis and opens up Peace River district to wheat—selling registered wheats in 1913—seed cleaning plant—scientific and academic noses out of joint—McGill collects Seager's publications—Henry Partridge marries—big loss from hail.

Events of the second decade of the century were unprecedented for Seager Wheeler, for his province, and for his country. Fate would put the unassuming farmer on an astonishingly high pedestal and yet try to knock him off a couple of times, immigrants would flood his province, and the whole country would be tested mightily by a world war followed by a crippling pestilence.

The little man had a low centre of gravity, and continued to conduct his life much as he always had. In 1909, Prof. John Bracken, then in charge of the agricultural department in Regina, had sent him some samples of alfalfa, red clover, timothy and Turkey Red winter wheat to be seeded in small plots for trial purposes. The agriculture department in Washington, D.C., sent him 13 varieties of red clover to grow. A Kansas experimental farm sent Kansas winter wheat to be tested. And he was busy developing several varieties of trees and shrubs. In 1910, he had been experimenting with Red Fife, Preston and Red Bobs wheat, and in 1911, with a wheat he had developed and named Kitchener; Victory oats; Canadian Thorpe and O.A.C. No. 21 barley; and Early Ohio and Nugget potatoes.

The alfalfa had brought him $300 in much-needed cash in 1911, when he took third prize in a best-field-of-alfalfa contest sponsored by the Saskatchewan government. In 1912, better off now with the money left after paying off his mortgage from the New York winnings, he built another granary, 12′ x 14′, for $150.

The 1912 season was a bad one for many seed growers. In the fall, crops were battered with heavy rains and high winds. Yet Rosthern, which for years had annually shipped the largest amount of wheat from a single point in the west, sent out 800,000 bushels. Wheeler won a few minor prizes at local fairs, but he didn't enter the big one. The world wheat king that year was R.H. Carter, Fort Qu'Appelle, Saskatchewan.

Each plant sending out roots and leaves was an experiment. A prodigious amount of record-keeping was required, but as he dodged in and out of the rows, he revelled in the task, which so matched his nature. In recounting the course he followed in developing a variety of anything, he sounded as though he had all of the tabulations in his head.

He "rogued" the experimental plots to pull out foreign grains or types, preferring to do this in morning or early evening. He would straddle the drill row and work towards the sun. "By looking toward the sun, one can see better if there are any bearded kinds of grain and other foreign grains. Everything depends on the purifying of the seed plot. When the plot is ripe it is time to hand-select the heads sufficient to seed another similar plot the following season."

Friends sometimes said, half in jest, that Wheeler knew his plants and their peculiarities even better than he knew the members of his own family—but that was not true. His daughters recalled how they loved it when their father made up songs about them. He would sing about what one of them had said or done, or what they were wearing and they'd burst into delighted laughter.

Like most driven people, Wheeler had great powers of concentration. One example was related by the late Larry Janzen, in an article from a study of tourism potential for the Seager Wheeler Historic Farm Site:

> "Seager would generally plough and pack with a four-horse hitch consisting of three blacks and one dappled grey. Usually, the grey was hitched to the left set of traces. One day one of the men decided to hitch the grey onto the right side. At the end of the day as Seager drove the team back to the barn, he remarked how much he liked this new team of horses. He obviously looked at the ploughing a lot more than he did at his horses."

Another incident, wrote Janzen, underlined his devotion to his plots of cereal grain:

> "Upon starting his workday at 5:00 a.m., Seager found a herd of cattle enjoying his head rows of wheat. Well, Seager viewed this as thieves stealing his lifelong earnings. Using language that he had learned from his sailor uncles, he chased the cattle down the driveway at a gallop, and they took off across the countryside. As Seager hurried back to see how badly damaged his precious plots were, one of his workmen asked him why he had driven his own cattle out. Seager, embarrassed, announced that nothing would be allowed to threaten his plots."

In January 1912, L.H. Newman, now the Canadian Seed Growers' Association secretary-treasurer, sent his protegé a letter thanking him for a report on his 1911 efforts, which had included seed samples and photographs. "We also wish to compliment you on your skill as a photographer. These illustrations will be able to be used to excellent advantage." Newman's organization was quite new, and eager to take advantage of such a promising member.

A month later, Newman thanked him for material that delegates at the last convention had admired:

> "We are particularly glad to have the splendid photographs … these will probably be published in our annual report. I have read your special report …and will record the various points mentioned so that we may be able to follow your work from year to year…When our annual report

comes out you will note frequent references of a very gratifying nature to your excellent work. I suppose there is no man in Canada at the present moment enjoying greater notoriety."

Enjoying it indeed. And the chances to talk! One cold January day in 1912, the Wheelers entertained yet more illustrious visitors, including W. Steedman, chairman of the East India Trust Co., London, and Sir George Whitehouse, a British engineer celebrated for his work in constructing the Uganda railway. A newspaper report commented, "Mr. Wheeler talked so interestingly no one noticed that the dinner hour had long since passed. He began about 11 o'clock and it was past 2 p.m. before his wife was able to catch his eye and telegraph the fact that luncheon had been ready and waiting about one and a half hours. Every one of his audience was fascinated and came away with the impression that not only was Mr.Wheeler an enthusiast in his work but that he thoroughly understood his subject (wheat raising) and had the ability to disseminate his knowledge to others."

Steedman and Whitehouse were so impressed with Wheeler's success that they invested more than $2.5 million in farmland in the area, planning to settle English farmers, according to the Reverend R.O. Armstrong in *The Christian Guardian*. Wheeler's guests always were genuinely glad to maintain contact. On January 26, Mr. Steedman wrote from the Royal Alexandra Hotel, in Winnipeg:

> "I am leaving Winnipeg today for the East with Sir George Whitehouse, and we sail from New York on Wednesday. Before leaving I want to thank you again for your and Mrs.Wheeler's kindness to us on our visit to Maple Grove. I will attend to the photographs etc. when I get to London and I look forward to seeing you again in the spring."

During these heady days, said Noel Dyck, in a report prepared for the Saskatchewan department of tourism in 1975, "It was not unusual for Maple Grove to be visited by upwards of seven hundred people on a summer weekend, for the farm was known throughout Western Canada, and even in the United States, as the home of the most accomplished farmer-agriculturist in North America."

When she married, Lilian had learned right away that although she was mistress of the house, the parlour was not exclusively her domain. Each spring, her husband planted hundreds of experimental headrows of wheat. When these ripened, he chose heads, cut them off with his pocketknife, put them in little bags, and hung them in the shed and in the parlour. He would examine these during the winter, discard what didn't show promise, and plant the superior grains the following spring, again in rows. This continued year after year and resulted in new varieties of wheat, oats and barley. A new variety had to go through six to ten annual tests before being accepted.

"The process is simple in theory," said John R. McMahon in *The Country Gentleman*, "as easy as it was for Michelangelo to chisel out a masterpiece that was inherent in a block of marble. To you and me a head of wheat looks like 10,000 others. To the plant breeder every head is different from the others and has a character all its own; verily, the grains in each head are numbered and each is weighed in the balance and many are found wanting."

Only a seed grower's wife knew what went on behind the scenes in the exhibition game, according to an article by Kathleen Strange, whose husband, Major H.G.L. Strange, credited the Rosthern farmer with showing him how to select grain. He went on to become a world wheat king, president of the Canadian Seed Growers' Association, and a good friend of Wheeler's. She quoted several other growers' wives who got together at a seed fair:

> "I always dread fair time … my husband brings all the sacks of grain into the living-room and piles them around the walls. You've no idea the dust and dirt it brings into the house, not to speak of the general disorder. People are always tripping and falling over the sacks and I have to move them every time. If I so much as spill a single kernel of grain on the floor, my husband nearly throws a fit."

Another:

> "That's nothing. My husband actually brought a full-size fanning mill into our dining room when the weather was too unpleasant for him to work outside. He had the pulley belt running through the front window to the engine outside on the veranda. We were almost frozen to death what with the open window and the door continually opening and shutting as the men tramped back and forth."

One husband's only reply to repeated complaints was: "Well, all the tidying up in the world won't bring in any income."

Lilian Wheeler was one of the wives Kathleen Strange wrote about. But Lilian faced an additional challenge: when grain bags weren't taking up space in the parlour, Wheeler's photo developing and printing equipment was. And the smell of chemicals. Fortunately, before long he could afford to have his film developed professionally.

Major Strange always said that he owed his occupation to Wheeler. At the end of World War I he was at loose ends and undecided what to do. He visited Maple Grove Farm and was inspired by Wheeler "as had many another with the idea that the production of good seed was a work worth while." All the later exhibitors, he said, owed a debt to Wheeler. He had shown them all the way and was still "Canada's best advertisement."

Better wheat varieties came along, and Wheeler stopped growing Fife and Preston in 1914. He had continued developing strains of Marquis and Bobs. Soon, he had 30 variations of Marquis in his trial plots, all from the seeds of one head his alert eyes had spotted and admired. By 1912, there were 125 head rows of Marquis, still all descendants of that single head, but there was considerable trouble in keeping Dr. Saunders's variety true to type—all except for one row, the tenth, which was outstanding. Wheeler named it Marquis 10B.

This is where history, perhaps, has been unfair concerning Wheeler's improvement of the Marquis strain. J.M.S. Careless, in *Canada: A Story of Challenge*, wrote of Marquis: "Its development by Charles Saunders … is one of the most fascinating and significant stories in Canadian history." This accolade should have been shared, at least, with Seager Wheeler.

Dr. Saunders, yes, had presented Marquis to the world, but it was unstable and tended to revert to earlier strains that had differing qualities and, therefore, would not permanently provide a uniform crop, which presented all sorts of problems. Wheeler's 10B Marquis, on the other hand, was a superior strain of Saunders's and almost guaranteed the wheat growing possibilities about 100 miles farther up into Canada's northland. For many years, new members of the Canadian Seed Growers' Association were started with

Marquis 10B. The organization had adopted it to form the standard pedigree stock for all registered Marquis. This was the strain directly associated with the rapid expansion of prairie wheat production in Canada and the northern United States after 1914.

Older varieties such as Red Fife fell out of favour as increasing amounts of Marquis seed became available over the next few years. As its use spread across the Canadian spring wheat country, it also was taken up in Australia, and by the northern growing belt of the United States. In 1913, 200,000 bushels of Marquis seed were shipped to the U.S. Three years later, as the U.S. prepared to enter World War I, 40% of the wheat grown in Montana, North Dakota, South Dakota, and Minnesota was Marquis 10B, a wheat that became the measure of quality into the 1960s. Before long, more than 80% of the hard wheat grown on the prairies was Marquis 10B, all of it—and that grown in the States—the variety selected and developed over the years by Seager Wheeler.

For decades, the main wheat grown in Canada was his Marquis 10B. Its use had increased the annual crop production in the country by an estimated 50 to 100 million bushels, an additional $100 to $200 million gross revenue in farmers' pockets, according to one estimate. And this wasn't like oil money, an exhaustible product; his added wheat production could go on forever.

From 1911 until today, Dr. Charles Saunders has been given all the credit for developing the wheat that transformed western Canada. To recap: Charles Saunders's brother Percy made the important cross of Red Fife and Red Calcutta; Charles Saunders selected from this, producing an offspring he named Marquis, that proved unstable; Seager Wheeler took this Marquis and improved it through selection to produce a stable variety he called Marquis 10B, which became wildly popular. And out of Marquis 10B, Wheeler made the selection he named Kitchener because, in his mind, it was straight and strong as Britain's soldier-hero Lord Kitchener; it was a variety he personally preferred to Marquis.

"Kitchener wheat was originated on my own farm in 1911, a single plant selection, which was made in a field of Marquis wheat… Kitchener is a mutant, or what is commonly called a 'sport.' It appeared suddenly and remained true and constant to type without breaking up into other forms, as is the case in natural or artificial crossings." A small field of hand-selected Kitchener yielded 80 bushels an acre in 1915. He figured it might have a place where earliness was not the chief consideration, such as the southern portion of the prairie provinces. Canadians didn't take to Kitchener, but farmers in Colorado loved it.

Wheeler admired Bobs the first time he saw it. To him, its potential was obvious. Rather than being a "sport," the parent of this variety was attributed to a cross between an unknown wheat variety and a barley called Nepal, made in Australia by William Farrar around 1900. It was called White Bobs when a sample was sent to the Ottawa experimental station in 1905. Wheeler got a sample from there in 1908, planted it, and found it matured 10 days earlier than Marquis, yielding at a rate of 60 bushels to the acre. That kind of earliness could be measured with dollar signs.

So Wheeler set out to change the color of White Bobs to red. Red varieties were more resistant to sprouting, and tolerated more successive days of wet weather; a greater number of varieties were possible. Red varieties were higher in nutrition and would store for many years. He kept planting head rows and regularly prowling them, his practised eye looking for a tell-tale change of color in individual heads. Eventually, he found some that were slightly yellow, and cut these out for propagation. After a few years, almost ready to give up his quest, he saw a lone head of wheat near the end of a row, darker than any yet, a tinge of red. When the grain was rubbed out, every kernel was a perfect red. Then he found three more similar heads.

From those 300 kernels he grew a plot in 1911 with many heads superior to the original White Bobs in straw strength, head and berry. These were his candidates for further improvement. More selections after seven years produced the first type of Red Bobs wheat, a fixed and distinct variety that reproduced true to type. Some heads ran as much as 95 kernels, when the average for most wheats was 50. The kernel was a little shorter than Marquis and flinty hard. It ripened on average eight days earlier than Marquis, which allowed it generally to beat the rust and escape the occasional August frost of the Canadian prairies. It outyielded Marquis ten to 18 bushels at a rate of 80 bushels to the acre at Maple Grove Farm, and rated No. 1 Hard Wheat.

When Wheeler began selling his Red Bobs, he listed two improved strains in his catalogue as Early Triumph and Supreme, which sold for $4 a bushel of seed. Red Bobs was popular in western and northern Saskatchewan and, particularly, in Alberta where it opened up at last the Peace River district to successful wheat farming. Alberta farmers profited from Red Bobs until well into the 1930s.

The Rosthern seed producer developed close contact with all his customers, always asking them to write and let him know how his seed performed for them. Most did. Of course, being a natural marketer, Wheeler often used their comments in his catalogues. The former mayor of Saskatoon, William Hopkins, bought Red Bobs seed at $32.50 a bushel, and Kitchener seed at $10 a bushel. "Results," wrote Hopkins, "have more than justified the expenditure." Three years later, the Red Bobs had yielded 45 bushels to the acre, and the Kitchener, 40 bushels. Hopkins still had not been able to thresh all of his Marquis, and it was yielding 15 bushels. Wheeler shrewdly pointed out in his catalogue that Hopkins the farmer thus was able to sell his spread at $80 an acre, "and with his family will spend the winter at Nice, in Southern France."

Wheeler began selling registered wheats in 1913, and included instructions for their cultivation. He sent seed samples to universities and other plant scientists in Saskatchewan, Alberta, Manitoba, Ontario, North and South Dakota, Montana, Minnesota, Kenya and Australia. As well, he experimented with wheats from Australia, Kenya and Russia. "All these I grew in head rows and rod row plots which I kept myself, seeding and harvesting by hand. My days were long and busy ones but I was keenly interested."

The cornerstone and great innovation, of course, of Wheeler's pioneering work was the seed cleaning plant, the "best example of innovation you will find in western agriculture," said Larry Janzen, when he was chair of the Seager Wheeler Historic Farm Site. The seed cleaning equipment was vital to his seed selection process, and production of commercial seed.

"When most other seed growers were using a single, hand-cranked fanning mill, Seager's seed plant consisted of five machines that cleaned and sized the seed. Since there was no electricity, the machines were powered by two stationery engines. The seed plant was state of the art in 1925 and it can still meet the standards of today," Janzen wrote in a 1992 report. Seager was the innovator, his brother Percy, the engineer. Seager told his brother what he needed, Percy built it.

His painstaking care was universally recognized. A 1919 story in *Campbell's Scientific Farmer* stated, "Seager Wheeler in all his experiments has gone slowly. He has not rushed his new grains onto the market for the purpose of making money as he might have done. In all his work he has been endeavoring to find the wheat best suited to the soil, climate, and general needs of western Canada and his discoveries are worth millions of dollars to the Dominion.

"Five of the most painstaking and reliable members of the Canadian Seed Growers' Association made growing tests (in 1918) of the Kitchener and Marquis wheats." in northern and southern Alberta, central Saskatchewan, and northern and central Manitoba. There was no difference in the dates of ripening, but "In four out of the five cases the Kitchener outyielded the Marquis."

The growing popularity and acclaim coming Wheeler's way was putting some noses out of joint. In 1918, dominion cerealist Dr.Charles Saunders wrote an article entitled "Wonder Wheat" for the *Farmer's Advocate and Home Journal*, in Winnipeg. He referred to "gambling spirit," and "many a farmer wastes time and money on comparatively worthless wheats which are advertised as new marvels." He issued "words of warning" and reminded his readers that he had "introduced more new sorts during the past few years than anyone else ... none of them has been introduced with any fantastic claims as to its merits... . Sensible people will also beware of all new varieties for which extravagant claims are made," he said, apparently referring to Wheeler who certainly was citing the performance of his wheats, based on trials, in his catalogues, and how one or two of them were earlier than, and outyielding, Marquis. Said Saunders: "I should never believe— without convincing evidence—that, in a series of tests fair to both sorts, a variety ripening a week earlier than Marquis could produce a higher average yield."

His piece ended with this patronizing comment: "Nothing in this article is intended to discourage or to reflect upon the exceptional grain-grower who delights in experimentation as a hobby. It would be a waste of time to advise such a man to stop doing that which gives him so much satisfaction."

But many scoffed at such criticism. F. MacClure Sclanders, commissioner of the Saskatoon board of trade, did not agree with critical professionals, and said in a letter to Wheeler that experimental farms and colleges "characteristically" sneered at "the man of the small patch." But, he added, Dr. David Fairchild, head of the Bureau of Plant Industry, Washington, DC, was in Saskatoon during the fall of 1915 and looking forward to seeing Wheeler, when he was called back home unexpectedly. "He was very sorry... He is enthusiastic over your work. He was the man who sent Hansen out to Siberia to collect wild fodder plants, among which were the Siberian alfalfas which we are all growing so successfully."

Rushing to Dr. Saunders's side was R.G. Thomson, in a letter to the *Farmer's Advocate*. He referred to an earlier article in the paper that stated "The names of Marquis wheat and Seager Wheeler are synonymous." He took strong objection to that statement

> "because the names are not synonymous, but also because it is giving credit where credit is not due, and detracts from the work of our agricultural investigational institutions, like our Experimental Farm system, which did produce Marquis wheat, and the Agricultural Colleges.
>
> Had the statement been that the names of Seager Wheeler and Red Bobs were synonymous, the statement would have been all right...I want to impress upon the readers of the *Farmer's Advocate* that the Marquis wheat

was originated by Dr. Saunders… I will admit that it was the means of bringing Seager Wheeler to fame through being one of the first growers and exhibiting at the New York Soil Products Show some years ago."

The library of McGill University was the Canadian bureau for *The International Catalogue of Scientific Literature*. It wrote Wheeler in 1914 to tell him it was collecting titles of his publications for inclusion in the catalogue, and to send copies of all future papers.

Another professional who respected the Rosthern farmer's work was John G. Rayner, one of the vast army of people who had been utterly charmed by him. They met in 1917, when Rayner was an agricultural representative of the Saskatchewan agriculture department. He was sent to Maple Grove Farm to inspect crops for the Canadian Seed Growers' Association. During that period, he said years later, he and Wheeler and others went out together as a team, lecturing at farmers' meetings and he grew to appreciate "the spirit and enthusiasm of this man."

Henry Partridge had been living in the original sod-roofed house at Maple Grove Farm since 1908. But when he brought Hettie, his bride-to-be, over from England in 1913, he and Wheeler tore down the soddy and added a two-room frame lean-to onto the back of the "wedding house." Their families increased, and before another house was built in 1925, the Partridges and their four children were crammed into the addition, the Wheelers and their four children lived in the main part of the 1908 house. But this was not a hardship for the children. "We were more like a family. We grew up like brothers and sisters," said daughter Isabelle Blatz.

Lilian Wheeler and Hettie Partridge spent a good deal of time together, working and talking, but they were unable to shake the English need for class distinction. A fine line was drawn which both respected: Lilian called her "Hettie"; Hettie always called Lilian "Mrs. Wheeler."

July 26, 1913, in *The Saskatchewan Valley News*:

SEAGER WHEELER'S BIG LOSS FROM HAIL

One of the greatest losses from Friday's hailstorm was that of Seager Wheeler. For the past 15 or 18 years Mr. Wheeler has been experimenting in hand-selected seeds and part of his farm is arranged into plots like an experimental farm … much of his seed is now pedigreed and very valuable. This year the plots were looking remarkably well but the hail totally destroyed them… However, Mr.Wheeler was quite optimistic and thought he would be able to gather enough seed to continue his work …it would be a national calamity if his work was even interfered with let alone being suspended…Mr.Wheeler had no insurance. Indeed, one could not insure so valuable a crop.

On the afternoon of July 25, a severe hailstorm had swept across the area, enveloping Maple Grove Farm. Branches were stripped from trees. Hail was ankle deep. Wheeler had sold $2,000 of seed in advance, and it was all gone. His total loss was estimated at $5,000. But he was relieved to find that some of the selected strains in plots had suffered less damage than others. His Marquis 10B showed little effects of the hail bombardment, and it was beardless; the bearded varieties, he realized, because they presented more surface to be hit, all were smashed. His Red Bobs, which was strong-stemmed, had weathered the attack reasonably well.

A report in the *Winnipeg Telegram* said Wheeler displayed the temperament of an artist following the hailstorm. "It is not the money loss which he bemoans but the destruction of all his grain experiments. He is as heavy hearted as a painter would be over the destruction of his masterpiece… Mr. Wheeler has some hundred plots where he was carrying on experiments, many of them the work of years, and they are practically all destroyed. Seager Wheeler is a sad man."

But he was a happier man when, a few weeks later, he found that in many of his small plots, "the stock being so vigorous … it came on again until it was not possible to say that they had received any damage."

E. Cora Hind, of the *Manitoba Free Press*, visited Maple Grove Farm and reported that "every farmer in the west will rejoice to know that Mr.Wheeler's hail loss is proving less disastrous than was at first feared." And, apparently, the neighbors were trying to keep up with the Joneses (Wheelers). "It is five years since I made an inspection of this district and the improved methods of farming … is remarkable."

Obviously, Wheeler could not compete in the international wheat competition that year, but he was proud that another Saskatchewan man, Paul Gerlach, from Allan, won the title of wheat king of the world. He struggled to get his scientific work back on the rails, and to keep the impoverishment of the old days at bay. It helped a little when he was appointed pound keeper for Division One. A fund was started in Saskatoon to "help him make a fresh start." "Less than $200 was subscribed," said *Saturday Press*, "a much smaller sum than was spent on an elaborate banquet tendered to Mr.Wheeler the previous winter by the local board of trade."

Soon, the daily routine had returned to normal, and then something else unexpected came along. The family had accepted that Wheeler's brother, now 47 years old, was a confirmed bachelor. So they were surprised, early in 1914, when Percy announced he was getting married.

SIXTEEN

The War Years

Brother Percy weds Julia Armstrong—Georgina Binnie-Clark publicizes problems of women trying to own and run farms—Seager joins Home Guard—writes articles urging special efforts by farmers—second world wheat title in 1914, three more by 1918—journalists label Seager "national treasure," urge government financial assistance—hailed out in 1916—almost dies of pneumonia—birth of fourth daughter.

Percy Wheeler took the big step and married on Feb. 25, 1914. His bride was a pretty brunette 21 years his junior—Julia Armstrong, daughter of Robert Armstrong, former Indian fighter and buffalo hunter in the U.S., and one of Louis Riel's captors. Julia was vivacious, with a good sense of humour, but considered by some to be flighty. The Maple Grove Farm children, as they grew up, found her to be a lot of fun and a talented artist.

A newspaper account by H.A. Kennedy, former war correspondent for *The Times* of London, claimed that Armstrong's adventures in the North American west, "if thrown on the movie screen, would hold a crowded house thrilled and breathless through a hundred reels. From Halifax to Victoria, you will find veterans of 'the 85' with lively recollections of Bob as scout and despatch rider with General Middleton's command." Few, however, knew much more about him than the fact that he played the chief part in trailing and catching the fugitive Metis leader.

Around 1899, he and his son, Dawson, were hired by Percy Wheeler as farmhands, and he showed up with his family of seven. It appears Robert Armstrong was not made for the domesticated life. He left the farm, while his family—wife Adelaide, Dawson, daughters Myrtle, Cora, Julia, Florence and Ida—remained at Percy's.

The two households didn't mix much, usually only at Christmas. Seager visited Percy's farm frequently, sometimes with one of his daughters; Percy showed up at Seager's every Sunday afternoon, often driven by Julia, who would go back home and pick him up later. Seager was the more talkative of the two, but once they got together, "They'd talk about wheat, wheat, wheat, things they had heard on the radio, about hockey and baseball and the Bible," recalled Elizabeth and Isabelle, "and they'd be contradicting each other. We used to get a kick out of it. We could hear them from upstairs."

An orgy of land speculation in Saskatoon had begun in 1910; two years later there were 267 real estate firms in the city. The province's population had jumped from 140,500 carly in the new century, to 675,000, with 27,000 in Saskatoon, according to *Saskatchewan: A*

History. More than 4,000 miles of railway lines had been added. There now were many more primary and secondary schools, and a university. Crop acreage had increased ten-fold. There were almost 1,200 more grain elevators. The settlers' attention was focusing on improving their society. Co-operative ventures were allowed to incorporate in 1913 and, by the end of the year, 113 agricultural co-operative associations were registered.

The isolation experienced by many farm women was diminished somewhat with the arrival of telephones. Homemakers' Clubs had been set up following a Regina meeting of activist women, including Lillian Beynon, women's editor of the *Grain Growers' Guide*, Cora Hind, of the *Winnipeg Free Press*, and Nellie McClung, author and champion of women's rights.

However, women were not equals before the law, even though the pioneer wife was a partner in the hard work of homesteading. In 1914, Georgina Binnie-Clark, a former British journalist and a would-be farmer, publicized the problems of the single woman attempting to own and operate a farm in *Wheat and Woman*. She could not obtain a free homestead, but had to purchase her land, depleting her capital and making an added interest charge on the income.

Binnie-Clark wrote: "She may be the best farmer in Canada, she may buy land, work it, take prizes for seed and stock, but she is denied the right to claim from the Government the hundred and sixty acres of land held out as a bait to every man. I talked to every man about it, and almost to a man they said: 'Too bad!'"

When war was declared on Germany in 1914, Seager Wheeler's routine remained largely unchanged, except for attending occasional meetings of the home guard.

The "wheat wizard" won his second world wheat king crown in October 1914, with his selected Marquis 10B, at the International Farm Congress, Wichita, Kansas. One of his prizes was a six horsepower portable oil engine.

The world wheat title was his again at the end of September 1915, at the Dry Farming Congress held in Denver, Colorado—again with Marquis 10B, his selection from the original five-pound lot of seed he got from Dr. Saunders in 1911. Prize money totalled $340, plus a John Deere sulky plough with cultivator hoe and midget weeder, a low-lift manure spreader, and a silver cup.

Saskatchewan's 1915 wheat harvest had been remarkable, amounting to more than half the total grown in all of Canada, in spite of a dry spring, some soil drifting, and June frosts. Average yield had been just over 25 bushels per acre, for a total crop of more than 300 million bushels for the first time. The farmers' faith in their land was confirmed. Canada had geared the grain trade to the war effort, to ensure deliveries to Britain, France and Italy. When the 1915 crop strained the delivery system, Ottawa built two new storage elevators in the province, but delivery still was slowed down. Most of the wheat grown in 1915 was Wheeler's Marquis 10B, and Saskatchewan saw it as the icing on the cake when that year Seager Wheeler won the world championship for the third time.

About this time a new sentiment began to appear in the press—concern for Wheeler's future. By his third world crown, the whole continent had realized that more than luck was involved. According to one article:

> "It is time this prophet of seed selection began to be properly recognized
> and assisted in his own country. Seager Wheeler has been carrying on his
> work under the most difficult conditions possible… A man of his bent and
> achievements should not be allowed to work without state assistance. He

should be picked up and taken out of there, and placed where he will be able to proceed with his work unhampered [Wheeler must have blanched when he read that]... Although he is winning world prizes, he is not winning wealth... Seager Wheeler should be taken hold of either by the Provincial or the Dominion Department of Agriculture, and given the opportunity to work and experiment to the top of his bent. If neither body is alert enough to do this, some private individual will come along sooner or later and capitalize Seager Wheeler, and make a lot of money out of his talent..."

Another newspaper article, by Dr. R.C. Manly, called for a research scholarship to be established:

"It was suggested that a scholarship of $500 would permit the winner to devote more of his time to special research and experiment without loss to himself. Mr. Wheeler would be the first logical candidate for such a scholarship and, if presented, it would enable him to realize a cherished wish by visiting some of the men who have devoted a lifetime of experiment for the improvement of grains, fruits and vegetables."

On a fine, sunny third of August morning, 1916, Wheeler strolled through his grain fields with George Chipman, editor of Winnipeg's *Grain Growers' Guide*. Both were struck by the rapid ripening of the tall plants during the past week. His Kitchener stand, which he planned to send soon to the International Farm Congress wheat competition at El Paso, Texas, "looked as solid as a wall, the finest field of grain I ever grew, and I am quite sure that some of the wheat would go between sixty and seventy bushels to the acre. I was particularly struck by the Red Bobs, which was beginning to turn, and promised to ripen earlier than my earliest Marquis."

A few hours later, it all was gone. The most destructive hailstorm in memory, accompanied in places by a cyclone, swept across part of the province, pounding a strip several miles wide, from the north of Rosthern, to six miles south. Crops on the Rosthern Experimental Farm and on the Seager Wheeler farm were destroyed. Neither place carried insurance.

Wheeler was at the Saskatoon *Phoenix* newspaper that afternoon when he got word from Lilian, telling him of the disaster. "I have had some very bad news," the paper reported him as saying. "It is very discouraging. I was hailed out in 1913, and now three years later, just when I was getting things well under way, everything is gone again. The work I am engaged in is a difficult one at best, and it is very hard to carry on my work of seed selection and at the same time earn enough money to make a living for myself and family, but with two such blows as these it comes very close to putting me down and out."

But his optimism prevailed. "Fortunately, I have some seed saved, and also have some small plots of most of my varieties or strains grown on the university farm, so that the work I have been carrying on is not altogether blocked, but I had no insurance, and depend absolutely on the sale of grain I raise for seed, for the means to carry on my experimental work."

"Seager Wheeler is one of our most promising 'natural resources,'" said a *Phoenix* editorial next day. "This is the time to do something for him and for the science of agriculture, to which he is so devoted, and in which he has labored so intelligently."

"Letters of a Farmer to His Son," a popular newspaper column of the time, referred to the hailstorm:

> "I thought my own loss was bad enough, but his is more than a personal loss—it is a public calamity … the little Rosthern wonder simply must be started going again, to win millions of dollars of good advertising for the Province to add, we do not know, how many millions to our wealth, and to win about thirty-seven dollars and fifty cents worth of prizes for himself… Apparently the kind of work Seager Wheeler is doing is its own reward, like virtue. I have even heard him criticized pretty hard, because his crops are not very large and he has not fine buildings and other outward marks of prosperity. Great Scott, man, Seager Wheeler has not time to be prosperous… . Seager Wheeler is one of the little bunch who hitch their chariot to a star, while I am trying to couple my wagon to a dollar."

The *Phoenix* predicted he would not be able to compete for the world prize that year. But he did. His 1916 crop of Kitchener ruined, he dipped into threshed 1915 Kitchener wheat that, in its first international exhibition, took the sweepstakes, beating everything in sight.

His 1916 El Paso victory was followed by another new selection on September 10— Isobel Lily, their third baby daughter. Many years later, the baby of the family, Elizabeth, laughingly admitted: "Oh, I was kind of like an Anne of Green Gables and I liked things to be fancy. I liked to dress things up. So I changed the spelling of her name to Isabelle." And the change stuck.

The 1917 world cup wheat competition was held in September, in Peoria, Illinois, but Wheeler's crop wasn't ready and he didn't enter. The wheat king title went to Samuel Larcombe, of Birtle, Manitoba. But Wheeler was enthusiastic about his exhibit of a bushel of potatoes. Once again his judgement proved sound: he was acclaimed best spud grower in the world with his Early Ohio, an extraordinary achievement as he was competing against the best potato districts in the United States. His Irish Cobbler and Early Ohio potatoes each won firsts. He won more individual prizes than any other Canadian competitor—one sweepstakes, nine firsts, three seconds and one third.

For many years now, western Canadian farmers—particularly those from Saskatchewan—had been cleaning up at these big U.S. events, often sweeping all the top prizes for wheat, and a substantial proportion of all prizes awarded for produce.

When Wheeler threshed his 1917 seed crop, he was able to command the equivalent of $48 a bushel for small lots of no more than 20 pounds. The *Grain Growers' Guide* bought 85 bushels of Red Bobs at a high price, and distributed it free to its readers when they brought in new subscribers. The same year, the first shipment of prairie wheat to the United Kingdom, through the Panama Canal from Vancouver, sailed on the freighter "War Viceroy."

In 1917, Wheeler wrote an article in the *Grain Growers' Guide*:

> "We must speed up production for 1918. The world is facing a food famine and the most important foodstuff is wheat. We are so far removed from the theatre of war that we do not in full measure realize the gravity of the situation … we must plant everything and everywhere it will grow or this time next year the food problem will be unsolvable and the world will face absolute starvation…

Wheeler continued in a pre-Churchillian cadence:

> "As a producer and tiller of the soil for the past 30 years, I am not unaware
> of the efforts that have been made to increase production. I know some-
> what of the toil in the field in the heat and the cold, the dust and the
> sweat. I am acquainted with that tired feeling at the end of the day's work
> when every effort is being made to get the crop planted in good time. I
> feel sure that the farmers of Canada have done their utmost to increase the
> acreage. We have not yet, however, reached a high place in production …
> the only real and satisfactory solution lies in better methods of cultiva-
> tion…it calls for but a little extra effort beyond what is usually given… The
> secret of success lies not so much in the time spent as in doing the right
> thing, in the right place…"

Wheeler almost missed the competition for the world's best wheat held in 1918, at the
International Soil Products Exposition, October 16–26, in Kansas City. That he was able to
compete there underlined the man's indomitable spirit, indeed, the spirit that drove most
successful western farmers. In early winter of that year, he nearly died of double pneumonia. For eight weeks he was confined to his room, seven of them in bed. Elizabeth Wheeler
said the Rosthern doctor, Archibald Blyth Stewart, tended him and reportedly claimed he
had put enough strychnine in his patient to kill more than one man. "Had it not been for
his strong heart, he would not have survived." A medical dictionary states "strychnine is a
convulsive poison formerly prescribed as a tonic and stimulant to the nervous system. Its
use has been discontinued because of its dangerous effects, especially on the spinal cord."

His recovery was very slow and he spent many days sitting outside in the spring sun.
He was still weak in late spring, and unable to do much work, when Henry Partridge, his
right-hand man, broke his collar-bone. He managed to find someone to do his seeding. But
during the summer, it was a challenge to supervise working of the land. The weather was
no help, hot dry winds during much of the growing season, just one good rain and then
early onset of cool weather, almost dropping to frost.

He had been able to get only a small acreage seeded. Despite everything, the crops
looked good and the harvest was reasonable. On his experimental plots, he harvested
more than 50 bushels an acre of Red Bobs, a good harvest any year, extraordinary under
that summer's conditions. Samples of Red Bobs and Marquis 10B were sent off to Kansas.

The morning of October 20, 1918, the four-time wheat king was told the astounding
news that he had won the sweepstakes cup (best in show) for the fifth time. And he won
the CPR $500 silver cup for his one-half bushel of Red Bobs hard red spring wheat—the
strain he developed and had great faith in—against a huge number of entries, 20 from
western Canada alone. For the best wheat in the show he won an eight-foot McCormick
binder. Winnings, including value of the cups, totalled more than $1,000.

Arch Dale, cartoonist for the *Grain Growers' Guide* (and later for the *Winnipeg Free Press*),
captured the moment. Under a drawing captioned "Bringing Home the Bacon," he depict-
ed Wheeler, a pig under his arm, a silver cup tied to its tail, walking towards "Canada's"
outstretched congratulatory hand. Leaning on the international border is a nonplussed
Uncle Sam, and an American farmer muttering "Shucks! What's the use of trying against
him? This is the fifth time he's cleaned us up!" The leading wheat growers of Canada and
United States had been battling for supremacy annually, and the Americans kept losing.

To top it all off, that same morning of his fifth win, Lilian had given birth to their fourth daughter, Elizabeth Rose, upstairs in the little house at Maple Grove Farm. He couldn't contain himself. "Winning the world's prize for wheat wasn't in it with the good news of a baby daughter," he told a Saskatoon newspaper reporter. He put out of mind his hopes for a son.

While he was doing his best to harvest the wheat crop, an outbreak of influenza was wiping out lives around the world. Deaths in Saskatchewan equalled those of the soldiers the province lost during the war in France. Dubbed the "Spanish Flu," it resulted in the Kansas International Soil Products Exposition being closed to the public. All Rosthern's businesses, churches and the school were shut tight, according to H. Ruth Neuman, in *Old and New Furrows*. The school was used as a temporary hospital; the front rooms as wards for the sick, a north room as a temporary morgue.

For most of his life, Wheeler was robust and full of energy. He was almost always in bed by 8 p.m., reading until he fell asleep, a dog on the mat at the foot of the bed. A believer in some herbal remedies and vitamins, he swallowed chlorophyll tablets for many years.

Wheeler was seldom ill, and complained little of aches or pains, but when he had the sniffles or a cold, said Lilian, it was such drama: "Oh, dear, oh dear," groaned the Wheat King of the World, "it's terrible, just terrible." On hearing this, Lilian Wheeler would tell the girls, "I'd rather be sick myself than listen to his moans and groans."

At the invitation of C.A. Dunning, Saskatchewan's agriculture minister, Wheeler spent two weeks at the Kansas City exhibition in 1919. He didn't win the grand prize, but was happy to take home several firsts, seconds and thirds, in wheat sheaf, oats, grasses, and potatoes.

— SEVENTEEN —

World's Most Famous Wheat Grower

Idolized by the press—editorials call for financial help—campaign in Parliament for recognition—CPR should fund Wheeler—*Omaha Daily News*: Wheeler and Luther Burbank outstanding figures of our time; *Christian Science Monitor*: Wheeler equalled CPR developing western Canada; *St. Louis Globe-Democrat*: Grows more wheat to acre than any other man; *New York Mail*: Ranked with great industrialists, engineers and artists—Seager yearns for a son—trip to California—Queen's University honorary doctorate—Give him a knighthood!

Seager Wheeler had become the most famous wheat grower in the world. He was a hero not just to the farmers, but to all the people of Saskatchewan. Most Canadians probably recognized his name. The press made a fuss over him—was it his accomplishments alone, or something else as well, perhaps his gentleness and his humility? Increasingly, writers took up his cause if they felt he was not fairly treated, generally caressing him with their praise.

Gerald M. Brown wrote this character sketch:

> "A visit to Seager Wheeler's farm near Rosthern is ever interesting, no matter how many times one has been there before. In 1911, when I was eight years of age, I was taken to see the $1,000 in gold that Wheeler had won at the New York Land Show. The following summer, a special writer from the Toronto *Saturday Night* visited Seager Wheeler in the interests of his paper. The boy of nine was allowed to squeeze into one of the cars that accompanied the Toronto man to the Wheeler farm. It is significant that the little wheat king devoted as much attention to the child as he gave to the journalist and his escort of local civic authorities. The boy's eager queries were answered as fully and as courteously as the questions put by the man who had made a special trip to the west for his information.

> That is Seager Wheeler. He is always willing to conduct anyone, agricultural expert or puzzled immigrant, the premier of the province or the inquisitive school boy around his farm, in and out among his plots and plantations, and to treat each with the same degree of unvarying courtesy. His time is valuable, but nothing gives him greater pleasure than to spend several hours explaining the purpose of his experiments and point out

every few yards the progress this tree is making under certain conditions, the failure of that plant to develop properly, and while you observe the particular growth, out comes his huge jack knife and Seager Wheeler is on his knees, digging away at the roots to illustrate his point."

By 1918, many newspaper editorials and subjective features were making an issue of the fact that, in their view, the Rosthern farmer worked so hard for fellow growers, and his country, with so little official acclaim or financial reward. A Saskatchewan MP, James R.Wilson, had opened a campaign in the House of Commons for parliamentary recognition of the achievements of the "Wheat Wizard of Rosthern."

The Saskatoon *Phoenix*, in the prolix manner of the time, said that titles and honours in Canada were "thick as autumnal leaves that strew the brooks in Valombrosa." Wheeler was a citizen who deserved honour. "It is understood that Luther Burbank (celebrated American plant breeder and horticulturist, whose career resembled Wheeler's, and whom the U.S. government endowed with $10,000 a year) has for some years been in a position of independence so that, unfettered by the cares of making a living, he has been free to solve the problems of nature. Seager Wheeler should be in the same carefree position. Hon. T.A. Crerar, the Minister of Agriculture, would be properly rewarding true merit and at the same time be doing a useful thing for Canada, if he made Seager Wheeler's farm a Dominion government experimental station, and let the famous wheat grower do his admirable work untrammelled for the future by the vexatious cares of money making."

After Wheeler's bout with pneumonia, the *Saturday Press*, of Saskatoon, printed a chiding "what if" editorial:

IF SEAGER WHEELER HAD DIED

If Seager Wheeler had died of pneumonia this week, he would have been lauded to the skies as one of the men whom even the king should have been delighted to honor. The flowers at his funeral would have been magnificent and his obituary notices would have been something impressive to behold and gorgeous to read…

Fortunately, Seager Wheeler is getting better and there is every hope that next spring he will be out at his miracle plots again, plugging patiently and persistently at his self-imposed task of improving the grain crops of Western Canada by improving the strains of seed sown, and discovering new strains and varieties by a keeness of observation which is nothing short of marvellous. And the province, and the Dominion will applaud his work, and do nothing to help him, as it has done nothing in the past…

What Seager Wheeler should have done was to have cornered the wheat market and made a million…If he had done this, he would have been drawn to the attention of Sir Robert Borden (PM) and when the next bunch of titles was handed out the Premier would have seen to it that he would have been made Marquis Bobs of Rosthern, and allowed to contribute to the campaign fund…

In the store of written material concerning Seager Wheeler, it was difficult to find many individuals who, after meeting the man, were not deeply impressed. Dr. A.H. Reginald

Butler, former eminent professor of botany at the University of Manitoba, described a visit to Maple Grove Farm in August 1918, in his Essays on Wheat:

> "As he passed from plot to plot, pointing out the qualities of the plants in each, it became evident that he was whole-heartedly absorbed in the task of raising new and improved cereals; and quite unconsciously in his conversation and manner he exhibited an other-worldliness to a degree not often met with in such practical men as farmers ... uppermost in Mr. Wheeler's mind was not the thought of monetary award but the hope of originating something of high value to western agriculture."

A "special" appeared in the Christian Science Monitor in 1919:

> "Perhaps it is because the efforts of Seager Wheeler, farmer of Rosthern, Saskatchewan, have not been spectacular, that his name is not found among the 'Makers of Canada,' but the fact remains that his efforts have done more to make western Canada, and particularly Saskatchewan, than anything since the building of the Canadian Pacific Railway... Tardy recognition has been accorded the Burbank of the west ... at Kansas City."

Professor P.G. Holden, director of the agricultural extension department of the International Harvester Company of Chicago, toured Canada in 1919, and addressed the Saskatoon chamber of commerce. The bloom was off, the boom times of high wartime wheat prices were gone, and the year had seen a near-drought that meant hard times for farmers (conditions which would persist to 1924).

That sunny Saturday afternoon, Holden asked the manager of the local Harvester farm machinery branch to drive him out to Rosthern to see the Wheat Wizard he had heard so much about, and to take note of general crop conditions and farming practices. Holden, former head of the Iowa Agriculture College, returned to Saskatoon, shaking his head with admiration. He said Wheeler's reputation was high in the U.S., and "he is breeding a wheat that will bring this country millions of dollars and outbid even the Marquis wheat."

The chamber of commerce, Holden suggested, could undertake the distribution of Red Bobs and stock the whole region with it. He was another who contrasted "the neglect" of Wheeler, with the generous treatment by the U.S. government of Luther Burbank. Wheeler would go down in history and be written about for centuries, he predicted. His farm should be taken over as an experimental station. In effect, he said, all the progressive farming techniques of Maple Grove Farm should be applied by all farmers if they wished to better their lives.

That same year, John R. McMahon, a writer for *The Country Gentleman* of Philadelphia, visited the Wheeler farm during the drought. His two-page illustrated article appeared in November 1920. He was another captive of the Saskatchewan farmer's charm.

"Right here, I would like to emphasize that the Canadian benefactor has accumulated no great wealth for himself and probably never will. Others are on the way of making small fortunes out of his creations." Wheeler, he wrote, hoped to get $15 a bushel for his Red Bobs seed that year. "All the wheat grown on his farm last year ... sold for about $5,000, and the expenses of the place were $3,000, leaving about the usual net wages for genius."

McMahon had been given the grand tour of the place and, "While he was showing his

SOURCE: ELIZABETH WHEELER COLLECTION

Undated family portrait (mid-1920s). Back row, left to right: May, Isabel and Ella; front row, left to right: Lilian, Elizabeth and Seager.

seed plots a quartet of little girls, including a toddling baby, advanced on Mr. Wheeler (May, 11, Ella, 9, Isabelle, 4, Elizabeth, 2). Unreprimanded they walked between narrow rows of precious wheat that represented the labor of years. One climbed to his shoulders; others clung to his hands. I asked their names and ages. The father hesitated a little in reply.

"'There is no trouble about remembering this one,' he said, patting a ribboned head. 'She is Ella Marquis and she must be nine years old. You see, she was named after a variety of wheat… Now the baby here ought to have been called Red Bobs. The name was all fixed for him. Then he turned out to be a girl and we couldn't call her Bobs. That's the way it happens.'" In a 1999 interview, daughter Elizabeth, the "toddler," said her father, after retirement, told her, "Oh, I always yearned for a son."

It was mid-July when McMahon visited Maple Grove Farm. Only one inch of rain had fallen since seeding. Most wheat in the region, he had noticed, was stunted by the drought, worthless. Maple Grove Farm was relatively luxuriant, and he put the difference down to Wheeler's farming methods.

The Wheeler daughters, as they came along, were not farm girls in the sense of doing dirty, sweaty work. They did household chores, making their own beds, ironing, setting the dinner table, doing dishes. Every summer Saturday morning, May and Ella took the kitchen chairs outside on the lawn to wash them.

During the spring of 1920, the family visited Wheeler's sister Alice, in California. On their return, he went through a pile of waiting mail and was surprised to find one from Queen's University, Kingston, Ontario, dated April 15:

> Dear Mr. Wheeler: At a meeting of the senate of Queen's University held yesterday afternoon, it was cordially and unanimously agreed that the honorary degree of Doctor of Laws be offered you in recognition of the great work you had done in promoting the scientific side of agriculture. It was recognized that there was no way of setting a value to those services other than by some recognition of this kind. You have added enormously to the wealth of Canada, and every settler is a gainer by your researches. What you have done can never be undone. It was felt that on no one could the LL.D. degree be more fittingly conferred than on yourself, and the degree is the highest honor that it is in the power of the University to grant.

On May 13, 1920, a small story appeared in *The Daily British Whig*, Kingston, Ontario, stating "Seager Wheeler, of Rosthern, Saskatchewan, was unable to be present to receive the degree of doctor of laws in person. His name was presented by Prof. Watson..."

Publications all over the continent—and several in Britain, including *Punch*—ran mention of the Queen's University honour bestowed on a farmer, a first in Canada. H.B. M'Kinnon, of the *Toronto Globe*, visited Rosthern and filed a perceptive, sensitive piece on the man he had met once before:

> "I found him just where I had expected—out in the fields—and, to my relief, I noticed that academic distinction had altered him not a whit. Away across the stretch of summer-fallow, he saw me making in his direction, and with the kindliness that is part of the man, he left his team and came to meet me. I had intended to greet him with his new title, but when he grasped my hand and instantly 'placed' me as one whom he had met, for the first time, on a sultry Sabbath evening last September—when he stood before me there, in one of his own fields, utterly unspoiled and unassuming, I forgot all about recent announcements from Kingston and the carefully prepared salutation went completely out of mind.
>
> We walked back together toward the patient horses and Dr. Wheeler—I must do him justice, at least once—beckoned me to a seat beside him on the implement to which the team was hitched. While he filled his pipe, thus graciously suggesting that he was not too busy to give to an itinerant newspaperman a few moments of his time...
>
> We rambled on in chatter for half an hour or more—small talk, about Red Bobs wheat, summer-fallowing, the Wheat Board, public school education, immigration; odds and ends of everything. The longer we talked, the more we delayed work of first and vital importance, so, unwillingly, I arose to take my leave. As my companion knocked the ashes from his pipe, I said: 'What do the neighbors think of you now? Will they call you Dr. Wheeler?'

Quick as a flash came the witty response, in good-natured jest: 'Oh, they're calling me Doctor, all right; they tell me it will be handy, with a doctor so near at hand, to get the popular form of prescription.' Wheeler liked to invite his friends to enjoy an occasional glass of his home-made wine on special occasions, such as his birthday. Sometimes, on a particularly hot day, someone from town might pop in with a cold bottle of beer. At Christmas, he trotted out his home-made dandelion and cherry wines.

As I walked towards the car, with its patient driver drowsing at the wheel, I heard Seager Wheeler, Doctor of Laws of Queen's University, giving very common-place directions to his team, now slowly turning at the end of the furrow. On one man, at least, I thought, sits very lightly the weighty dignity of cap and gown."

D.B. MacRae wrote in the *New York Evening Post* that Wheeler was too busy on his quarter section on the prairie, or winning world's championships, to have time to "work himself into the limelight. It was for Queen's University…to recognize the value of his services to wheat-growers the world over."

"What conquering general has ever done more, or done it half as well?" asked the *Ottawa Citizen*.

"A Prophet Is Not Without Honor," said a Saskatoon headline, "Save In His Own Country." Public recognition finally had been given, said the newspaper. "But did that recognition come from Mr.Wheeler's own province, or from some one other of the agricultural provinces of the west? It did not! It remained for the province of Ontario, which is termed 'the home of manufacturing in Canada,' to lead the way in this matter."

Omaha Daily News: "Men like Wheeler and Luther Burbank will be the outstanding figures of our time, when a really civilized posterity rewrites history and puts wars, kaisers and Fatty Arbuckle (a Hollywood actor involved in a sex scandal) where they belong—on the back seat."

An editorial in the *St. Louis Globe-Democrat*: "There is nothing legal about wheat growing, or illegal for that matter, yet there is a man in Saskatchewan, Canada, who enjoys the title of doctor of laws, because of his success in growing the berry from which the staff of life is made… Growing more wheat to the acre than any other man and thus giving a practical demonstration that the United States average of not more than 14 bushels should be considered a national disgrace, is a service of more benefit to mankind than that for which most men are honored with this degree…"

From an editorial in the *New York Mail*: "In honoring such a man Queen's University has honored itself. For Seager Wheeler—we imagine he would look hurt and annoyed if anybody addressed him as 'Doctor' Wheeler—has conferred upon the world a benefit of inestimable value. He deserves to be ranked with the world's great builders of industries, great engineers, artists and musicians."

The House of Commons record of votes and proceedings, "Hansard", shows that on May 14, 1920, J.R. Wilson, Saskatchewan MP, re-opened the debate he had initiated a year earlier about government recognition. "I think the Department of Agriculture should…put him at all events beyond the necessity of worrying about financial matters so far as his experiments are concerned."

MP J.F. Reid, in the House of Commons on May 30: "I think the Government should do something to encourage Mr. Wheeler in carrying on his work… I understand his health is breaking down… I mention these facts so that the minister may give his careful consideration to the matter."

Thomas Crerar, agriculture minister: "I know Mr. Wheeler personally, and I have known for many years of the splendid work he has been doing and the advertisement, to say the least, that his wonderful series of prize-winning achievements in international expositions has given to Western Canada. This proposal that his work should be recognized… I gave considerable thought to it. There is, of course, one difficulty. In matters of government, precedents are always dangerous to establish and while I fully recognize the value of the work Mr.Wheeler has done, I have not been able up to the present to convince myself that that recognition should come from the Federal Department…"

One other Canadian, Herman Trelle, from near Grand Prairie in the Peace River district, won the wheat king distinction five times, starting in 1926. He was a young man whose first win was with Wheeler's Marquis 10B. In 1926 he wrote to "My dear Dr.," saying Marquis 10B seed he got from Wheeler had better results than similar seed obtained from the University of Alberta. "It is my intention to pass out a few one-pound samples of your grain to some promising young farmer boys, whom I am interested in—so will you please send them along no later than April first—thanks!"

Despite now being a world wheat champion himself, Trelle addressed Wheeler as a mentor: "Well Doctor, if I do not stop I will be taking up too much of your valuable time in telling you 'stuff' that is old and worn out, to one of your wide scope of knowledge and experience—but it helps to relieve a little pressure on my part—I thank you. P.S. When my plum trees bear, I will send you the first fruit."

Other winners of the world wheat championship during Wheeler's time were:

Henry Holmes, of Raymond, Alberta, at Lethbridge in 1912;

Samuel Larcombe, of Birtle, Manitoba. He came to Canada in 1889 and settled in the Bird Tail Valley. He did selection work and attempted to develop new varieties, coming up with Axminister, which was claimed to be more rust resistant, but never caught on. He won the world championship in Peoria, in 1917;

J.C. Mitchell, of Excelsior Farm, Dahinda, Sask., won the world crown three times in Chicago, 1919, 1920 and 1924, with Marquis 10B. Coming from Manchester, in 1905, he experienced much bad luck in his farming career through fires, hail and drought. As with other winners, his neighbors were impressed by his successes in Chicago and all wanted to plant Marquis 10B;

Major Harry G.L. Strange, long-time friend of Wheeler's, came from London, England. He was an engineer, served in the Boer War and four years in France during the Great War. He settled in Fenn, Alberta, won in Chicago in 1923. He became president of the Canadian Seed Growers' Association;

Joseph H.B. Smith, of Wolf Creek, Alberta, 130 miles west of Edmonton. Also born in London, England, he came to Canada in 1907, won the wheat king championship in 1929.

It was perhaps coincidence that all of these winning wheat growers had emigrated from England. But they had something else in common: they were universally esteemed by their fellow westerners, who valued accomplishment—and their work was adding to Canada's stature, and topping up the bank accounts of a diverse group of people. This esteem could become evident in admirable ways. Mitchell and his wife, in 1925, were given the gift of a trip back to England by appreciative business friends and neighbors; Samuel Larcombe, dubbed by some the "John Bull" of Canadian agriculture, was so popular in his own province that, when his house burned down, Winnipeg business associates provided him with a brand-new, furnished house.

Perhaps Larcombe's Winnipeg friends had read the earlier newspaper pleas in Saskatchewan for practical appreciation of Wheeler's efforts. Dr. Robert Harvey wrote in *Pioneers of Manitoba*:

> "The westbound train stopped at the Birtle, Manitoba, station platform on October 15, 1929, and discharged 500 passengers from two special Pullman cars. They were Winnipeg businessmen and heads of provincial government departments…" The Hon. J.D. McGregor, lieutenant-governor of Manitoba, presented a brass tablet with the inscription: 'This house was built and donated to Samuel Larcombe by his business friends in Winnipeg as an appreciation of his self-denying efforts on behalf of Canadian agriculture.'"

But no winning of the world title ever had the impact of Wheeler's. His first victory had focused attention initially on Marquis and on Saskatchewan; hundreds of thousands of people had flocked to the province from United States and Europe to see if they, too, could enjoy a life of farming. And nearly everyone, both sides of the international boundary, wanted to plant Marquis 10B.

— EIGHTEEN —

Discontent in the Wheat Belt

A place to serve the East—"farmers' parliament" sounding board of Farmer's Revolt—Union Government's stifling controls—New National Policy—*Grain Growers' Guide* farmers' mouthpiece—bombastic advertising for Seager's seed—his book on growing is first by a farmer—backlash, protective reader response—rust investigation—"historians overlook importance of Red Bobs"—jealous American exhibitors contaminate Canadian exhibits?

All the market levers were in the hands of outside entrepreneurs, and the farmers' resentment simmered throughout World War I. When peace returned, a huge discontent roiled the wheat belt. Farmers were angry, gathering to complain about their lot. Seager Wheeler was sympathetic. Their demonstrations were easily dismissed as the work of "socialists" or "Reds." Undoubtedly, there were people with those political views involved, but men such as Wheeler were as conservative as you could get.

No, the problem resulted from a perception of the West that had been there from the beginning, and exists today—that it is a place to serve the East, a hinterland to be exploited. Some farmers, and writers, complained of "capitalists" and "big bosses," but the core lament simply was that farmers didn't have the heft to protect themselves from what they saw as unfair practices.

Ottawa's union government had been set up under the *War-Time Election Act* to foster a united war effort by having Liberals and Conservatives run the show together. This brilliant move by the established parties planted the idea that opposition to them was unpatriotic; as a result, farmers' candidates for Parliament often were asked to step down in favor of one representing the two main parties. So formation of a farmers' party never took root. But after the war, annual conventions of the Saskatchewan Grain Growers' Association became a sounding board of the so-called Farmers' Revolt, a protest in favor of "progressive action" against the stifling controls exerted by the federal government.

In February 1919, the grain growers' convention had been held in Regina, and Rosthern's 262 members made it the largest local in the association. The happy farmers, proud of their world-famous associate, had come down to town in grand style. They had hired a special train decorated with red-white-blue bunting, carrying Wheeler's vast cache of trophies, and crowded with boisterous delegates from Tisdale and other locals of the Prince Albert district.

The first day of the "Farmers' Parliament" of 1919, the largest attendance ever had registered at the Metropolitan Methodist Church, Regina. Wheeler was called to the podium to "three cheers and a tiger," and praised to the ceiling for his improvement of wheat, oats and barley, and for originating Kitchener and Red Bobs wheat.

At least once, Wheeler was asked to be a political candidate, according to his daughter Elizabeth. It seems likely that it would have happened in this pre-1920s period. But Wheeler had chosen the path of scientific agriculture, and believed all his efforts must be directed that way to make his contribution to Canadian society.

The farmers' dissatisfaction had steeped more than four years, and bubbled over with demands for a role in shaping their world. They called their federal platform the New National Policy, with abolition of high tariffs its main goal. No longer admired as the nation's economic foundation, the farmers realized that now they were regarded simply as complainers; they felt downgraded, cut adrift as a second class of Canadian citizens.

The agriculture minister in the Union Government, Manitoba's Thomas A. Crerar, president of the farmers' business arm, United Grain Growers Ltd., resigned from government in 1919 over a budget that did not reduce tariffs. He crossed the floor to head a group of "progressives." This group was supported by organized farmers in Ontario, Manitoba, Saskatchewan and Alberta. A federal election was expected in 1921, and Crerar, at a February 26 House of Commons caucus of farmer MPs, was named leader of the National Progressive Party.

"The Progressives had earlier been dubbed 'Liberals in a hurry,'" said John H. Archer in *Saskatchewan: A History*. "There was a radical wing which could rightly be described as the forerunners of the Farmer-Labor and the Co-operative Commonwealth Federation. There was also a strong conservative strain evident in its leadership and stemming in part from the older provincial rights tradition. All the Progressives were oriented to reform but many had a conservative social bias...."

The mouthpiece of the farmers' revolt was the *Grain Growers' Guide*, a specialized publication aimed at educating farmers to feel they were owners of their land and their produce, to have self-respect and to be self-thinking, self-reliant. It was produced in Winnipeg at a subscription rate of $1 a year, and was edited and managed by George Fisher Chipman, who was in complete sympathy with the farmers' movement in Western Canada.

He had seized on Wheeler right after the 1911 world wheat king victory, asking him to write of his accomplishments. As they got to know each other, they found they had sympathetic views on the farmers' lot.

Chipman's interest in, and use of, the wheat king's talents over the years bolstered Wheeler's national image and promoted circulation of the *Guide*. Its editorial policy showed disenchantment with the old-line parties, in a time of political change and confusion. It supported a more orderly system of grain marketing, claiming farmers were at the mercy of fluctuating prices on the Winnipeg Grain Exchange, and the whims of the railway system. It backed wheat pools and completion of a railroad to Churchill, Manitoba; it supported votes for women.

In 1920, Chipman wrote a piece in the *Guide* attacking special interests and charging that they were withdrawing advertising from his magazine to force it to shut up. "For many years past, the protected interests have been accustomed to having the tariff made to suit themselves. They have had secret dealings with governments, both Liberal and

Conservative and the tariff has been arranged quite satisfactorily ... it is the farmers who pay the big bulk of the enhanced prices due to tariff protection." He compared Canadian manufacturers to "German War Lords ... men who believe that they have the Divine Right to make the tariff laws..."

Although seed distributor Steele Briggs was the first to use Wheeler in an advertisement, running his picture with sprigs of his 1911 Marquis, along with quotes, it was nothing compared with the bombastic advertising that ensued in the *Grain Growers' Guide*. Full page ads, always with Wheeler's picture, shouted the Wheeler name in 72-point type and larger. "**82 BUSHELS OF WHEAT, IT CAN BE DONE! SEAGER WHEELER DID IT!...** 500 Dollars in Cash to the person who produces the most bushels on one acre, seeded with *Guide* seed." Seed was available to readers who rounded up new subscribers. Most editions of the *Guide* carried long articles written by Wheeler on different aspects of farming, such as "Grain Rust and Smut," "The Soil and the Seed," "Conserving Soil Fertility."

Various versions of this advertising campaign went on through the years, altering as Wheeler's triumphs built, and his winning wheats changed. Then, in 1919, Wheeler's articles had proven so popular, the *Guide* published a thick book by him, including most of his articles and some new ones.

The book was titled *Seager Wheeler's Book, Profitable Grain Growing*. Wheeler was not talking about money when he used the word "profitable," said Victor Friesen in a 1996 article in *Saskatchewan History* magazine. He meant "beneficial," or "useful," Friesen reasoned, "the practice of growing the best crops in order to feed a hungry world."

This claim was borne out by statements in the book: "One may be cropping more acres than can be cropped profitably. What is wanted ... is not more acres in crop, but better producing acres... The soil is ours to make or mar, and we should aim to leave it ... in as good or better condition than when it first came under our hand."

The book was available at first only from the *Guide*, and once again was tied to collection of new subscribers forwarded to the magazine. It was the first known attempt by an agriculturist to lay down certain laws that govern grain growing, said O.R. Mooney, agriculture representative for the northwest district of Saskatchewan, in 1955. "Many of Dr. Wheeler's theories are still applicable today."

Praise for Wheeler's work was widespread from grain growers' officials, professors and other professionals; but it also came from the man in the trenches, the farmer, in letters preserved by the Seager Wheeler Farm Historical Society, at Rosthern. From Robert Kirk, Climax, Saskatchewan, in the province's southwest: "I would like to convey to you how I have appreciated your book. I have also read Prof. John Bracken's book on crop production, but I must say I did not receive the same benefit as from your book."

Bracken's book was sympathetic to the difficulties of farming, but perhaps Mr. Kirk didn't get as much out of it because Wheeler's book was a practical guide for the prairie farmer, written in plain language and much less academic. His book gave precise details on all aspects of dryland farming, and put particular stress on methods of deep ploughing and seed and root-bed preparation. It has been written that the revolution that turned the semi-arid Canadian prairies into viable farmland had been accomplished through the "application of scientific methodologies to the art of farming." John Bracken and Seager Wheeler were two of the leaders of this revolution.

A farmer's widow, Mrs. S. Cooper, Vera, Saskatchewan, wrote in 1946:

"When I saw your picture in the *Star* I felt my son and I were looking at an old friend.

Your book *Profitable Grain Growing* was read and re-read by my late husband and used as a guide very often. This spring, when my eldest son, farming alone for the first time, had breaking to be worked down, I was pleased to see him get out your book for guidance…We often intended writing you this just by way of a 'Thank You.' We were glad to hear of honors which came your way at various times for the work done for the good of Agriculture. There are many men farming in Sask. But too few real farmers."

The *Guide* jumped onto the Red Bobs bandwagon with a small book telling of the new wheat variety's development by Wheeler. "RIPENS Six to Ten Days Earlier Than Marquis; YIELDS More Per Acre Than Marquis; MILLING VALUE Equal to Marquis; GRADES NO. 1 HARD"

Daily newspapers, such as the *Star* in Saskatoon, were trumpeting Wheeler's new wheat with stories and pictures. Even an Isle of Wight newspaper ran a small piece about Red Bobs.

The *Guide*'s flashy, aggressive marketing was becoming too much for its opposition publications, and for those who were suspicious of anything not produced at an official government experimental station by scientists with university degrees.

An editorial in the *Farmer's Advocate and Home Journal* on December 1, 1920, warned readers to "Beware of 'New Varieties'." Red Bobs had "failed most decidedly to live up to the claims made for it by those who are advertising it," the Winnipeg magazine said, basing the warning on a report of the Brandon Experimental Farm's superintendent. "Some persons have failed in their duty to the farmer in allowing the same to be 'put over.' Many farmers … have not been getting value for their money. During the last two or three years Red Bobs has been sold for $10 to $30 a bushel, which is far in excess of its true worth… Don't be misled by those whose main aim is to sell a particular variety for one or two seasons."

The *Nor'-West Farmer* said on December 6, 1920, that both of Wheeler's most recent developments, Red Bobs and Kitchener, "have not proved equal to the other wheats… It is not advisable to seed either." A year-end report from Indian Head Experimental Station said "Red Bobs yielded fairly well but showed susceptibility to rust. It also showed evidence of not being well fixed as to type."

Reader response to such criticism was swift and highly supportive of Red Bobs, and of Wheeler's products and reputation generally, although some admitted Bobs rusted too easily in their areas. Letters flowed in from British Columbia to Manitoba, and from down as far as South Dakota, where one writer reminded readers that there had been no claims that Red Bobs would not rust. Most devoted to Red Bobs were wheat growers in Alberta, particularly those in the Peace River district in the north, who were enjoying boom times.

Red Bobs was described as one of the most promising wheats by officials in Montana. Later, the U.S. department of agriculture collected reports from all American and Canadian experimental stations from 1919 to 1924 and released a compilation of how all varieties in the spring wheat belt withstood rust. "It is surprising to note that Red Bobs, a variety which has been condemned by empirical observers as being peculiarly susceptible to rust, stood up better than Marquis, although the difference was not great."

The next spokesman for the scientific establishment to criticize Wheeler's product was close to home, W.A. Munro, superintendent of the Dominion Experimental Station at Rosthern. He said Red Bobs growing in his plots showed a susceptibility to rust, while a variety of Dr. Saunders's, Ruby, showed no rust. Munro asked Gerhard Ens, William

Wiebe and several other respected district farmers to conduct an investigation. They tramped around Wheeler's farm and then the experimental station, looking for rust.

They checked 40 acres of Kitchener at Maple Grove Farm, slightly affected by rust in a couple of depressions. The Supreme Red Bobs, in stook for seven days, was "the best wheat on the farm," again a little rust in depressions, but the heads were fine. Some Marquis, sown before the Red Bobs, was not yet ready for cutting. In Seager's experimental plots, the Red Bobs showed no rust.

Ens and his group went on to the Rosthern station and checked the one-fortieth-acre plots of Red Bobs, where the controversy had started. The stooks were dry, they found, because they could have been cut earlier. There was a slight depression running through the plots and this was where they found the most serious rust. Other wheats in the depression also were rusted. "Accepting the principle that grain on low land is more subject to rust than elsewhere, there was absolutely nothing, in the opinion of any of the party present, to indicate that Red Bobs wheat was more susceptible to rust than any other variety of wheat." All farmers in the district growing Red Bobs declared they were sticking with it.

Writing of her western crop inspection tour, E. Cora Hinds, the *Winnipeg Free Press* agriculture editor, said she saw "some especially good patches of Red Bobs and Kitchener wheat…"

No doubt there were some early problems. Red Bobs did tend to lose type, but this problem eased with the introduction of Wheeler's strains Early Triumph and Supreme. Many of the rust complaints could have come from farmers who were not as fastidious as he in his planting methods and preparation of seed.

Newspaper commentators could work themselves into a real tizzy when defending Wheeler and his Red Bobs, their logic occasionally flying wild. "W.J.H.," who wrote the column "Heliograms" in the *Manitoba Free Press*, offered the following in reaction to adverse headlines about the new wheat variety:

> "Seager Wheeler's name isn't in that fat, red and gold volume of 1,427 pages, Who's Who and Why in Canada. He is a plain unpretentious man, an Englishman by birth, who on his homestead of one hundred and sixty acres near Rosthern in Saskatchewan, has done, and is doing, patiently and perseveringly, work of incalculable value to Canada and to humanity.
>
> We have in our mind's eye Horatio, a moving picture of several snobs of the Sudden Rich variety, whose portraits (furnished and paid for by themselves)—pages of indecent self-exposure puffed up, snobbish little souls, and of their consuming hunger and thirst for cheap admiration and envy. Any one of these snobs would, without doubt, regard Seager Wheeler, if he came within their ken, as a poor boob."

It appears that the "campaign" against Red Bobs scared off enough farmers that it had no chance to supplant Marquis 10B as *the* wheat to plant on the prairies. Certainly, where it appealed most—in the shorter-season areas of northern Saskatchewan; Alberta, particularly the Peace River area 430 miles north of the international boundary; and Colorado—it had a long, successful life.

When Wheeler began experimenting with Red Bobs, he could not have known that he would save up to 80 million bushels of wheat a year from early frost damage, A.W.

Erickson wrote in the August 14, 1940 edition of *The Northwestern Miller*. That year, he said, there were millions of acres of Alberta wheatland sown to Red Bobs.

In 1946, the *Free Press Weekly Prairie Farmer* reprinted a piece from the *Windsor Star*. The writer observed that the Red Bobs varieties Early Triumph and Supreme still were going strong in large areas of North America, particularly Alberta, and "How many dollars that wheat has meant to the prairies cannot be estimated."

It is likely that there was an element of fashion in the popularity of a particular wheat during the years of the wheat economy, as there is with any product. Renown came to be considered an excellent wheat by the CSGA, but farmers ignored it. For Red Bobs in particular, it is also possible that the publication of so much negative comment may have held it back.

We'll give the last word to the late Larry Janzen, Rosthern seed producer and founding director of the Seager Wheeler Farm Historical Society: "Seager, with his introduction of Red Bobs wheat, shortened the growing season significantly. Many historians have overlooked the importance of Wheeler's Red Bobs wheat on the central and northern prairies. Perhaps they felt that due to the accidental cross of White Bobs and Marquis on Seager's farm, that this was a non-event. Well, a non-event it was not...a one-week shorter growing season. One week may not sound like much, but it was enough to add a one-hundred-mile-wide strip of the most productive parkland soil from Manitoba to the Alberta Rockies into wheat production."

Rust attacked the wheat stem, perforating it so that life-giving moisture could not reach the ear. It was a parasite disease and, in Wheeler's words, "The conditions so favorable for the spread of this disease are warm, close, murky or muggy weather, accompanied by heavy dews and fog, which often comes at night and hangs over the crop, particularly the lower portions of the field...." He considered rust to be close to an insoluble problem, but still the holy grail he pursued for many years was a wheat variety that resisted rust. His hopes had been high for Red Bobs to be rust resistant. But he had never claimed that quality for Red Bobs.

The first rust-resistant varieties to be developed, in the 1930s, were Thatcher (which would end the era of Marquis domination), Apex and Renown, and their significance to western wheat growing equalled the development of Marquis two decades earlier. An even greater discovery, in 1953, would be Selkirk.

On December 17, 1924, Randolph Patton, editor of the *Saskatoon Star* (later an editorial writer with the *Winnipeg Tribune*), began a series of articles dealing with "the extraordinary accomplishments of Dr. Seager Wheeler." They subsequently were reproduced in a catalogue, "Special Prices on Seager Wheeler's Selected Seeds, 1925":

> "Seager Wheeler doesn't believe in luck. His neighbors think he's lucky. He isn't. They're the ones that have the luck, and it's pretty rough on them sometimes... So he doesn't have crop failures. He is in the middle of the worst wild-oat district in Saskatchewan. One of his neighbors got 700 bushels of wild oats out of 3,200 bushels of wheat. We didn't see a wild oat on his whole farm. 'We've got 'em,' he admitted, 'but they aren't as thick as they used to be.' The saw fly was busy in every field we examined until we got to the Wheeler farm. There are no saw flies in the Wheeler crop..."

Patton's references to luck and crop failures had been lifted from an article by Wheeler in the *Guide*. The adulation was just too much for H.A.C. Brown, of Carnegie, Manitoba, who had read Wheeler's article too, and wrote a letter to the editor signed "A Manitoba farmer." He challenged the statement that luck should play no part in crop production.

"Can Dr. Wheeler or anyone else side-step at all times such things as rust, hessian fly, saw fly, frost, lack of rain, too much rain, dry scorching wind, heavy windstorms in spring and harvest, grasshoppers, inability to do certain work at the right time and the consequences that flow therefrom, not to mention the weed menace?... It is absurd to say that farming is not a gamble, it is, and it always will be.... It is statements like these from such men as Dr.Wheeler that leave the impression, so general with those not conversant with ordinary farm practice, that farmers are a poor lot and simply do not know their own business."

The *Guide*'s associate editor, P.M. Abel, sent a copy of Brown's letter to Wheeler on Jan. 3, 1925, suggesting he send a reply that could be run beneath Brown's critical letter. The few controversies in Wheeler's life were always met head-on. He was sure of himself, was never cowed. On January 7, he penned his reply:

> "By a perusal of all the articles I have ever written in the past, the evidence is quite clear—when I made the statement that I have never had a crop failure or even a poor crop, it is a fact. In the 28 years that I have been on the farm, the only year that I had no crop was in 1916, when one of the finest stands of all crops was totally destroyed (by hail), and that certainly could not be considered a crop failure. This is the one factor that Mr. Brown omitted...
>
> Rust has never injured my crops to any appreciable degree, as in most cases the crop was near or at maturity or sometimes in stook before rust could do any damage, owing to the introduction of earlier-maturing varieties of grain... Hessian fly I do not know as it has not appeared on my farm. Saw fly does not attack my crops and never has... Frost, owing to the introduction of early maturing varieties is practically eliminated... I have had my own share of lack of rain, as in the past season, and still produced a good crop. I have had my share of scorching and heavy winds. Grasshoppers have never appeared in my fields.
>
> Despite all these drawbacks mentioned by Mr. Brown, my statement as published in the *Guide* stands... I do not intend to be drawn into any controversy over the matter and the above statement is final on the subject."

Wheeler never won the world wheat championship again, although coming close— close enough that it is possible claims of devious contamination of exhibits by American exhibitors, who resented the lock Canadians had on so many prizes, robbed him of another win.

In a 1923 letter, J.C. Mitchell of Dahinda, Sask., then two-time world wheat king himself, said he had kept an eye on Wheeler's exhibit at the Chicago exposition that year because he suspected "unfair play. I personally rogued your exhibit twice and then found kernels very detrimental to first prize in them. The hard red spring was worse. I did all I could ... but I could not sleep with the exhibits... I think we as grain exhibitors should ...

at least have some person down there always on deck."

An Alberta exhibitor at the same show wrote to say he had called a meeting of all exhibitors while there "for the purpose of correcting a number of loopholes which I observed by which an unscrupulous and unfair man might take advantage of an honest person, and I am told that in the past people have actually done this."

Yearly, there were claims from Canadians of exhibit tampering. As late as 1926, M.P. Tullis, field crops commissioner, said:

> "Certain it is, there was some tampering with wheat exhibits at Chicago, whether intentional or not I am not prepared to say … it is purely a question of it happening and, in order to prevent a recurrence of such a possibility, departmental representatives from Manitoba, Saskatchewan and Alberta, and those from many states of the union, took the matter up with the exposition authorities of the grain section, and we received a definite promise that all chances of tampering with grain exhibits would be cut off."

SOURCE: ELIZABETH WHEELER COLLECTION
Five-time international wheat champion Seager Wheeler, with some of this trophies.

If American wheat growers too often found themselves in the chaff at these international competitions, their chagrin would not be surprising. Their standing was very visible. A 1933 article in the *Western Producer* stated:

> "at the International Grain and Hay Show in Chicago a huge map of the United States and Canada hangs on the wall of the grain show building and as soon as a championship is decided, a gold crown is placed in the state or province from which the exhibit comes. The grower thus becomes a Wheat King, Oat King, Corn King, etc. The province of Saskatchewan can boast many such Kings…"

Who can challenge the claim of western Canadians that they grew the world's best wheat? Records of the 54 world championship competitions held from 1911 to 1968 show that Canadian exhibitors won the top title 49 times, western Canadian exhibitors 48 times.

— NINETEEN —

Experimental Orchard

Develops hardy fruits, *Guide* markets stock—publishes own seed and plant catalogues—orchard supports experimental work—new buildings—bigger house in 1925—preferred horses to machines—Partridge his chauffeur—works sunup to sundown—newspaper campaign for federal funding resumes—his daughters—new barn.

Back in 1918, Seager Wheeler had decided to put down new roots with an experimental orchard in which to grow, test and originate hardy fruits suitable for western Canada.

He branched out because there were indications that the Dominion Experimental Farm would assume increasing control over experimental grain seed development and no longer work hand-in-hand with private growers. This it did after 1920, according to Edward Mills's agenda paper for the Historic Sites and Monuments Board of Canada, circa 1994. Members of the national seed growers' association, including Wheeler, shifted to commercial seed stock selection and distribution to wheat farmers.

Once again a pioneer, he began the experimental process—a patient pace he was used to in grain selection—of developing a hardy fruit orchard, the farthest north ever attempted on the North American continent.

"I came to Saskatchewan from the south of England in 1885," he would say later, "and for forty years in Saskatchewan I did not see a single apple or crab or any other fruit tree in blossom or fruit until I saw it on my own farm."

By now, commercial fruit from Ontario and B.C. was not a rarity on Saskatchewan farm tables. But he was convinced that species of fruit showing promise in southern Manitoba, and some of the northern States, could be developed to hardiness for Saskatchewan, even as far north as Maple Grove Farm.

So, early in 1918, he contacted A.P. Stevenson of Morden, Manitoba, and asked for some of his crab, bush cherry, and plum trees that had been growing successfully at the dominion experimental station there for many years. He started an eight-acre "house orchard" just southeast of the 1908 house that the Wheeler and Partridge families still shared. Over time, he noted those trees that fruited well and ordered more of them from Stevenson, and similar varieties from North and South Dakota and Minnesota, as well as raspberries, currants and grapes. Eventually, he found that many of these were unsuitable and discarded them.

By 1919, his and Henry's industry had expanded the experimental orchard to include 60 varieties of apples, 80 of crabapples, hundreds of plums, raspberries and other small fruits, and sunflowers and rhubarb. As Wheeler became more proficient at increasing his fruit tree stock by the budding process, he averaged three to four hundred buds a day. Even though he had to cut and prepare new buds the same day they were used, one record day he budded 500 apple and crabapple stock.

That same year he bought an adjacent quarter-section and was able to shift some of his wheat growing there, freeing up more acreage for fruit and tree growing. Before long, he was selling stock throughout the prairie provinces. Sizeable orchards sprang up throughout the Mennonite district surrounding Rosthern and Waldheim, with farm wives putting down from 50 to 200 sealers of fruit for the winter. Much of the foundation stock came from the Wheeler farm.

As it had with his grain, the *Grain Growers' Guide* marketed his fruit stock during his early years of commercial production. The *Guide* continued to run his photographs and stories about his successes and techniques with fruits at Maple Grove Farm. An article by horticulturist Percy H. Wright, likely in the 1920s, pointed out that Wheeler had tried many varieties of standard apples and still could not recommend any. "At any rate, however long the north must wait for hardy large-size apples, the test begun on the Wheeler farm in 1917 reveals that there are a number of crabs in which we may place a great deal of confidence.

"The Oka cherry, in which Maple Grove Farm gets betters results than most... The quality of the Wheeler strain is high, so high as to suggest that it may differ from some of the other strains of Oka in commerce... The experience at Maple Grove, then, in showing how far we can go, and where for the present we must stop, under farm conditions, should be made widely known, since it is able to save a great deal for the buyers of fruit trees."

In 1922, Wheeler still was filling orders from the *Guide*, for bushel sacks of Marquis 10B, Kitchener, Canadian Thorpe Barley, and Victory Oats. But by the mid-1920s, said Edward Mills, Wheeler "assumed direct control of his commercial distribution and began publishing his own annual seed and plant catalogues. These publications, in combination with magazine articles and his book, drew increased attention to Maple Grove Farm as the site of Wheeler's accomplishments... Wheeler's reputation attracted a steady stream of visitors to his farm throughout the 1920s and 1930s."

More than 1,000 trees of many varieties were planted in 1924. Most farmers were getting shelterbelt seed and nursery stock from experimental farms, free except for any delivery charges. But they usually limited their planting to windbreaks around their farmstead; Wheeler "used them to define and enclose his growing network of gardens, test plots and fields, enthusiastically introducing new trees and shrub varieties as they became available," and further developing many of them. "The extent and diversity of Wheeler's tree and shrub plantings became a distinctive and enduring landscape feature." Russian poplars were planted extensively as shelterbelts, in combination with natural aspen bluffs; some trees he planted, such as the Ohio Buckeye, are uncommon on the prairie even today. He introduced the Siberian silver leaf willow to Western Canada from the U.S. He grew and sold elm, ash and willow trees. A black walnut from Manchuria was described in a newspaper article as "much hardier than previous walnuts from the experimental stations in North and South Dakota."

Wheeler earned fame as a horticulturist, particularly with his Wheeler poplar. Les Kerr, superintendent of the Forestry Farm at Indian Head, visited Maple Grove Farm to ask the master for advice. Wheeler had planted a shelterbelt of poplar seedlings in the early days and they had survived the hazards of canker, rust and dry weather. In the 1940s, Kerr took seed from the hardiest tree in the shelterbelt and propagated it on the forestry farm. Soon, thousands of these Wheeler poplar seedlings were being shipped out each year for planting throughout Canada. "By introducing fruits and trees," said Kerr in a 1955 speech, "Dr.Wheeler contributed much to welfare and happiness in the West."

Lilian (always "Lil" or much later plain "Ma" to her husband, sometimes Lily to others—she signed her name "Lilian" to a legal document in Victoria, B.C.) was in charge of selling berries at the farm. She paid the Wheeler and Partridge children 5¢ for each quart basket they picked. Customers who picked their own were charged less. But she expected recognition of her status, and when the local doctor's wife telephoned to tell her how many baskets of berries she wanted delivered, Lilian in her soft, gentle voice, replied that she did not *peddle* berries, and hung up. The doctor called later and said he would come around for the berries.

A string of new frame buildings began to rise. A combination granary and seed mill built in 1918 was modified in 1922–23 to facilitate his commercial seed grain operation. Between 1918 and 1923, the farm saw a new smithy workshop go up (farm manager Henry Partridge sharpened ploughshares and did small jobs here, but bigger work was done in Rosthern), a large machinery shed, car garage, granaries, chicken coop and workshop. He built a long shed, running east-west, south of the house and leading into the house orchard. Here he stored horticultural stock over winter, and from here he and his employees prepared the stock for marketing in the spring. His daughter Isabelle, who took more of an interest in Maple Grove's operations than her sisters, recalls packing stock there as a teenager. She was said to have her father's ability to predict weather. Isabelle ended up running the farm, along with her husband, and later her son, for several decades.

It's easy to imagine the excitement at Maple Grove Farm when the Wheelers decided in 1925 to build a bigger house. Henry and Hettie Partridge had shoe-horned their family (daughter Esther, sons George, Leonard and Edward) into the addition built onto the back of the 1908 house. The Wheelers then had only two bedrooms; May and Ella shared one, and Isabelle and Elizabeth slept in their parents' bedroom.

Charlie Wilkers, of Rosthern, was hired to build the third house—about 300 feet south of the 1908 building—for a total cost of $5,000. Looking ahead, Wheeler had it wired for electricity, although that wonder didn't appear until the 1950s. It had indoor plumbing, a septic tank, and was heated with an oil furnace fed from an outside tank. There was a full-height basement, but with a sand floor as was the custom at the time. A hole could be dug for storing vegetables over winter.

The two-storey, wood-frame structure was typical of farmhouse design throughout the grain-growing regions of western Canada and the United States. It was distinguished by three narrow windows on the front and back elevations rather than the usual two, broader windows. The back door led into a kitchen, then a hall into the living room and dining room on the left. Wheeler's den was on the right, through an archway. There were four bedrooms upstairs; one for the parents; the other two each accommodating two girls; and the fourth for a hired hand, or company. Isabelle and Elizabeth loved to spend time in the attic, where there were shelves for books and toys.

Wheeler's personal indulgence was a small balcony atop the front veranda, accessed from the main bedroom. When first built, the veranda was open, and the balcony uncovered. Soon, the veranda was enclosed and a roof put over the balcony, a special private vantage point on which for years to come he would relax. He smoked his pipe and admired his domain—particularly when dark storm clouds scudded overhead—"until a big clap of thunder came and then he'd run inside."

How spacious the old house must have been for the Partridges as they spread themselves and their belongings upstairs and down. Living in the same, but divided house, the Partridge and Wheeler children had grown up together "like brothers and sisters... We had a happy childhood. You know, I always thought how sad that must have been," mused daughter Elizabeth. "Almost every time Mrs. Partridge had a baby it was a son. In later years, I thought it must have hurt him. My mom told me that every time she had a child, she always hoped it would be a boy. But he loved his girls."

Although Wheeler didn't read to his girls, he made sure there were plenty of books for them. Every year he bought them the traditional English favourite, *Girls' Annual*, and *Boys' Annual* for the Partridge boys. Christmas was special. "Oh, yes, we always had a tree and lots of presents, plenty of dolls. In the old house, he never put up the tree until Christmas Eve. And we were not allowed to see it until Christmas morning, its branches bearing lit candles," Wheeler standing close by, in case. "I remember one time when the door was a little bit ajar and I saw the tree, I felt I was committing a sacrilege by seeing it before Christmas morning." On the morning of the big day, the girls would wake up and find bags of presents at the end of each bed, and more under the tree.

Wheeler loved to give presents at any time of year, but at Christmas there was no stopping him. "He used to send to Eaton's and Simpson's and order toys for us. I still remember that big, wooden crate coming in. And they'd take it into Dad's den and Mom and Dad would shut the door and they'd be unwrapping things. She told me once 'I'd be ashamed to tell people how much he spent.' And then he'd say 'I don't know, Lil, we don't seem to have enough for the girls somehow.' And he'd go and send in another order."

"He did things for people," said Elizabeth. "Our young cousins in Maymont said they'd never forget. They would never have known what Christmas was like if not for their Uncle Seager, because my auntie Maud was very, very poor. She was left a widow and lived in the house that my grandfather Martin had built. She didn't even have a Christmas tree and Dad would send a big packing case full of things for them."

Maud's youngest, Ethel Boskill, living in North Battleford in 2001, recalled those times: "There was never much money for extras, such as Christmas. Always a big parcel arrived from Uncle Seager with gifts for everyone. There would be a five-pound box of chocolates which mother took charge of. Every evening we would get two or three chocolates until the box was empty."

Wheeler would climb the stepladder to decorate the room with crêpe paper chains festooned from a big bell at the center, to the corners. The grand feast featured turkey and Christmas pudding, and Wheeler always muttered: "Oh, pooh, we never had turkey in England. We had roast beef, good roast beef. Turkey is an American idea."

Isabelle recalled neighbors visiting at Christmas and her father whispering to his good friend, B.J. Friesen, "Stay back, just for a minute." He would have gifts for the Friesen children. "And he would open a bottle of his home-made wine and give him a drink."

In a way, Wheeler had sons. The Partridge boys were part of the family and ended up working in his orchard for a time. Elizabeth remembers her mother occasionally helping in the field when they were short-handed. The younger children were frightened of her then, perspiring, dirty-faced, so unlike her usual well-groomed self.

In summer, later on, there were as many as six hired men, four in the orchard and two in the fields. At threshing time, meals were taken out to the fields. The work was hard, but according to one hand, almost idyllic at times. Each man knew his job, how the boss wanted it done. The late John Martens, of Rosthern, was hired as a 21-year-old in 1945, and stayed on for three summers. "I ... thought if I could work for him it would be the greatest thing in the world," he said in a 1988 interview in *The Saskatchewan Valley News*.

He recalled the beauty of the big orchard in blossom "just like a white and pink cloud... It was so different from anything else anyone had ever seen. You couldn't see the house from the road. Mr.Wheeler had planted trees along both sides of the driveway so that you drove through a tunnel of trees and you had to be almost at the house before you saw it. There was no other farm like his around." Everything was ordered and well cared for, the employer never raised his voice, there was plenty of shade on hot afternoons and, Martens recalled, he found it relaxing to sit milking five cows after a day's work in the fields or the orchards. "Mr.Wheeler expected nothing but perfection. He never rushed you, but he expected that you would do the job well. He was always cheerful, organized and punctual... Breakfast was at 6:30; lunch was at noon sharp; dinner at 6:30 ... he had strict rules and he lived by them. I was so impressed with Seager Wheeler when I worked for him, because when I was a kid and went to school, our teacher said Seager Wheeler is the greatest man to ever set foot on Canadian soil. He said he will go down in history as the greatest man of the century."

Seager respected the time and effort Lilian spent cooking for them all, and made sure the men stopped work at the same time each day so they'd be washed up and at the table when the meal was ready. There was plenty of milk, cream and butter for the Wheelers, the Partridges and for the hired men. John Martens recalled Wheeler telling him that it was healthier to eat just a little meat and lots of vegetables and fruit.

The staple meat at Maple Grove Farm, as on most farms, was pork. With so many people living at home, and several farmhands, pigs were slaughtered several times a year. Pork chops and roasts were pickled in salt brine or frozen outside. A small frame smokehouse built early in the century provided hams, bacon and, sometimes, sausages.

By 1922, Wheeler had revamped the approach to his farm. The long, winding maple-flanked trail from the main road was displaced by a much shorter, 40'-wide driveway. Both sides were lined with several rows of Colorado blue spruce, his favourite jack pine, balsam fir, Black Hills spruce, Prince of Wales maple, Russian olive, white willow, ash and elm.

At 54 years of age, stockier, bald on top and displaying an experience-lined face, he still worked from just after sunup to sundown. Not all of his day was devoted to the fruit orchard; that year, he had planted more than 300 varieties and strains of wheat in his head-row plots. He also had under observation oats, barley, fodder plants, grasses, vegetables and shade trees. He made his rounds of every plot, stopping to check and work. If he wasn't working at night with his seed and wheat sheaf selections, and jotting notes, he might don the earphones for his new battery-powered radio and tune in Saskatoon or Regina.

During the 1920s and 1930s, Wheeler continued to run a large wheat selection nursery, testing cereals from many parts of the world. Always searching for a better wheat variety that would not be vulnerable to rust, he would send scores of plants to Dr. J.B. Harrington, head of the University of Saskatchewan's field husbandry department, to test them under a different environment, exposed to attack by wheat stem rust. He collaborated with Harrington for nearly 40 years. And he was trying to develop an 80-day wheat.

The newspaper campaign for federal funding to support Wheeler's work was resumed by the *Saskatoon Phoenix* in late 1922. An in-depth article about his work in the fruit orchards wound up with an impassioned plea for financial recognition:

"The world has beaten a path to his door: government officials, agricultural officials and prominent citizens have visited him at his obscure little farm near Rosthern, and have gone away with sentiments of the deepest admiration and respect for the little toiler; they have praised him in public and in private; he has been lauded as a benefactor of his country, and he has no doubt been the greatest advertisement Canada ever had, but through all the years of his surpassing achievements, he has been forced to depend on his own slender private purse to finance a work from which the public has profited."

The "greatest man of the century" had joined the automobile age in 1918. He built a small garage to house his crank-start $700 Ford Model T; a few years later, he bought another garage and had it hauled to the farm for a Star automobile that Henry Partridge owned. In 1918, he also bought his first tractor, a Fordson, but he was suspicious of their dependability. Wheeler was not for machinery born; he preferred horses until well into the 1930s, while his brother Percy was a natural with machinery, and liked tractors. Seager soon realized that he didn't like to drive, or couldn't, and eventually things found their own level: Henry Partridge drove him to town and anywhere else he wished to go, becoming his unofficial chauffeur.

"He just thought he could drive," recalled his daughter Isabelle, laughing. He and Lilian were out driving soon after he purchased the narrow-wheeled, flapping-fendered Model T, and he couldn't help showing off when they came to a sharp turn on the road, with bushes on either side: "Watch me, Lil, I can go through the eye of a needle," he boasted. He swerved and they landed in the ditch.

Elizabeth added: "He'd be driving and smoking his pipe and he'd be pointing with his pipe saying 'That's a good crop,' or 'That's a poor crop,' and my Auntie Maud would shout, 'Never mind the crops, just keep your hands on the wheel.'" One of Wheeler's best friends in Rosthern was Ralph Fleury, who operated a pharmacy. He had been an officer in Sir Henry Pellatt's militia regiment in Toronto, was sharp-minded and flamboyant. He had caught the automobile bug early and had a reputation for continually changing cars— McLaughlin, Durant, Reo, Auburn. In the late 1930s he bought a huge Studebaker, a limousine really, with back, middle and front seats. Late in the decade, Wheeler bought the Studebaker from Fleury and, of course, Henry would drive Wheeler and members of the family.

"I was embarrassed riding in it," recalled Isabelle. "Everyone would look at us."

"I hated that car," agreed Elizabeth. "I guess Mr. Fleury talked Dad into buying it. It was terribly hard on the gas. And those blinds, ugh!"

Historian Victor Friesen, one-time neighbor of the Wheelers and acquaintance of the younger girls, wrote of the car with gratitude. "And years later when a sudden death among our kinfolk made it necessary for my mother to go to Prince Albert, it was Wheeler who kindly arranged that she be driven there in his own Studebaker (as a preschooler I was taken along)."

That Wheeler was a pioneer in western Canadian fruit growing was made plain in the

Saskatchewan Valley News edition of March 4, 1926. Its front page's seven columns, and much of the back page, were devoted to a talk he gave on his work to that time.

Wheeler described himself as "freelance" horticulturist, "not tied down by red tape." One value of his work, he said, was in finding out what wouldn't grow under prairie conditions so time wouldn't be wasted on them. Until recently, raspberries had to be laid down and covered before winter, but now there were varieties that needed no protection.

In his passion to develop fruit trees for Saskatchewan farmers, Wheeler was tantalized by reports from South Dakota, where weather was only a little less severe. There, one orchard alone shipped out more than 40,000 cases of apples. He was always careful to emphasize that no claims could be made for a standard-size apple tree for the prairie region. He had good success with crabs. Eventually, he would be successful in selecting many fruit varieties suitable to Saskatchewan conditions. These would be distributed throughout the prairies, Yukon and Alaska.

Although he never did develop a full-size apple, he did in time develop the Amur and Saska crabapples, strains of Opata, Mammoth and Assiniboine plums, Prolific and Ruby cherry-plum hybrids, Tom Thumb cherries and the Advance sandcherry.

His 1927 catalogue offered Marquis 10B, Red Bobs, Kitchener, Garnet and Kanred winter wheat, and was the first to list a Horticultural Section, just more than a page. He mentioned now having 12 acres devoted to fruits, apples, raspberries, rhubarb and sunflowers. The next year, he listed three pages; by 1942, the cover bore pictures of fruit and there were 10 pages, and the only wheat seed listed was improved, now "rust-resistant" Renown. For the first time, his catalogue did not offer seed of the wheat that had been the foundation of the "wheat economy" of Canada, Marquis 10B.

As each season's harvest of more varieties of fruits and berries grew, so did Lilian Wheeler's kitchen research. At least one batch of each variety of the orchard's bounty of crabapples, plums, cherries, currants, raspberries and strawberries was preserved and the texture and flavour noted. Of course, any fruit or berry could be made into preserves, jams or jellies, but the Wheelers of Maple Grove Farm would recommend only the best.

"We have at home," he said in the *News*, "some 300 quarts of home grown fruit, canned, sufficient to permit us to have fruit preserves on the table practically every day in the year; in fact, we did not use up all the fruit that we had canned during the previous season. And this was not all. We had all the raspberries and strawberries and other small fruit during the fruiting season, from July until the end of September, whenever we wanted it, on the table as fresh fruit."

He had found that in developing fruits in the north, it was best to grow them in bush form, with lower branches coming out about a foot from the ground; they were less likely to fall victim to sun scald or cold, and could be picked more easily. He cut older branches back on his plums to encourage new spring growth, which fruited the next season. He promulgated dos and don'ts of fruit growing, based on his own experience.

Wheeler's old friend John Bracken, the field husbandry professor and long-time activist with the farmers' protest movement, became premier of Manitoba. He had moved there in 1920 to become principal of the Manitoba Agricultural College. The Manitoba Grain Growers' Association had adopted the "Farmers Platform," and created the United Farmers of Manitoba. In 1922, the UFM—which insisted it was not a party as such—had won 28 seats in the legislature, without a leader. Bracken was asked to take the helm, and finally agreed, reluctantly.

Bracken favoured return of the Canadian Wheat Board, a temporary federal agency that, from 1917 to 1920, had controlled grain marketing. It made one payment on delivery of grain, and the last one at year's end. After 1920, the Progressive Party gained strength in Ottawa because of agrarian discontent with a drop in grain prices. In 1922, the governments of Charles Dunning, Liberal premier of Saskatchewan, and the United Farmers of Alberta premier Herbert Greenfield, passed legislation allowing reinstatement of the board. But this required approval of all prairie provinces, and in Manitoba, although approved by Premier Bracken, his 27 populist farmer "delegates" rejected the idea.

In September 1928, Wheeler received a letter from W.D. Albright, superintendent of the Dominion Experimental Farm at Beaverlodge, Alberta, stating he would send some Saskatoon roots "with great pleasure for your experimental orchard... The best part of your letter is the intimation that you may possibly accompany Mr. Newman on his visit to the Peace River district next summer. You may be sure of a very hearty welcome as our guest."

That summer, Charlie Wilkers built a gambrel-roofed barn to replace the primitive 1909 stable; it was enlarged through the years. Following general practice of the time, the barn was never painted, and eventually developed a weathered grey patina. Isabelle Blatz said Wilkers did most of the building on the farm, except for the 1908 house. The barn housed draft horses and dairy cows.

Canada's agriculture minister, Robert Weir, wrote in November 1931, thanking Wheeler for 200 two-year-old English white willows. "I will appreciate the gift more than you realize. Nothing could be a more appropriate remembrance of yourself to me than these trees especially if they do well and I can assure you we will give them every chance. We are planting them in a well cultivated piece of land, in fact in our garden. I had a letter from my brother stating what full instructions you had sent him and that he was taking every care to conform with your instructions."

Wheeler still was being recognized for his work with grain production. In January 1931, he was given an honorary life membership in the Saskatchewan Agricultural Societies Association for "the contribution he has made to the cause of pure seed."

From W.R. Leslie, superintendent of the Morden experimental farm, in March 1932: "When you advise that you have 16 acres of fruit to look after, I am amazed in wondering how you manage same, this all the more so when you are obliged to spend so much time receiving visitors in your kindly, helpful way...

"Your seedling plantations should be of very great interest in 1932. We have many good seedling plums, which have sprung from such mother parents as Assiniboine, Pembina, Cree, Compass Cherry and Opata. If you can get down when the fruits are ripe, I hope you will decide that a number of these Morden selections are worthy of being included in your trials. We will be pleased to hear from you any time we can send material or help in any way. You are doing mighty good work in central Saskatchewan and one which is sure to bring you permanent blessing of the peoples, who shall from generations to generations dwell upon Canadian prairie plains."

A 1933 newspaper story pointed out that wheat and fruit were doing well at Maple Grove Farm despite a serious drought, and "Dr. Helge Nelson, of Sweden, a visitor last week, felt a thrill of national pride when he saw the magnificent crop of oats from the variety introduced by Nillson-Ehle, of the famous Svalof plant-breeding station in Sweden..."

From the *Western Producer*, June 8, 1933: "In spite of his sixty-four years, he is exceedingly active and when he has conducted his visitors over his farm and through the horticultural section, they are all glad to get back to the house for a breathing spell and a drink of refreshing cold water."

Elizabeth Wheeler remembered her mother telling her that if it hadn't been for the income from the orchard and tree nursery, her father couldn't have carried on his experimental work.

— TWENTY —

The Roaring Twenties

500 million bushels a year—Seager's wheat basis of "wheat economy"—grain economy rests on family farm—competitive inferiority of farming—thistles tumble with prices—Hudson Bay Railway to Churchill—home life—crystal radios, sports—CSGA honour—Ottawa makes Seager's farm first private experimental sub-station—federal official reminds him who is boss—term extended beyond retirement age.

The freedom of the automobile age was well established in the farm belt, but other common features of the Roaring Twenties such as electricity and running water still were limited mainly to urban dwellers. One fashion—the flapper look—soon was adopted by the style-conscious girls and women of rural Canada. Lilian Wheeler bought the latest patterns and Mrs. Blatz, a Rosthern widow, turned out slender, long-waisted dresses for May and Ella on an upstairs sewing machine at Maple Grove Farm. The older girls were cropping their hair. But Lilian laid down the law when she admonished them: "I don't mind powder, but don't let me catch you putting on rouge."

Lilian's sister Maud now was a frequent visitor to Maple Grove Farm. Her husband Percy Barrett was Wheeler's cousin and good friend, and he and Maud had moved to Maymont about 1909. In 1925, Percy was following a walking plough when the share caught on a stone. The handles levered upwards and struck him in the chest. The Maymont history claimed, "he developed tuberculosis and after spending several months in the Saskatoon Sanatorium passed away in August, 1925." Maud was left to raise four children. "I think she got a widow's pension of about $8 a month," said Elizabeth Wheeler. "Had it not been for Dad, and her brothers, I don't know how she could have survived." Maud died in 1950.

Maud's daughter, Ethel Boskill, recalled, "Mother was always interested in gardening, especially fruit trees. When at Rosthern she would be out in the orchard with Uncle Seager learning all she could. He supplied her with many fruit trees, cherries, plums and raspberries. They did very well in our sandy soil and mother sold fruit to neighbors for quite a few years."

In the evening, Wheeler would sit in his big armchair and read, or perhaps play his concertina and sing. "He had a little black terrier dog that would howl along with him," said Ethel. Then he went to bed to read. Lilian sometimes played the piano and sang, and Maud would join her, two light sopranos together. The girls crowded in to sing in chorus.

"I remember," said Elizabeth, "we used to be playing the piano and singing later at night when Auntie Maud was there and Dad was upstairs in bed, and he'd holler 'Quit that noise!' and Auntie Maud shouted back 'Oh, Seager!' and we all laughed and went on playing and singing."

The little girls were tickled by their father's bantering manner. If they ran into the house calling out "Where's Mommy?" he would reply, "Your mother's gone to see a man about a dog," or "She's gone looking for a soldier." Getting ready for a long trip, he would tell them "I'm going around Robin Hood's barn."

In the last half of the 1920s, the area of improved land on the prairies had increased to 60 million acres, and wheat production was at a plateau of between 300 and 500 million bushels a year, 40% of the world's export market, and mostly grown from Wheeler's Marquis 10B and Red Bobs. The "wheat economy" was firmly established—with the farmers at the base of the pyramid. After collapsing in the early 1920s, wheat prices rose near the end of the decade, then dropped in 1930–32. Wrote Gerald Friesen in *The Canadian Prairies*:

> "A cycle in prairie agricultural history had been completed by 1930. The grain economy rested on sure foundations. The family farm and the rural village were functioning as their architects would have wished. The complex structure of the grain production, handling, and grading systems was similarly accepted on all sides. But the onset of a world depression made evident the one crucial unresolved issue in farm politics; as V.C. Fowke, the pre-eminent scholar of the wheat economy has written: 'One of the most significant features of the national policy has been a persistent disregard of the competitive inferiority of agriculture within the price system. The major era of the national policy which ended in 1930 witnessed no serious attempt on the part of the government to ameliorate or even to assess that inferiority.' The crisis of the 1930s was so great, however, that the federal government and the Canadian people were forced to reconsider their reliance on the competitive market for agricultural exports."

When stock markets around the world collapsed with a thud in 1929, western farmers did not yet realize what was to come, partly because of the naivety of their prime minister, Mackenzie King, who maintained: "While a number of people have suffered owing to the sharp decline, the soundness of Canadian securities generally is not affected. Business was never better." Bank spokesmen were equally unruffled. The next year, throughout the country, many families were destitute. But Manitoba won compensation of $4.6 million from Ottawa when it finally won control of its natural resources, a windfall also enjoyed by Saskatchewan and Alberta.

The Canadian prairies had produced a record crop in 1928. The next year, drought hit some areas and, by 1930, was spreading ominously. Strong winds, hot and dry, were stealing topsoil, thistles tumbled, and so did produce prices. Farmers with big debt loads were scared stiff. They were told by agricultural experts to be smarter land managers, not to concentrate solely on growing wheat, not to expand acreage too much, not to neglect summerfallow so that moisture could be conserved—all methods advocated by Wheeler for many years.

A 1998 report by Canada Heritage said: "although Seager Wheeler's superior seed

samples were readily adopted by prairie farmers, often his messages regarding soil conservation and husbandry of the land were not, and the proof that they both needed to be
used together was established in the 1930s when the prairies turned into a dust bowl due
to poor soil conservation practices while Maple Grove Farm was producing 40 bushels to
the acre and other farms were producing only five to 10 bushels per acre, which was mixed
with Russian thistle."

In the federal election campaign of 1930, Liberal leader Mackenzie King said there was
no major unemployment problem. He would call no special meeting of federal and
provincial officials to discuss jobs and relief. His Conservative opponent, R.B. Bennett,
promised to end unemployment. After winning, the Bennett government passed an unemployment relief bill, which would spend $20 million on "make-work" jobs such as high-
ways, railways, wharves and other public projects, with just $4 million of it for direct
relief. The same year, some farm groups demanded cancellation of tax sales of property in
arrears, "in time of the present capitalist economic crisis."

The next year, Bennett announced purchase of two million bushels of wheat as part of
the relief program for starving people on the prairies. He said it was "practically a national calamity" that 98 per cent of residents in some municipalities in Saskatchewan were on
relief and some were near starvation. The Red Cross reported that southern Saskatchewan
faced "the most serious emergency Canada has ever known." More than 150,000 people
lived on the 3,385 square kilometres affected by drought and were desperate for food,
clothing and fuel.

In 1931, two dust storms dumped about 6,000 tons of topsoil on Winnipeg, a legacy of
faulty land practices of farmers in southern and central Saskatchewan. A dozen years earlier, Wheeler had written prophetically about the causes of soil drifting in his book
Profitable Grain Growing:

> "Under our western conditions where the prevailing high winds in the
> spring, especially during the month of May, not only evaporate consider-
> able moisture but carry away soil into the atmosphere, into the lower
> parts of the field, into the wayside, the fences, not only the soil grains
> proper but also valuable humus is carried away… Burning the stubble is
> responsible for much of the loss… For an immediate return from a finan-
> cial point of view the soil is being put out of condition."

Meanwhile, partly due to Prime Minister Bennett's relief program, work had pushed
ahead on facilities at the Port of Churchill, in Manitoba, which the Hudson Bay Railway
now had reached. In September, the Saskatoon chamber of commerce sponsored a special
train carrying 300 observers, including Wheeler, to inspect the new port.

He made copious notes of all he saw—man-made and natural—and when he gave a
speech on his return, he was prescient in his prediction that Churchill would become a
great tourist attraction; he was less accurate in his belief that Churchill would become one
of the world's great ports and a popular shipping site for prairie wheat.

By nature and necessity a meticulous man, Wheeler didn't like anyone to disturb anything in his den. "Everything had to stay the same," said daughter Elizabeth. "Every time
he went away on a trip, he would say: 'Now don't you touch anything. You leave things
as they are.' And we'd say 'No, Daddy, we won't.' And we'd just tidy up a bit (laughter),
but not touch anything of his. He didn't like anyone touching his personal things. I

remember one time I took an aspirin from out of the bottle he kept by the side of his bed. And when he came home, he said to me: 'I'll buy you a bottle of aspirins but don't touch mine.'"

He always dressed up on Sundays, suit, black boots and best hat. He didn't like the brown suits in vogue at the time, preferring black, grey or navy blue. His best suit was a navy serge. He would drawl in Isle of Wight dialect, "Me faaaather wore a navy serge, me grandfaaather wore a navy serge, and I wear a navy serge."

Sunday was a day of rest at Maple Grove Farm, but Wheeler couldn't resist putting something right if it caught his attention. He was in the orchard turning some earth over with a shovel when Lilian good-naturedly cautioned him: "God will punish you!" "I'm not working, Lil, I'm just puttering around."

Since there was no Anglican church nearby, Lilian arranged for the girls to receive Sunday school material by mail from the diocese office in Prince Albert. "They were nice little picture cards with scripture," said Isabelle, "I still have my copy of *Peep of Day*." "So do I," added Elizabeth, "and also *Line Upon Line*. They were illustrated Bible lessons."

Wheeler was a great sports fan. He was active with his hometown baseball team, the Wheat Kings, which won the Saskatchewan championship three times. In 1936, the hockey team was renamed the Wheat Kings as well, in his honour. They were provincial champions in 1938, and Wheeler, as team president, was included in the championship photograph.

Whenever big hockey games were on in the 1930s, particularly the Toronto Maple Leafs, he sat in front of the radio, which he always placed on the piano bench, Foster Hewitt's "He shoots, he scores" commentary bringing the game to life. And he would have Lilian place his supper beside the radio when baseball's world series was being played, so he could eat and cheer on his favourite team. This year, 1931, the Montreal Canadiens beat the Chicago Blackhawks three games to two to win the Stanley Cup. Often they all listened to the battery radio: *Lux Radio Theatre, Amos and Andy, Charlie McCarthy, Fibber McGee and Molly, The Nightingale of the Airways*. Sometimes he would invite neighbors in to listen, and almost invariably there would be static drowning out the program and he would mutter "It's not usually like this!"

"When the World Series was on, he always stuck up for the underdog team," said Elizabeth. "He'd come in from his work and we'd have his dinner ready at noon. We'd have to set it on the piano bench and he'd sit there chewing and sometimes he'd say 'Oh, the boys aren't doing very well, I'd better get out my pipe!'" "Or his Havana cigars from Christmas," added Isabelle. "And you know, so many times, they'd score after that."

Wheeler had a lasting effect on those he met. W.C. Martin, who worked for him briefly in 1905, had taken a homestead west of Rosthern, at Petroffa (no longer on the map) and occasionally he and his son Ernest visited Maple Grove Farm. The Martins and Wheelers had become fast friends. "He gave my Dad a sample of 10B Marquis wheat about 1931. Dad kept and cherished this sample until he passed away in 1979. He had given me the sample and I have had it ever since," Ernest wrote in a letter accompanying the sample of Marquis 10B when he donated it to the Seager Wheeler Historic Farm Society. In a 2000 interview, Ernest Martin said he and his father "were almost a part of the family. We would travel by horse the 35 miles to the Wheeler farm. Often we spent the night at their house. We used to walk all through those 40 acres of orchard. Seager Wheeler just lived agriculture. A great man! My Dad thought he was just everything."

In 1931, Wheeler's peers honoured him at the annual convention of the seed growers' association held at the Kemptville, Ontario, agricultural school. He was the first of 10 growers elected to an honour class to commemorate founder Dr. J.W. Robertson. Writing of the event in *Farm and Ranch Review*, Kathleen Strange said, "For many years it was mainly upon the shoulders of Wheeler that the production of elite stocks of wheat depended and there is no better strain of Marquis than his."

The seed growers' recognition was followed by another the same year, one that couldn't have come at a better time. A letter dated December 14, 1931, arrived from Robert Weir, agriculture minister in the year-old Tory government of R.B. Bennett. He wrote that Wheeler would get some official financial recognition at last.

> "After a great deal of delay we have passed an Order-in-Council creating the position of Experimental Sub-Station Superintendent in the Experimental Farms Branch in Saskatchewan. I am enclosing an application form for you to fill in and return. This is just a matter of form. The remuneration attached to this position will start at $2220.00 a year. The work will not make any difference in your operations, not the slightest. It is the only way, with our present Civil Service arrangements for positions, that I could work out so that we could extend to you in a tangible way, small as it is, something of our appreciation of what you have contributed to Agriculture in Western Canada.
>
> I feel that this sum is much too small and yet no sum could quite pay you, not only for what you have contributed in grains, fruits and flowers, but more particularly for the inspiration that you have been to so many people for many years. Every person that one meets who has visited your farm makes similar statements, first, the great work that you have done and are doing, second, the inspiration that you were to them in their visit, third, and perhaps most noticeable your absolute unselfishness in the time and advice that you give to your visitors.
>
> This action of the Government was not in any way brought about by requests from people on your behalf. I thought you would be pleased to know this…
>
> Remember that this is not to entail any extra duties on you. It means simply that you carry on the way you have done in the past as a true experimental station with not only the free advice you have always given but again, if I may repeat, that inspiration that has meant so much to many…"

At age 63, Wheeler would start getting a government cheque as sub-station superintendent. An initial press report got it wrong, stating the government had bought Maple Grove Farm.

Wheeler was used to record keeping, but now he became acquainted with government red tape. The Canadian Civil Service Commission, in January 1932, wanted "a list of positions held to date showing clearly the nature of the duties involved." Wheeler replied: "During the past thirty (30) years on my own farm… I have carried on private experimental work and plant breeding of farm crops, principally cereal crops and the production of pedigreed seed grains, also experimental horticulture during the past 13 years."

The agriculture department notified him of a temporary certificate of appointment from December 31, 1931, and asked him to complete an Establishment Record Enquiry Card and Particulars as to Employees form. This covered birthplace, conjugal status, racial origin, military service, pension number, previous government service, was he a British subject?

On January 15, Wheeler wrote to his old friend George Chipman, editor of the *Grain Growers' Guide*:

> "I am also enclosing Mr. Weir's letter to me. While this was marked Confidential, I feel I would like you to read it as you are one of three men who have for so many years past been of real assistance to me in many ways.

> Mr. L.H. Newman since I first met him some 23 years ago as Secretary of the Canadian Seed Growers Association, and since he was made Dominion Cerealist, has at all times kindly co-operated with me in my seed growing operations, and in testing out some of my recent grain selections, and also yourself in our several transactions in the past which has been of real assistance to me in a financial way as well as your friendly co-operation at all times. And also Mr. Weir's efforts to secure for me this appointment which comes at a time when it will be appreciated."

Newman wrote near the end of January: "This recognition has been a long time coming, but this was due largely to the difficulty of doing anything for any one person without establishing a precedent and also without leaving oneself open to having to do the same thing for a lot more…"

His first cheque, for $190.97, came at the beginning of February, sent by E.S. Archibald, director of experimental farms, Ottawa.

The same day, he got a letter from G.D. Matthews, superintendent of the experimental station at Scott, Sask., saying he had been advised by Newman that Wheeler had 16 selections of wheat he wanted tested at the Scott station, and he would be pleased to carry out the tests.

Farmer W.L. Martin wrote from Maidstone, Saskatchewan, "Will you kindly send me your catalogue of hardy fruits? Have you any sand cherries? And also Siberian crabs? Allow me to congratulate you on the arrangement made with you by the government re future use of your farm for experimental purposes under your direction. This meets with my approval and is in line with what I have considered for some time was coming to you."

Then the director of experimental farms sent a letter March 8, 1932, which gently set out the fact that he now was Wheeler's boss:

> As a newly-appointed official of the Experimental Farms Branch of the Federal Department of Agriculture, you will naturally be expecting to receive from me as Director of the above Branch an intimation as to the course of procedure you are to follow.

> As your work will naturally be confined largely to activities which are related to the work of the Cereal Division, the Forage Crops Division and the Horticultural Division, I have obtained from the Chiefs of these Divisions their opinions as to how they may best assist you in your efforts

to enlarge upon your contributions in these three fields. It is the opinion of these officials, and in this I heartily concur, that in view of the splendid work you have already done and already have under way, that it would be inadvisable to suggest any radical change at this time. Rather is it our opinion that you should proceed as you have been doing but that you consult these men with a view to insuring that you are not unnecessarily duplicating the work done at some of the other Branch Farms or Stations. These men will endeavour to visit you at least once each year and will always be prepared to go over your work carefully with a view to assisting you as much as possible. As time passes they may be able to suggest lines of work which you might possibly be able to take up without burdening yourself unduly. Similarly, they may be able to assist you in weeding out certain lines in order to make room for others which appear more promising."

This was a typical letter sent by a civil servant to a person imposed upon him by a politician. Archibald had to balance himself on the fence, the good of the service on one side, the wishes of politicians on the other. He said all the things the politicians wanted to hear, but at the same time, asserted the authority that was his to wield.

But Archibald's message wasn't quite what Wheeler wanted to hear. Since he strode into the unknown 45 years earlier, an optimistic boy determined to make good, he had worked unfettered save for the dictates of his scientific discipline. He had done it his way. Now, he felt eyes staring over his shoulder, and this bothered him.

Three weeks later, another letter from Archibald informed him that a certificate of permanent appointment would be issued "when the necessary evidence regarding his age, health and character is on file…"

On April 15, another letter from Archibald, this time informing Wheeler the permanent appointment certificate as Experimental Sub-Station Superintendent had been issued by the Civil Service Commission. All he had to do now was to complete an Oath of Allegiance and of Office form before a Justice of the Peace, and return it to Archibald.

In 1933, when he was 65 years old, a civil service ruling set retirement age for all civil servants at 65. An appeal was made on his behalf and an extension of his employment was granted.

Life at Maple Grove Farm became more straitened during the Dirty Thirties, but because of the visionary aspects of his farming methods—and the timely income from Ottawa—Wheeler got through the depression and drought years far more easily than most of his neighbors, some of them complaining that he "made them look bad." His former employee, John Martens, remembers Wheeler saying: "Everybody looks good in a good year, but you can tell a good farmer in a bad year."

The Wheeler girls' lives at Maple Grove Farm were hardly ruffled by the desperate conditions around them. Elizabeth remembered nothing of hardship on the farm, although she had heard people who went through the period say they had to have outside help:

"We were an oasis in the desert. I remember I asked for something from my mother and she said 'Your daddy's a poor man now,' but I don't remember us being poor. She just meant that he had to be careful now. But we always had a big vegetable garden and all that fruit. Mother canned food and we had an icehouse. The butter she made and the cream were stored there. We had animals for milk and meat, we had chickens and eggs. Mother made bread, and sometimes we bought bread. The only difference I can see is that he bought the south farm at that time, and where he would have paid cash for it, he had to pay something on it each year."

One farmer from this period never forgot Wheeler's generosity. Elizabeth Wheeler was at the farm site in 1996 to make a speech at a ceremony designating it a national historic site. An elderly man pulled at her sleeve, saying he had been a friend of her father's and wanted to tell her a story. He had come out from England many years before with his wife and five children, and lived in the bush not far from Maple Grove Farm.

Wheeler had said to him, "You know, you can't live out here in the bush with five children and have nothing, no means of support. You've got to have some means of livelihood." Not long after, the old man said, Wheeler came to see him with a cow, some chickens and some eggs. "There now, you've got something to go on."

Half way through a decade that was seeing prairie farmlands destroyed, and harsh economic conditions around the world, Wheeler's friends in high places got together and in the winter of 1935, notified him that he was being presented with a gift—a trip to England.

TWENTY-ONE

Trip of a Lifetime

Packing for England—leaves Henry in charge—Isle of Wight, reporters, well-wishers crowd him—pageant in Sherwood Forest, Experimental Station, Cambridge University, London, the old school, Naval Review—new Wheat Board guarantees minimum wheat price—*Guide* editor killed—hockey and baseball—Coronation Medal—retired by Ottawa—70th birthday banquet—Henry Partridge retires.

The Wheeler household was in a whirl early that spring of 1935. What should they buy, what should they pack for almost two months abroad?

For the last few years, Wheeler had been having clothing tailor-made in England. He now ordered a suit and an overcoat from Egerton Burnett's Ltd., Somerset, and a couple of weeks later another order, "a lounge suit made up of this pattern cloth … tasteful tailoring … made to measurements of my former order … buttons outside on trousers." He wanted side pockets, inside pocket and watch pocket, all deep, trousers "lined, but not heavy lining, cuff bottoms." He enclosed a money order and directed that they be delivered to his niece at 86 Somers Road, Southsea, "…because I expect to be in England."

Seager and Lilian had long discussions about their itinerary because CPR officials had to be told where they planned to go, and for how long, so arrangements could be made. Elizabeth was going too, although her father would pay her passage and travel expenses.

Harry Strange, now a director of the Searle Grain Co. Ltd., wrote: "We were all more than glad to read in the paper that you had been tendered a gift trip to England through the medium of a number of your friends and the Canadian Pacific Railway. This is splendid and only, however, what you deserve. We hope that you will have a most pleasant trip and come back refreshed, ready for many more years of the good work you have been rendering to Western Canada."

On May 5, he was a happy man. He had just been to Saskatoon to pick up tickets; his harvest of fruit trees was all sold; he had shipped a freight-car load of first generation registered wheat. He was past his 67th birthday, but the approach of old age in no way blunted his enthusiasm for life and for his first extended holiday after 50 years of hard work.

The Maple Grove Farm operation was left in the capable hands of Henry Partridge who, after 32 years, knew exactly what was required. They left Saskatoon by train on May 10, arriving in Montreal four days later. The S.S. *Montrose* sailed May 15, at 9 a.m.

The ship was a destination in itself, an enjoyable time with nothing to do but be waited on by courteous stewards while eating multi-coursed delicious meals, read, play deck games, get acquainted with other passengers. They were wakened each morning with pots of tea and biscuits. Breakfast was at 8 a.m., lunch at 1 p.m. and dinner at 7 p.m. At 10 a.m., a cup of soup and biscuits were served on deck or in the lounge; at four in the afternoon, tea, cakes and buns. There was a masquerade ball one evening, and on Sunday morning, church service. Every evening, there were card parties.

Elizabeth wrote: "'There you are my girl, take your first look.' My father has his arm around me as we watch the outlines of the English coast come into view… My mother is not with us. She has not been a good sailor. While she lay too ill to lift her head from the pillow, he has been wishing for a storm at sea… His luggage is labelled 'Dr. Seager Wheeler, Proprietor, Maple Grove Farm, Rosthern, Sask., Canada,' and he's wearing King George V's Silver Jubilee Medal given this year 1935 to citizens of outstanding accomplishments."

When the ship docked at Southampton, reporters, photographers, relations and the CP Steamship agent were waiting for them. Wheeler exclaimed to a reporter, "Didn't I get a thrill when I saw the Isle of Wight an hour or two ago. I couldn't keep the tears back. It's been 50 years since I left, you know." Next day, the *County Press* trumpeted: "Seager Wheeler Comes Home; Island Newsboy Became Wheat King; The Island Is Indeed Proud Of Its Native Son." One interviewer, "Patoc," referred to him as "Wheeler the Conqueror."

Eventually, they got away from the crush, through customs and aboard a train for Southsea, where they stayed with his niece Daisy, before crossing to the Isle of Wight for a nostalgic three-day visit with family and friends. Seager Wheeler's arrival in England was news, and mail found him wherever he travelled, letters of the do-you-remember kind; asking him to make speeches; invitations; seeking farming and emigration advice.

Next, they took a steamer back to the mainland, and on to Swanage, in Dorset, to meet his mother's relatives. And Lilian, of course, was eager to see her family again, so they travelled north by bus to Loughborough, near Leicester, where they spent two weeks visiting and sightseeing with her eldest sister, May and family, and several other relatives.

The old temperance man noted a decided change in drinking habits in England. "In the towns and villages there are numerous public bars where beer and spirits are consumed. I noted how orderly they were kept in passing and during my stay I did not once see any person under the influence of drink, so different to what it was when I was there as a boy. They take their drink soberly and quietly."

May took them to an historical pageant on the grounds of Sherwood Forest, near Nottingham. For the finale, the costumed characters from the 10 episodes mingled with the audience as they all sang *O God Our Help In Ages Past*. "This was one of the most impressive moments spent during our trip, and not easily forgotten," wrote Wheeler.

After touring the Rothamstead Experimental Station, he went on to Cambridge to visit its agriculture department, and to visit with George Chipman's son, Robert, studying there.

While in London, they were invited aboard the Empress of Britain to have lunch and a tour of the ship and marvel at the rotunda's roses, hydrangeas, rhododendrons, flowering shrubs and small trees all growing in soil, and as healthy as if they were growing outdoors.

London was a terrible place for strangers, Wheeler decided. He spent much of his two days there trying to find their way back to the hotel. "Nothing but enquiring of people my

way, and not finding it!" Friends showed them the city's historic landmarks and the botan-
ical gardens at Kew. Then, back to the Isle of Wight, where they stayed at Heath Cottage,
once occupied by his father Henry, and now by his half-brother, Ernest, and wife Alice.
Cliff Terrace, where Seager was born, was gone, swept away by the sea after land slippage.

In Ventnor, he noted that "the houses, shops, hotels, streets... the house we once lived
in was just the same, the euonymus shrub hedge still there—I used to take cuttings and
get them to grow when a boy. The same school across the street is there...the same shops
selling the same kinds of goods—butcher shop, fish shop, candy shop. I was agreeably
surprised. I met some of my old schoolmates and talked over school days." He was disappointed to see that the Pelham Woods he frequented as a boy, now was replaced by houses and gardens down to the highway.

Outside his old school, they could hear children inside reciting their lessons, Elizabeth
recalled. Her mother asked, "Why don't you go in and introduce yourself?" He demurred:
"Oh, no, I don't want to push myself forward."

During their farewell visit with Daisy, just before sailing home, they were thrilled with
the review of the fleet by King George V and the princes. The Wheelers stood three hours
waiting to see them in a crowd packing the road for six miles, waving small hand flags.
Next day, they boarded a steamer and, to Wheeler's delight, spent two hours moving
around and through the warships moored for a stretch of 20 miles along the coast.

"As soon as it was dark," Wheeler wrote, "a rocket went up from the King's yacht at
one end of the line, when instantly every one of the 150 warships was outlined in electric
lights showing the size and shape of each warship. After an interval each ship sent up
rockets high in the sky which burst in falling colored streams lighting up the whole sea
front. After another short interval, each ship sent up high in the sky searchlights, weaving
back and forth. This was all repeated once more and then, instantaneously, everything was
dark... it was estimated there were half a million people on Southsea beach, and another
large crowd on the Isle of Wight side as well... the following morning at daylight, not a
warship was there."

On their return to Canada, there was more sightseeing in Ottawa, Toronto and the fruit
country of the Niagara Peninsula. Back at Maple Grove Farm, Wheeler weighed himself.
He had gained 20 pounds.

The year ended with a tragedy. On Boxing Day, 1935, Wheeler's good friend George F.
Chipman was killed. Editor and manager of the *Grain Growers' Guide* for a quarter of a century, the 54-year-old was out with his hired hand shooting rabbits, which had been chewing his fruit trees, when his gun accidentally discharged.

Robert Chipman wrote: "I want to tell you how grateful Mother and Sally and I were
for your kind letter of sympathy after our recent loss. Your friendship with Dad must have
been one of the first he formed in the West and I know it has always been a close one
involving very high mutual regard."

Wheeler, of course, always kept track of events back in England, and in 1936 he sat fascinated many times in front of his radio as a royal tableau played to the world. In a 12-
month period, three kings sat on the throne—George V died, Edward VIII ascended, then
abdicated for the love of an American divorcee, and George VI was crowned. In 1937, he
received a letter bearing the Buckingham Palace crest. Enclosed was a medal commemo-
rating the Coronation of the previous May 12.

Later in the year, a letter from Ottawa was far less pleasing: E.S. Archibald, director of experimental farms, reminding him that in 1933 a special appeal had been made in Wheeler's case against the compulsory retirement age of 65 years, but

> "Extensions of employment of persons over sixty-five years of age are only granted until the employees reach the age of seventy years, which is the definite date of retirement. According to our records, you will be seventy on January 3rd next, hence I have no alternative but to recommend that you be retired as from that date."

He was entitled to seven months' pay after retirement.

Robert Weir, now a private citizen, wrote from his Weldon farm on March 30: "Has the Department of Agriculture reinstated you on your original standing of $2,250.00 a year, or have they left you still on pension: and if so, what is the amount of the pension? If they have not put you back on the original basis, I am writing Mr. Mackenzie King a confidential letter."

And from his friend Harry Strange, on April 2: "I heard a rumour the other day that the contribution which you were receiving from the Dominion Government had been cut off. Would you kindly let me know as quickly as possible whether this is true or not, or if any reduction has been made in the grant."

Wheeler thanked Strange for his interest. He pointed out that, "I have never yet in any way solicited from anyone any favour. Anything that has come to me in honours or awards has come to me voluntarily and naturally. At the time Mr. Weir established my farm as sub-experimental station, I was given to understand by him that I was a free agent and that it was along the lines of a grant without any responsibilities. I can assure you that at the time this was done it did very materially help me financially in my work on the farm … but I always felt I was under an obligation in a way. And now at my time of life I am not able to carry any more responsibility other than I am doing, in fact I will have to give up the propagation and sale of nursery stock after this fall, as the amount of work involved in a nursery business and carrying on the production of registered seed on a three-quarter section of land is too much for me. If I gave up the fruit nursery business I would… have a little more leisure time… I thought it best to let you know if anything was done along the lines you mentioned in your letter, I would want to be a free agent." He added he needed more relaxation, not work "day in and day out."

Wheeler was the guest of honour at a gala banquet in Rosthern to celebrate his 70th birthday in January 1938. Dignitaries included the provincial agriculture minister J.G. Taggart, MP Walter A. Tucker, and Dr. L.E. Kirk, dean of the agriculture college. Kirk told the cheering diners that "Doctor Wheeler accomplished probably more than any other agriculturist in the world." Wheeler was visibly moved, then got up and talked for a long time, telling the story of early difficulties and grain-growing efforts that so many had heard before, but still enjoyed. "I would not close without mentioning that Mr. Henry Partridge has worked for me the past thirty-five years. This Christmas, he and Mrs. Partridge celebrated their Silver Wedding on the farm … married twenty-five years ago. He is present with us tonight."

But not for much longer. His farm manager and friend had decided it was time to retire. It was an emotional day when Henry and Hettie said goodbye and moved to Regina. The Partridges kept in touch, visiting the Wheelers at Maple Grove Farm and, later, in Victoria.

On February 16, 1938, Wheeler got his last government cheque, for $1,242.50, his gratuity.

His third daughter, Isabelle Lily, had married a Rosthern man, Edward Blatz, a couple of years earlier. The young couple had lived in Meadow Lake, 120 miles northeast, until Wheeler asked his son-in-law if he would work at Maple Grove Farm. He was so pleased with Blatz's work that, in 1940, he promoted him to farm manager, a vacant position since Henry Partridge had retired. The workload was piling up now, because several of his hands had joined the armed forces.

He was growing Himalaya wild blackberries, which he loved in jellies. He was planting more flowers than ever before, pink heather and, as a reminder of the Isle of Wight, foxgloves. Isabelle recalled that her parents' favourite flowers were peonies, gladioli, shirley poppies and delphiniums.

The sunlit sitting room, and his den, displayed trophies—one more than two feet high—reflecting his many agricultural successes. He liked to take visitors there, to talk surrounded by the glitter of his accomplishments.

Wheeler's one-time benefactor and former federal minister of agriculture, Robert Weir, was killed the winter of 1939 when a sleigh overturned and pinned him not far from his Weldon farm. Wheeler had, to his sorrow, lost several good friends recently, but he had his family and work to keep him in good spirits.

— TWENTY-TWO —

Honours to the End

Depression ends—wheat economy's golden years over—wheat surplus—government should buy at price satisfactory to farmers—inadequate farm policy—Royal Commission finds farm homes in serious financial plight—MBE from the King—1943 record cold destroys orchard—brother Percy dies—Lilian's health suffers—last crop—farewell banquet—Wheelers move to B.C.—Elizabeth and Isabelle—keeping a journal, watching the waves, planting flowers—television—reunion, Maple Grove Farm provincial historic site—Salvation Army—home mecca for visitors—50th wedding anniversary—slowing down, 1961 dies in sleep, close to the sea, at 94.

The economic misery of the Depression eased in 1939 with the outbreak of World War II and, coincidentally, the end of the drought and low wheat prices. Unlike during World War I, the demand for Canadian wheat fell as Hitler's armies invaded so many former customers. But the land continued to produce, in 1942 the biggest wheat crop ever at 550.7 million bushels.

The wheat surplus was a national concern, and the golden years of Canada's wheat economy were over. A year earlier, Harry Strange had written in the *Canadian Countryman* that Canada would have in storage 500 million bushels of wheat. "The truth is that providing storage is the least of all the difficulties connected with wheat… The one simple thing that needs to be done is for the government to declare that it will buy the wheat at a price satisfactory to the farmer, and then the grain companies will do the rest. The government actually need not concern itself about storage at all."

The June 1941 edition of *National Home Monthly* magazine, published in Winnipeg, contended there was a grave world famine. Millions of food producers had quit the farms to fight the war. Since Strange's article, the federal government had announced a policy of paying farmers for "not growing wheat." Four dollars per acre was to be paid for wheat land summer-fallowed, and $2 per acre for prairie wheat land which was put into coarse grains.

The president of the Canadian Federation of Agriculture, H.H. Hannam, who represented 350,000 farmers, was quoted: "This wheat program is a good example of the folly of trying to carry on without a national agricultural marketing and production program… The lack of an adequate farm policy for the Dominion means that agriculture becomes the victim of a series of ill-advised, last-minute emergency measures which cannot be regarded in even our most generous moments as the product of competent leadership or good statesmanship."

In a presentation to the Rosthern area's MP, Prime Minister Mackenzie King, the federation stated that "Victory cannot be achieved without sacrifices… It is vital from consideration of national unity that no one class shall be called upon to carry an undue share of the burden and that there shall be equality of sacrifice."

Far from equality of sacrifice, the Rowell-Sirois Commission on Dominion-Provincial Relations found Canadian farm families in a serious financial plight. Figures released by the commission had shown that average annual farm income for 1930–40 was $473. Average income for a city worker was about $1,400 a year, working eight hours a day, six days a week, with no personal investment.

Canadian farmers were again "busting their butts" for Britain, as they had during World War I. But the slavish doffing of the cap to Britain was no more. In the late 1940s, another Anglo-Canadian Wheat Agreement was signed, but Canadian farmers said it turned out badly for them, and blamed Britain. The symbiotic relationship between western Canadian farmers and Britain, it was said, had faded. When the agreement was signed, farmers had thought they were doing something for the United Kingdom that would be appreciated. But, said one farmer, they had no reason to believe "that the British people have the slightest conception of the sacrifices farmers had made, compared with the prices they could have got from other countries. They would never again let sentiment enter into it."

One of 285 Canadian civilians named in the English Honours List of 1943, Wheeler now was Dr. Seager Wheeler, MBE. A federal seed inspector in Saskatoon, S.B. Gilmour, wrote to congratulate him, and added: "At this time, I should also like to take the opportunity of telling you of the admiration that I have always had for your work, and since coming to know you, of the great respect and high esteem that I have had for you personally."

He received congratulations from, among others, his MP, Walter Tucker; Dr. L.E. Kirk, dean of agriculture at the University of Saskatchewan; Harry Strange, of Searle Grain; The Canadian Society of Technical Agriculturists; The Saskatoon Industrial Exhibition; M. Champlin, of the Saskatchewan Field Husbandry Association (Wheeler was on the board of officers in 1944); S.H. Vigor, of the Canadian Seed Growers' Association.

Miriam Green Ellis, Western Editor of the *Family Herald and Weekly Star*, of Montreal, sent a letter: "What with your birthdays and the King's birthdays, I seem to be able to keep up a fairly regular correspondence with you. I just want to say how pleased I am that you have been included in the King's Birthday List, and I presume from now on that you and the little dog will not be crawling under the currant bushes and plum trees any more. I don't think that it would be quite correct for an M.B.E. to grub around in the dirt the way you have been doing in the past."

In the depth of winter, 1943, nature—which had co-operated with Wheeler for more than 50 years as a silent partner—turned on him with wrath. Temperatures plummeted to -67° F, freezing the trees' inner wood. That spring, he found that most of the fruit trees had been mortally wounded. For a year or two, they fruited only on the new bark, then died. All 60 acres, which he had been developing for more than 30 years, and had survived drought and depression, were wiped out. He was 75 years old and, "At my age, I could not start all over again planting a new orchard."

On February 1, 1944, Percy Wheeler went to Calgary to visit his daughter. On February 9, he became sick and was taken to hospital. Alice sent Seager a telegram and, horrified, he exclaimed, "Oh, I must go to him!" and started packing. "But before he left," said

Elizabeth, "a call came from Alice saying Uncle Percy had died. Dad broke down and wept." Seager was devastated. He and his brother had been inseparable for most of their lives. Percy often was mistaken for Seager's son by people who had not met them. He would get, much to his amusement, letters from people in the grain business saying they knew his father well.

Percy had died of "circulatory collapse." Percy Henry William Wheeler was 77 years and 11 days old. Funeral service was held in St. Paul's Evangelical Church, in Rosthern. His obituary noted he "was an associate member of the Canadian Seed Growers' Association for some years and a recent winner of the Robertson trophy for producing prize seed grains." Interment was in the Bergthal Cemetery, not far from his mother. He left his wife Julia and their two children, Alice and Maurice.

Percy never farmed more than a quarter section because he planted with one purpose in mind, to produce registered Marquis 10B for seed. The late Larry Janzen, along with his wife Doreen, founder of the historic farm site, said Percy perhaps was better liked than Seager by many of German ancestry in the area because he learned to speak low German. This pleased and impressed his Mennonite neighbors who worked with and trusted him. "Seager was more remote, a researcher who saw himself as keeper of the holy grail. In early years, local people didn't understand what he was doing. If you have a band, and want a big audience, play in the next town."

Harry Strange, of Searle Grain, sent his condolences, saying the seed growers' association had lost one of its ablest and most trusted members. He asked Wheeler for details so he could write a piece about Percy in his next grain market letter. He would place a wreath on the grave when he visited that summer.

"You and Percy have made the most distinguished contributions to your adopted country, Canada. I was chatting with Mr. Vigor the other day and with Dr. Newman; also a number of scientific agriculturists assembled here in Winnipeg. We all agreed that there were probably no two men in the whole of the agricultural history of Canada who had done more for agriculture than yourself and Percy…"

On Wheeler's 76th birthday, January 3, 1944, W.T.G. Wiener, secretary-treasurer of the Canadian Seed Growers' Association, wrote to congratulate him: "Your individual record is probably the longest of any living grower in Saskatchewan. The Kirkham family has been growing seed for a longer period, but the record of this family is the result of three generations of effort. According to the old annual reports, you were apprenticed in 1908, and established as a member in 1909. In 1944 you will have been an operating member of the Association for a period of thirty-six years, thirty-five of which you have held full membership in the Association."

Wiener pointed out Wheeler's unique place among western Canadian seed growers at the annual meeting of the Saskatchewan branch of the association. The larger proportion of the really good grain of any variety in Canada, he said, traced usually to one or two sources. Most of the good Marquis wheat could be traced to the 10B strain produced by Wheeler. Most of the good Victory oats were traceable to Wheeler's strain of this variety. "Mr. Wiener might have added," said the newspaper report, "that the Red Bobs wheat becoming the most popular variety in Alberta originated, and much purification work was done, on the Wheeler farm."

For some years, Lilian Wheeler's health had not been good. Her daughter Elizabeth said, "This is why Dad retired earlier than he planned, because of mother."

Wheeler grew his last crop of registered seed grain in 1946, and that winter he and Lilian decided to move to Victoria, B.C. He wrote to tell W.G. Wiener that he was retiring as an active member of the seed growers' association. Wiener replied: "The Association is not unmindful of your contribution of Marquis 10B, Victory, and Red Bobs. The excellent stocks of these varieties prepared by you were made available to our members at a very critical period in the development of the Association. Had these outstanding stocks not been made available the work of the CSGA would have been much less successful."

Harry Strange was glad for him. "As you sit in your chair sometimes and enjoy a glass of your nice wine you make from wild grapes—I shall never forget how nice it is—you can reflect on the great good that you have done in many ways to all the farmers of Canada, not only by cereals, but in making their homes more liveable and more attractive by means of the splendid … trees and shrubs that you have made available to them."

Seager and Lilian went to Victoria on May 26, 1946, apparently to find a suitable house, returning August 10. He went to his Rosthern bank four days later and paid off a loan of $4,000 he had made while in Victoria, presumably to pay for a house.

On November 7, the same year, he wrote to Angelus Temple, Los Angeles, to cancel a subscription to *Four Square Magazine*. Brought up in a non-comformist religious tradition, he had always been drawn to such movements; his radio had introduced him to Aimie Semple McPherson, the hugely successful Canadian-born evangelist who founded the Foursquare Church. She had conducted a preaching and healing ministry at the temple, and on the airwaves via her own radio station.

In a whimsical mood, Wheeler occasionally attached a horse to an old wagon and drove it into town; he called it his Bennett Wagon, recalling the Bennett Buggies of 1930s Depression days when farmers who couldn't afford gas hooked horses to cars. He did so on April 15, 1947, and drew bank drafts of $500 each for May, Ella, Isabelle and Elizabeth; he called this "gift share," apparently a desire, now that he was growing old, to distribute some of his meagre wealth to the daughters he loved.

Harry Strange wrote May 7 to tell Wheeler he deserved retirement. "You have worked long and hard for the people of Canada … the fruits of your efforts have aided untold thousands of farmers and they have achieved a much better living because of all that you have done." He thanked him for a book; in recent years, Wheeler had been sending many books from his collection to close friends.

The evening of June 1, the Wheelers left by train for the West Coast, on coach tickets, $53.20 return. Presumably they prepared the new house for their occupation, returning on June 29.

A farewell banquet, sponsored by the Agricultural Institute of Canada, was held on October 8 at the Bessborough Hotel, an evening of praise, memories and laughter. Presentations were made by the Saskatchewan Field Husbandry Association; Saskatchewan Agricultural Societies' Association; Saskatchewan Horticultural Societies' Association; Saskatoon Board of Trade; Canadian Seed Growers' Association; Saskatchewan Branch, Canadian Seed Growers' Association; North Saskatchewan Branch, Agricultural Institute of Canada; and the Saskatchewan Registered Seed Growers' Association.

A novel feature of the evening occurred when a radio was turned on and the dinner guests listened to their honoured guest, seated beside his wife, in a recorded interview on the country-wide program CBC "News Round-up." Then everyone sang *Seager Wheeler*

Had a Farm. The seed growers' association secretary pointed out that Marquis 10B and Red Bobs wheat stock "were landmarks in the development of this association."

Professor John G. Rayner recalled:

> "Dr. Wheeler was always a charming conversationalist, and when the topic was one in which he was vitally interested, his enthusiasm knew no bounds. At such times, it was always a source of unalloyed pleasure to us to see him try to light his pipe. He would light a match and hold it to his pipe, but could not stop talking long enough to take more than one or two hasty draws. Of course, nothing happened and he had to drop the match to avoid burning his fingers, so the same thing occurred again and again and again, and all the time we were laughing more at this performance than at the ready wit and enthusiasm of the man."

SOURCE: ELIZABETH WHEELER COLLECTION

At his retirement banquet, Wheeler fooled his friends—who always laughed at his fumbling attempts to light his pipe with matches—by using a lighter.

When Wheeler rose to thank Rayner, his eyes twinkled as he drew out his famous pipe, tamped with a finger, and then held a lighter to it, drawing until clouds of smoke surrounded his head. He grinned: "Fooled you." He was presented with a pen-and-pencil set, a purse containing $80—one dollar for each year of his life—and a tri-light lamp affixed with a plaque commemorating an important prairie agricultural event. The inscription read: "From this spot on October 21, 1876, the first shipment of wheat from Western Canada started by Red River Steamer, 857 1/6 bushels of Red Fife at 85¢ per bushel, Consigned by Higgins & Young Wpg., 10 Steele Bros., Toronto, for use in Ontario as seed." It named the shippers. Mark-up was high; the seed sold in Ontario for $2.50 a bushel.

After dinner, the retiring farmer was interviewed by the regional correspondent for *Time* magazine. This article, with photograph, was the lead item in the Canada section of the magazine's October 20 edition.

The Alberta Wheat Pool sent appreciation of his research. "We wish particularly to mention Red Bobs wheat, which has made and will continue to make, a substantial contribution to the welfare of the wheat growers of Western Canada and the bread consuming people generally." Saskatchewan Pool Elevators in Regina, which had handled Wheeler's grain for so many years, took a load off his mind by buying several hundred bushels of First Generation Thatcher seed and other wheat that he had left, relieving him of the burden of marketing it. Wheeler wrote thanks for the years of service the pool had provided, saying Edward Blatz was taking over the farm and "He is a good man to carry it on."

On October 2, 1947, Wheeler had gone to the Imperial Bank in Rosthern to arrange the transfer of his cash and bonds to a branch in Victoria; the dozen war bonds totalled $7,500. After a few days, a truck arrived at the farmhouse and loaded 11 boxes, two trunks, eight cartons, one crate containing a cabinet radio, and one bale of garden boots, and left for the West Coast.

He paid $195 in outstanding debts, and on the October 13 he, Lilian and Elizabeth left Maple Grove Farm for Victoria and their comfortable, white-stuccoed house at 316 Linden Avenue, just a couple of blocks from the water. There he tended flower and vegetable gardens, listened to the gulls complaining and, on stormy days, could hear the waves. On a clear day, to the south he could make out Mount Olympus in the state of Washington. He now was receiving annuity cheques, $100 a month.

One would think Wheeler must have felt a pang at leaving the "oasis" he had established over so many years. But, as his daughter Elizabeth pointed out, it was his way never to look back, never to pine. He was too optimistic, too caught up with the present, and soon settled happily into a new life, an islander again, back by the sea he loved. The climate agreed with Lilian and she felt "completely different, back to normal, except for arthritis in her knees."

In 1951, May, now 42, moved to Victoria where she worked as a secretary. Although she lived in her own apartment, she often visited her parents and sister and enjoyed outings with them.

Prior to the move west, Elizabeth worked at *The Western Producer*, in Saskatoon, as a stenographer and then as secretary to the "Mighty Mite," Mrs.Violet McNaughton, early crusader in the farm women's movement. In Victoria, she was employed by the provincial government. Years later, she went back to the *Western Producer* in Saskatoon and became Youth Editor. At home, Elizabeth wrote poetry, preserved her father's papers, and in later years wrote articles, gave speeches in connection with her late father's life work, and self-published monographs on her father and on her mother.

Newspaper stories and national television featured Elizabeth Wheeler in 2005, when a man offered her father's 1915 world wheat championship trophy for sale on the Web. When the man discovered that the trophy had been stolen from Maple Grove Farm years earlier, he cancelled the sale and returned the trophy to Elizabeth. He had bought it in an antiques store a decade before. "It's so great, I think I'll hug it," she told reporters. Then she handed it over to the Western Development Museum, in Saskatoon, where other Wheeler trophies are displayed.

Daughter Isabelle and her husband Edward Blatz had moved into the 1925 house and continued to operate Maple Grove Farm's three quarters, raising four sons there. Edward ploughed the dead orchard and planted grain. In 1959, he died, just 44 years old. Her eldest son, Rodney, who had worked with his father, ran the farm until his grandfather died, then rented it from his mother and her sisters for 38 years. In time, Isabelle was alone. In 1973, following a break-in at the farmhouse, she moved to Rosthern. In 1998, the last quarter section of land was sold.

Wheeler had started keeping a daily journal back in 1905, and kept at it for half a century, a terse record of temperatures, precipitation, farm work and the comings and goings of family members and visitors. In a hurry, he scribbled, and much of the handwriting is barely legible. Faithfully, he watched World Series baseball games, noting the scores. As he grew older, he made more mention of aches and pains, a couple of nasty falls, visits by his family doctor, and hospital stays for Lilian. He talked a lot now about Percy and about his mother. But each day had to be filled with effort and accomplishment, as they had all through his life, and he was always busy, always planning; a log entry on a day he had gotten up "feeling poorly," or "aching from the fall," added that he had been out digging, or planting or pruning or at the park for a ball game.

These entries show that he continued his life-long habit of meticulous planning and record-keeping in Victoria, even though the scope of operations was so vastly reduced. His vegetable garden was 120' long and he dug it by hand right into his 90s. He packaged vegetable seeds for neighbors. He sent away to seed companies and he grew seeds sent to him by his daughter, Isabelle. Flowers grew all around the house, and on the boulevard; he planted bulbs, perennials and annuals. Particularly, he was thrilled by the variety of roses he could grow. Many varieties of fruit and specimen trees that grew about the house were pruned carefully each year. In between roses and baseball games, he was writing a brief memoir.

His old friend Miriam Green Ellis wrote in the *Family Herald*: "He likes his new home in Victoria, which is only a block or two from the ocean, and at first he spent many early morning hours watching the waves roll in. But now, he is just too busy planting roses, pulling out the weeds, splitting wood for the kitchen stove. He always did like reading, but things are difficult now, for the Victoria broadcasts bring in the news at 10 p.m., and then comes the seventh inning of the baseball games, and presently it is midnight, and he has to get up at 5:30 a.m. to get started in the garden. And if it isn't baseball it is hockey. So far as Seager Wheeler is concerned, baseball and hockey are all that matter; cricket is too slow, football is a bit complicated; but he will go to a baseball game if it is within reach, and if not he will take it canned from the radio. Some of his neighbors go over to the park to watch the bowling or the park checkers, but so far as Seager Wheeler is concerned, they are just old men's games.

"He will be going back to Rosthern in a week or two to take a look at his farm... However it will just be two or three weeks on the prairies and then back in time to stake up the glads and asters." In 1948, before he returned to his Victoria flowers, he was given a scroll in recognition of 20 years as a director of the Saskatchewan branch of the Canadian Seed Growers' Association.

In 1954, the 50th anniversary of Saskatchewan's entry into Confederation just months away, the provincial government's historic sites committee commemorated Wheeler's work at Maple Grove Farm by erecting an inscribed wooden plaque stating that one of his greatest contributions was the "breeding of the rare Marquis 10B." The message included his maxim: "The soil is ours to make or mar, and we should aim to leave it, when the time comes for us to pass it on, in as good or better condition than when it first came under our hand." He stood by this plaque the next summer, a hot July day, to pose for press photographers, a picture of contented retirement from life's demands, a man who had "passed it on." The Rosthern-Duck Lake Masonic Lodge was hosting a reunion picnic of more than 250 people on his farm.

After a baseball game involving younger picnickers, a short ceremony was held. The site couldn't have been more fitting, the dignitaries' platform a hay rick standing in the shade of trees planted by Wheeler, and close by a fine stand of Marquis 10B planted by his son-in-aw, Edward Blatz, waving in the warm breeze. The whole saga of Wheeler's trip through time in the Territories and then Saskatchewan, and all his accomplishments and honours and good works were pieced together as speaker after speaker from agricultural and governmental disciplines stood, watching their balance as the wagon shifted and swayed under their weight.

Press reports of the picnic resulted in another of the touching tributes so often sent to Wheeler, this time from (Mrs.O.) May Beamish, of Marshall, Saskatchewan:

"I had read with pleasure of your homecoming ... at Rosthern and last night when we were pulling crabapples off our Linda tree in the headlights of the car, I decided to write you and offer a long-delayed thanks—I hope you won't mind, even though I have never had the pleasure of meeting you.

"Some sixteen years ago, we sent to you for some apple tree seedlings—you sent them—and also a Linda crab and a very nice letter, telling us that we would have to wait many years for our apples but in the meantime the Linda crab, which you sent with your compliments, would provide us with plenty of crabapples. How many crabapples it has produced, no one could imagine—no matter how often the others failed to produce, the Linda always gave us our winter jelly supply—the yields have increased—until it now supplies jelly and fruit for all our neighbors—this year the boughs are bent to the ground with their weight of fruit—it has truly been a wonderful tree.

"I often thought through the years, that I would write and thank you but somehow never got it done—though I never miss a fall without thinking of your kindness to perfect strangers. My father was the artist "Gus Kenderdine"—though he came to this country much later than you, he too was a pioneer in his own line and like you, has left good work for the future generations. He told me that he once met you on the train, and said you were a "fellow you would like to know." I can imagine you would have much in common. So I would like to add my thanks to the many well deserved honours that have been bestowed on you."

A lifetime affinity with the Salvation Army blossomed in Victoria. Wheeler attended meetings most Sunday evenings and donated to its causes. As he grew older and couldn't attend meetings, the SA sometimes came to him on Sunday mornings to play hymns outside the Linden Avenue house. Neighbors would open their doors to stand and listen. When members knocked on the door to collect money, Wheeler waved them in and played old Army songs on his concertina.

As the years eased by, the old gentleman enjoyed their summer visits to Maple Grove Farm. Age didn't slow him down much, and passing years failed to separate him from admirers. Their home was a mecca for visitors, particularly from the prairies.

On December 17, 1958, Seager and Lilian Wheeler observed their 50th wedding anniversary. They entertained the whole afternoon and evening, a continual flow of guests offering congratulations, cards and gifts. Telegrams were delivered to the door, and wine from the Searle Grain company.

Vectensis wrote once again, in "An Islander's Notes" in the *County Press*, Newport, Isle of Wight, that a neighbor, F.W. Kemp, had sent a letter about the anniversary celebration:

> "Surely Dr. Wheeler, with his efforts and tireless energy, has contributed
> his share to the world's work, and it was a pleasure to sit and hear him

recall old times with his friends. The walls of his den are covered with photos of his beloved island, especially of the area around Chale Bay, where he was born. I often chat with him about the old wrecks and tales of life-saving. When I drop in to see him nearly always his first words are 'Did you bring me a Chale Bay mackerel?' On January 3rd he celebrated his 91st birthday and is anxiously awaiting the spring, when he can once again get to work in his garden. A wonderful man for his age, the Isle of Wight should be truly proud of producing a native son like him."

By 1959, Wheeler's journal entries showed he was slowing down. "Not feeling too well," was followed for days with "About the same," or ditto marks. This apparent lassitude continued from March into September. He noted Dr. Reid had checked him over and "said I was doing pretty good, left medicine for passing my water." Then, on September 18, he picked up a little, remarking, "Listening to Kruchev talk." Nikita Khrushchev, leader of the Soviet Union, was in the United States on a whirlwind tour after the sensation of Sputnik's space travel.

On October 6, he recorded "Chicago 1 run, Dodgers 0, 10 innings, a close game." An entry October 19, in what appeared to be someone else's handwriting: "Went to Jubilee Hospital at 4:30 p.m. by taxi." Then, November 1, "Returned home from hospital 11 a.m. by taxi." November 3: "About same," this time in Wheeler's hand again. He would make just one more entry.

When she was a little girl, Elizabeth always went into her father's bedroom where he sat reading by lamplight, to kiss him goodnight, and he would smile "Goodnight, my pretty." In Victoria, she said, "I always went in to say goodnight and kiss him because you never knew, he might die in his sleep or something."

On the night of December 15, 1961, close to the sea he loved, Seager Wheeler died in his sleep from pneumonia, "the old people's friend." He was just under three weeks short of his 94th birthday.

His last journal entry wandered across the page, a scrawl: "Home again, home again. From Victoria. From Victoria, B.C., yesterday evening, home again. Starting a new book."

— TWENTY-THREE —

A Farmer's Legacy

Legacy: better farmers, better farming—tributes—Sally Ann funeral service—by rail back to Rosthern—Bergthal Cemetery, near farmstead—Lilian dies in 1965—daughters sell Victoria house, back to Saskatchewan—Canadian Agricultural Hall of Fame—U of Sask. student residence named in his honour—Saskatchewan Agricultural Hall of Fame—declared national historic person—Maple Grove Farm designated National Historic Site—Seager Wheeler Farm Historical Society runs farm to continue "the vision the man had"—Seager Wheeler Lake, Red Bobs Lake.

Arguably the most important Canadian farmer to that time, or perhaps any time—the man whose work put more wealth into his country's coffers, farmers' pockets, businessmen's bank balances, who raised the quality of Canadian wheat on world markets, who helped populate Canada's West—died to muted notices in most other parts of Canada. Publications in the United States and Britain noted Seager Wheeler's death as funeral arrangements were being completed in Victoria.

The *Winnipeg Free Press* commented on his passing on December 21, 1961:

> "The name, Seager Wheeler, is often overlooked in Canadian histories. It does not appear in Canadian Who's Who. Yet few, if any, have contributed more to the agricultural development of western Canada and few have been more deserving of honour. His death in Victoria last Friday recalls the significance of his achievements in developing new strains of wheat that helped make the Canadian west one of the world's great wheat-growing areas.

> ...While funeral services have been held in Victoria, to which city he retired in 1947, it is fitting that his last resting place will be the little cemetery at Rosthern, near the farm that was the scene of his agricultural triumphs."

The Western Producer, on December 28, said Seager Wheeler's legacy to Canada was better farmers and better farming on the prairies. "No less important is the great number of friends who mourn the passing of a truly great man, a good farmer, and a gentleman in the finest sense of the word."

On January 10, the Searle Grain Company ran a tribute in the *Winnipeg Free Press* under the heading, "Western Canada's Debt To The Late Seager Wheeler." It included a quote from Dr. A.H. Reginald Buller, one-time professor of botany at the University of Manitoba: "Seager Wheeler's success has been achieved because it has arisen from the wellspring of service—an earnest desire to use the gifts of application and scientific understanding and research for the welfare of his fellow farmers, to accomplish something which would be good."

A few got facts mixed up, even in Saskatchewan. There were many accolades in the newspapers, but he was not, as one writer claimed, "the father of highly disputed Thatcher wheat."

The Salvation Army's Brig. B. Purdy conducted the service at McCall Bros. Funeral Chapel, Johnson and Vancouver streets, on Monday, December 18, at 11 a.m. Besides his wife and four daughters, he was survived by seven grandchildren and three great-grand-children, as well as his half-brother and other relatives in England.

Wheeler's body was returned by rail to Rosthern. Although a man of deep religious faith, he had belonged officially to no Rosthern congregation, so services were held at daughter Isabelle's church, St.Paul's Evangelical United Brethren.

The funeral procession made its way along Provincial Road 312 from the town east towards Maple Grove Farm, stopping on the south side of the road just half a mile short of the farm where Seager Wheeler had lived his dedicated life. Here was Bergthal Cemetery, where his mother and his brother were buried. His grave with a headstone is just off centre of the grounds, near the southern boundary—about 40 feet from his moth-er, Mary Ann Wheeler. His wife Lilian died in 1965 and she lies beside her husband, near the place where they passed such a full and happy life together. He had died on their 53rd anniversary and, wrote Elizabeth, "She was never the same … she grew silent." Daughter May joined them at Bergthal Cemetery 23 years later. Daughter Ella, who had lived with her family in Alberta, was buried in Edmonton.

A team of single-minded oxen would take perhaps 15 minutes to wander from the unprepossessing cemetery over to Maple Grove Farm, now entrusted to the Seager Wheeler Farm Historical Society, a locally-based, non-profit group of "friends of the farm." Chaired in 2001 by Larry and Doreen Janzen, themselves local seed producers, the group wished to "continue the vision the man had," dedicated to the site's preservation and development as a heritage and educational facility through such live farming and hor-ticultural events as Demonstration Day and Direct Seeding Day, some of them under direction of the University of Saskatchewan's crop development centre. "The Wheeler farm is all about educating, learning by seeing and doing. The farm is a stage, the visitors part of the audience," the late Larry Janzen said at the time. "You can't get closer to the grass roots than on the Seager Wheeler farm."

The society secured public, private and corporate funding to develop what is possibly the most significant piece of farmland in western Canada, and to publicize Wheeler's dominant contributions to Canada's prairie agriculture. The Historic Sites and Monuments Board of Canada considers the farm significant as a "representative farmstead established during the Wheat Boom period," defined as the period from 1900 to the begin-ning of World War II—the golden years of the wheat economy in this country. The farm will be preserved forever, because it was designated a National Historic Site by the feder-al government in 1996. The commemorative plaque states:

"Maple Grove is a living testament to Seager Wheeler's career as a distinguished agronomist. Established in 1898, it was typical of Prairie farms of the wheat-boom era in its buildings and layout. Here, Wheeler undertook his pathfinding research to develop wheat and fruit strains suited to the climate of western Canada. Significant vestiges of this work remain, including hedgerows, shelterbelts, test beds for seed selection experiments, and a distinctive range of plant material. The result is a landscape which speaks to Wheeler's achievements and to a major period of Prairie settlement."

The Janzens and their board began devoting time to the project in 1992, and it is considered one of the west's most prized, but still underdeveloped, agricultural sites. They wanted to see the farm project become a major adjunct to, and competitor of, existing tourist attractions at Fort Carlton and Batoche, all three situated in a surpassingly historic trail- and water-route section of western Canada.

After Seager Wheeler left Maple Grove Farm in 1947, no changes were made, except for installation of electricity in the mid-1950s. Edward Mills said in his study for the Historic Sites and Monuments Board of Canada that, "Tree and shrub planting ceased, and the existing building stock was left unaltered. Wheeler's numerous tree plantings matured and, in some areas, became severely overgrown. His various seed and garden plots were either untended or converted to wheat production, although the hedge margins were left intact...The buildings also reflect a pervasive regional characteristic borne out of prolonged periods of financial insecurity; a predisposition to live in extremely modest circumstances in the interest of building up the capital base of the farm...While most vestiges of the orchards have disappeared, along with some of the adjacent shelterbelts, the farmstead, along with many of the tree plantings and field patterns remain substantially intact."

Mills stated that a 1975 nurseryman's inspection identified 22 different species of trees and shrubs dating from Wheeler's occupancy; a 1992 inspection said at least 20 of these species survived, and "The Seager Wheeler Society took preliminary steps to stabilize and protect the plantings in 1993 with the assistance of Green Plan funding."

The site officially was opened to the public in June 1996. An annual seeding trends demonstration was established. Slowly, renovations are taking place. The house lived in by superintendents of the Rosthern Experimental Farm has been moved onto the Wheeler farm to be used as an interpretive centre, gift and coffee shop. This building is graced by a life-size statue of Seager Wheeler carved from laminated local aspen. The old barn has been restored with a new loft floor and shingles. Wheeler's seed-cleaning plant, including some of his own seed-cleaning equipment, were being renovated. Perennial and annual English flower gardens were redeveloped, plans for the beds drawn up by Sara Williams, author, landscape designer and one-time editor of *The Gardener*, Saskatoon. Acres of nursery were being replanted by the horticultural division, University of Saskatchewan, for fruit production and shelterbelt stock.

A "tourism opportunity study" of the Wheeler farm was published in 1992. "It is intended that eventually all the existing buildings, including the 1925 house, would be completely restored to their original appearance. The log house would likewise be completely reconstructed. Period furnishings would be used throughout the houses. The grain-sorting machinery shed should be restored and made operational. The barn and barnyard would be used to re-create a working farm, with maintained livestock representative of Wheeler's original farm operation."

A larger parking lot was developed for the increasing number of visitors. Grain plots and orchard probably will be expanded as more people visit the site. Two main groups are being considered: the general touring public; and school classes searching for a feeling of the past. A museum display already set up in the visitor centre deals with interesting aspects of Wheeler's awards, experiments and innovations. Displays also are planned for other seed growers of the time, and the work of such contemporaries as Dr. Charles Saunders. Development of the site, of course, depends on the ability of the farm society to network with, and continue raising funds from, interested governments, corporations, individuals, and agricultural and historical groups.

A plaque placed at Maple Grove Farm in 1955 by the Saskatchewan government commemorated it as a Provincial Historic Site. After Wheeler died, steps gradually were taken to honour his deeds and his memory. He was inducted into the Canadian Agricultural Hall of Fame, in Toronto, in 1967.

May Wheeler unveiled a plaque in her father's honour at Rosthern Centennial Park on August 15, 1967. She said that, "as a family, we knew him as a kind generous loving father, and a Christian gentleman… He never sought fame or desired to be in the public eye. We knew that he loved his work and had a keen zeal to accomplish his goal—to better his country for the benefit of his fellow man. We were proud of his lifetime, and we are proud of the memory he left us."

A University of Saskatchewan student residence was named in his honour in 1970. In 1972, he was inducted into the Saskatchewan Agricultural Hall of Fame, in Saskatoon. He was declared a person of national historic significance in 1976.

The railway station in Rosthern was renovated in 1990 to become the Station Arts Centre/Seager Wheeler Place. That year, an annual performance of *Harvest Moon* was inaugurated, a play written by Rod McIntyre about the past, present and future of Saskatchewan and agriculture, through Wheeler's eyes. About 80% of audiences were from outside Rosthern.

The Seager Wheeler Harvest Festival, held in Rosthern in September, was inaugurated in 1989. The two-day event featured threshing and stooking demonstrations, fiddle playing, and townspeople got into the act by wearing period costumes.

Two lakes in northeastern Saskatchewan honour Wheeler and his work—Seager Wheeler Lake and Red Bobs Lake.

As Canadians drive to the old Wheeler farm site, few might notice the little cemetery they pass as they near their destination. The graveyard is unpretentious, showing adequate care, nothing more. But it is difficult to imagine a more fitting resting place for such a man as Seager Wheeler. His spirit is lasting, and this place suggests the openness, modesty, and natural dignity of this extraordinary person. Here is simplicity on a spot of now weakly-remembered undeveloped prairie, waving wild grasses and flowers, dry heat of summer and ice of winter, all within sight of the old farmstead and, all around, the continuing business of producing grain crops and top Canadian seed.

Bibliography

Anderson, Charles W. *Grain: The Entrepreneurs*. Winnipeg: Watson & Dwyer Publishing Ltd., 1991.

Appleton, Thomas E. *Ravenscrag: The Allan Royal Mail Line*. Toronto: McClelland and Stewart, 1974.

Archer, John H. *Saskatchewan: A History*. Saskatoon: Western Producer Books, 1980.*Barber's Picturesque Illustrations of the Isle of Wight*. N.p.: Simpkin & Marshall, c. 1831.

Bercuson, David J. and J.L. Granatstein. *Dictionary of Canadian History*. Toronto: Collins, 1988.

Binnie-Clark, Georgina. *Wheat & Woman*. Toronto: University of Toronto Press, 1979.

Bliss, Michael. *Right Honourable Men*. Toronto: HarperCollins, 1994.

Brannon, A. *Brannon's Pleasure Visitor's Companion in Making the Tour of the Isle of Wight, Pointing Out the Best Plan for Seeing in the Shortest Time Every Remarkable Object*. Newport: The Author, 1868.

Briddon, James. *Illustrations of The Isle of Wight*. N.p.: Ventnor, 1863.

Careless, J.M.S. and R.Craig Brown (eds.). *The Canadians: 1867–1967*. Toronto: The Macmillan Company of Canada Limited.

Charlebois, Peter. *The Life of Louis Riel*. Toronto: NC Press, 1978.

Chronicle of Canada. N.p: Chronicle Publications, 1990.

Clinch, George. *The Isle of Wight*. London: The Little Guides, Methuen & Co. Ltd., 1921.

Donaldson, Gordon. *Sixteen Men: The Prime Ministers of Canada*. Toronto: Doubleday Canada Ltd., 1980.

Donkin, John George. *Trooper in the Far North-West*. Saskatoon: Western Producer Prairie Books, 1987.

Dunae, Patrick A. *Gentlemen Emigrants, From the British Public Schools to the Canadian Frontier*. Toronto: Douglas & McIntyre, 1981.

Fisher, Graham and Heather Fisher. *Monarchy and the Royal Family*. London: Robert Hale, 1979.

Foster, John E. (ed.). *The Developing West*. Edmonton: The University of Alberta Press, 1983.

Francis, R. Douglas. *Images of the West*. Saskatoon: Western Producer Prairie Books, n.d.

French, Doris. *Ishbel and the Empire: A Biography of Lady Aberdeen*. Toronto: Dundurn Press, 1988.

Friesen, Gerald. *The Canadian Prairies: A History*. Toronto: University of Toronto Press, 1984.

Friesen, Victor Carl. "Seager Wheeler, Wheat King," *Saskatchewan History* (Fall 1996).

From Sod to Solar, Story of Fielding, Lilac, Maymont and Ruddell. Maymont: Maymont Library Board, 1980.

Gray, James H. *Men Against the Desert*. Saskatoon: Fifth House Publishers, 1996.

Great West Before 1900, The. Edmonton: United Western Communications Ltd., 1991.

Grun, Bernard. *The Timetables of History*. New York: Simon & Schuster, 1991.

Harvey, Robert. *Pioneers of Manitoba*. Winnipeg: The Prairie Publishing Company, 1970.

Hibbert, Christopher. *The English: A Social History 1066–1945*. Chelmsford, Essex: Grafton Books, 1988.

Hill, Douglas. *The Opening of the Canadian West*. London: Heinmann, 1968.

Koester, C.B. *Mr. Davin M.P.* Saskatoon: Western Producer Prairie Books, 1980.

Levine, Allan. *The Exchange: 100 years of Trading Grain in Winnipeg*. Winnipeg: Peguis Publishers Ltd., 1987.

MacEwan, Grant. *The Sodbusters*. Toronto: Thomas Nelson & Sons Ltd., 1948.

——. *Fifty Mighty Men*. Saskatoon: Western Producer Prairie Books, 1958.

——. *Harvest of Bread*. Saskatoon: Prairie Books, 1969.

——. *Grant MacEwan's West: Sketches from the Past*. Saskatoon: Western Producer Prairie Books, 1990.

——. *Mighty Women*. Vancouver: Greystone Books, 1995.

Manitoba 125: A History. Winnipeg: Great Plains Publications, 1994.

Marquis of Lorne, The. *Canada 100 Years Ago*. London: Bracken Books, 1885/1985.

McCourt, Edward. *Saskatchewan*. Toronto: Macmillan, 1968.

Mew, Fred. *Back of the Wight*. Newport: The County Press, 1953.

Moorhouse, Hopkins. *Deep Furrows*. Toronto/Winnipeg: George J. McLeod, Ltd., 1918.

Morgan, Dan. *Merchants of Grain*. New York: Viking, 1979.

Old and New Furrows—The Story of Rosthern. Rosthern: Rosthern Historical Society, 1977.

Russell, B.W. *Ventnor and the Undercliff*. N.p.: The Advancement Association, Ventnor, 1935.

Sloan, Eric. *Our Vanishing Landscape*. New York: Wilfred Funk, Inc., 1955.

Stegner, Wallace. *Wolf Willow*. Toronto: Macmillan, 1977.

Stone, Percy G. *Songs of the Soil* (Isle of Wight dialect). Newport: The County Press, 1933.
Strange, H.G.L. *A Short History of Prairie Agriculture*. Winnipeg: Searle Grain Company Ltd., 1954.
Thomas, Lewis G. (ed.). *The Prairie West to 1905*. Oxford: Oxford University Press, 1975.
Tour Through the Isle of Wight, A. Portsmouth: J. Welch & Sons, c. 1905.
Trevelyan, G.M. *English Social History: A Survey of Six Centuries*. London: Penguin Books, 1984.
Walder, David. *Nelson*. New York: The Dial Press/James Wade, 1978.
Wells, Ronald A. *Letters from a Young Emigrant in Manitoba*. Winnipeg: The University of Manitoba Press, 1981.
Wheeler, Seager. "How I Grew My Best Wheat," The Farmer's Advocate of Winnipeg (January 24, 1912).
——. *Profitable Grain Growing*. Winnipeg: The Grain Growers' Guide Ltd., 1919.
Wilson, C.F. *A Century of Canadian Grain*. Saskatoon: Western Producer Prairie Books, 1978.

Articles

Saskatchewan Valley News, Rosthern, SK
Western Producer, Saskatoon, SK
Saskatoon Star-Phoenix, Saskatoon, SK
Time Magazine, Canadian Edition
Punch, London, England.
Grain Growers' Guide, Winnipeg (January 16, March 1, 1928)
MacLean's Magazine (June 25, 1925)
The Country Gentleman, Philadelphia (November 27, 1920)
Farmers' Magazine: Canada's National Farm Magazine, Toronto (July 1, 1919)
The Grande Prairie Herald (September 29, 1933)
National Home Monthly, Winnipeg (June 1941)

Other Sources

Agriculture Museum of Canada, www.science-tech.nmstc.ca
Ethel Boskill, North Battleford, SK
Keith Dryden, retired editor of *The Western Producer*, Saskatoon, SK
1881 British Census and National Index, Family History Resource File, CD ROM Library, supplied by The Church of Jesus Christ of Latter-Day Saints, Salt Lake City, UT, USA
Victor Carl Friesen, Rosthern, SK
Doreen and Larry Janzen, Rosthern, SK
John Martens, Rosthern, SK
Bonnie Milman, Maymont, SK, correspondence, 2000
Royal Naval Museum Library, HM Naval Base, Portsmouth, England
Dan Wheeler, Chale Green, Isle of Wight, correspondence and family tree, 2000
David Wheeler, Steephill Cove, Ventnor, Isle of Wight, correspondence, 2000
Elizabeth Wheeler, Saskatoon, SK and Isabelle Blatz, Rosthern, SK, daughters of Seager Wheeler, taped interviews, December 3, 1998 and October 6, 1999
Seager Wheeler Farm Tourism Opportunity Study, final report, 1992
The Seager Wheeler papers, Saskatchewan Archives Board, Regina—Autobiographical sketch, correspondence, addresses and articles, scrapbooks and miscellaneous documents. Guide No. GR 201; Call No. Micro R-2.246.
Margaret Zulkoskey, Anglican Synod Archives, Prince Albert, SK.

Index

Date I